THE NOTEBOOK OF A
COLONIAL CLERGYMAN

THE NOTEBOOK OF A COLONIAL CLERGYMAN

Condensed from the Journals of

HENRY MELCHIOR MUHLENBERG

Translated and Edited by

THEODORE G. TAPPERT
and
JOHN W. DOBERSTEIN

FORTRESS PRESS   PHILADELPHIA

COPYRIGHT © 1959 BY FORTRESS PRESS

First Paperback Edition 1975

Library of Congress Catalog Card Number 59-10536

ISBN 0-8006-1804-1

5216F75   Printed in USA   1-1804

Preface

A thirty-one-year-old clergyman, Henry M. Muhlenberg, arrived in America in 1742, called as pastor of three small Lutheran congregations in the Philadelphia area. He labored forty-five years among German immigrants who came to the New World in ever-increasing numbers, and was something of a bishop among American Lutherans in the colonial period.

Muhlenberg kept a day-by-day record of what he saw and did. He had a sharp eye for human-interest detail. During the winter the Continental Army camped at Valley Forge, he had a front-row seat at the skirmishes fought in the Philadelphia area, and described the situation of civilians between the lines.

For almost two centuries only a handful of scholars were acquainted with this valuable story of life in eighteenth-century America. Muhlenberg's Journals were left to posterity in two dozen volumes of manuscripts, scattered among descendants of the Muhlenberg family. As far back as 1881 the collection of these documents in the library of the Lutheran Theological Seminary in Philadelphia was begun. Several volumes were found in an attic in Reading, Pennsylvania, as recently as 1954. Transcription and translation were undertaken by Dr. Theodore G. Tappert and Dr. John W. Doberstein in 1939. Muhlenberg, under date of October 4, 1781, referred to his journals as "mixed straw and grain" and suggested that after his death others "may winnow or sift it and separate from it the grain, if they deem it worth the trouble." The present volume represents such a sifting. Actually, there is more grain than has here been selected, for Muhlenberg's journals have been severely reduced in these pages to less than one-twentieth of the total bulk. The object has been to put into the hands of the general reader only a few of the author's observations and reflections which will furnish intimate glimpses into the life and manners of American colonists in the eighteenth century. Readers who desire more of the "mixed straw and grain" must consult the three large volumes of *The Journals of Henry Melchior Muhlenberg* (published by Muhlenberg Press, 1942-58, and now out of print), from whose 4,502 columns of text the original editors and translators culled these jottings.

The author of the entries which are here reproduced was in a position to observe life in his times as an active participant in it. Sent from Halle, in Saxony, in 1742 to minister to German Lutherans in southeastern Pennsylvania, he extended the field of his activities and influence to embrace the whole Atlantic seaboard, supplementing his journeys with correspondence which reached from Nova Scotia to Georgia. Although he was more immediately concerned with Lutheran colonists of German, Dutch, and Swedish backgrounds, he had associations of many kinds with Reformed, Presbyterian, Anglican, Moravian, Mennonite, Quaker, Baptist, and other religious groups. His observations were not limited to ecclesiastical matters, however, for he had a keen interest in the social, cultural, economic, and political life of his day, which he saw from his own peculiar point of view. Apart from the fact that two of his sons were active in public life (Peter Muhlenberg was a brigadier general and Frederick Muhlenberg was the first speaker in the United States Congress), Henry Melchior Muhlenberg was involved in the Revolution and the birth of the American republic if for no other reason than that he lived through these eventful years.

Muhlenberg wrote his journals in German, and they have been preserved in manuscript just as he wrote them. The textual apparatus and the footnotes of this three-volume edition of the journals have been omitted in the present condensation, but words and phrases which Muhlenberg wrote in a language other than German and whose meaning will hardly escape the reader are printed in italics. A brief index is included in this volume. A complete index may be found in Volume 3 of *The Journals.*

The Year 1742

SEPTEMBER 22. Early in the morning we tripped anchor, sailed past the fortress of Charleston, arrived at the city about eight o'clock, and fired our cannon as a salute of happy arrival.

SEPTEMBER 23. Had myself transported to the city in a boat, looked for German people, and found several who said that they had no lack of physical nourishment but that they were gravely in need of spiritual nourishment, namely, the Word of God and the holy sacraments in their language. Went back to our ship in the afternoon.

A pair of the black heathen, who are sold as slaves to the white Christian people, came on board our ship. I questioned them concerning various matters, but they knew nothing of the true God, nor of him whom he sent. The heathen slaves are so numerous here that it is estimated that there are fifteen for every white man. They occasionally rebel against their masters in the country, a thing which occurred just two years previous, when they gathered together as a mob and mercilessly killed a number of English people and their children. One also finds here many slaves who are only half black, the offspring of those white Sodomites who commit fornication with their black slave women. This goes on dreadfully, and no one dares to say anything to the blacks concerning the true religion because the so-called Christians object that the blacks would kill them all and make themselves masters of Carolina if they accepted the Christian religion. This, however, is an absurd and contradictory opinion, resting on corrupt reason. For the so-called Christians lead a more evil life than the heathen, and for this reason they are not willing to let the blacks acquire knowledge so that they will not be punished or disturbed in their sin. This is a horrible state of affairs, and it will entail a severe judgment. A short time before, several

1

Englishmen had made an effort with the heathen and instilled some knowledge of Christ in them, but they were persecuted and punished by the authorities.

Today our captain contracted for a boat for me and the Salzburgers, besides one of General James Oglethorpe's drummers, which was to travel by way of the coastal channels to Georgia, since he was bound by contract to transport us to Georgia and must remain here with his ship for fourteen days longer. I could waste no more time, so I decided to go along.

SEPTEMBER 24. I took leave of our ship and rode over to the Georgia boat with the Salzburgers, accompanied by the captain and the jurist. The captain gave us some bread to take along; other provisions I had to procure on the way, and very dearly too. We left Charleston about eleven o'clock. A black heathen girl, twelve years old, had secretly slipped into our boat and seated herself between the Salzburg children. She belonged to the colonel in the city of Charleston and intended to escape from her master. The skipper of our boat thought she belonged to the Salzburgers, since the Salzburg children were burned almost as black by the sun. The Salzburgers, on the other hand, thought she belonged to the skipper. When I happened to ask whom she belonged to, nobody knew. The skipper of the boat dragged her out and gave her a sound thrashing to make her admit the escape and returned her to her master. All of us on the boat might have been subject to arrest if we had inadvertently taken her along. So it was a good thing that she was discovered when we were only a few miles away, though we were somewhat delayed on our journey.

Since there is a tide in these coastal channels, we got only about eight miles from Charleston and had to lie by most of the afternoon. While we were lying by, the drummer and I went ashore and through the woods on St. James's Island, where we found a house occupied by some English folk. They thought we were spies, but when I told them I was a preacher, they exhibited great friendliness and could not do enough to show their kindness.

2

SEPTEMBER 29. Ice formed during the past night, which is very unusual here at this time and generally ruins the rice still standing in the fields. Such sudden cold here causes acute maladies and sudden deaths. The dear God, however, preserved us and let nothing injure us. If there had been no cold we would have had an even greater plague, namely, insects. There is a sort of gnat which during warm weather attacks the hands and face in countless numbers and torments human beings frightfully. To be free of them one has to have a smudge on board made of cow dung or something else. Toward evening we had a good wind which drove us forward.

SEPTEMBER 30. During this night the wind carried us as far as we had gone in the past six days. About eight o'clock we arrived at the town of Beaufort, on Port Royal, where the skipper of the boat lived. I had heard that there was an English preacher in Beaufort named Jonas, who was an upright man. When we reached the town I visited Pastor Jonas and was kindly received by him. He refreshed me with food and spiritual discourse. He was also acquainted with the two preachers in Ebenezer and gave a good account of them. On this day I wanted to buy victuals for our further journey but could get nothing in the town.

OCTOBER 1. The skipper put us on a smaller boat to take us the rest of the way to Savannah. Before we set out, the worthy Pastor Jonas sent us bread and meat gratis for our subsistence, for which may the Lord repay him. About 9 A.M. we pulled away from Beaufort. About twelve o'clock the tide went out, so we went into the woods on the bank and ate our noonday meal. As soon as the tide came back we continued rowing until six o'clock in the evening, when we again entered a thick forest and prepared our supper. About seven o'clock we sailed on until eleven o'clock at night, when we met with a trading vessel anchored near the ocean. The captain of the trading vessel took us in, gave us some refreshments, and permitted us to sleep for several hours on his ship. About 3 A.M. we continued our journey, passing several dangerous spots where water spouted high in the air.

OCTOBER 2. About 8 A.M. we arrived safely at Savannah, Georgia. I went directly to Colonel Stephens in Savannah and reported that I had brought with me a Salzburg family recommended by Mr. Verelst to Pastor John Martin Bolzius in Ebenezer. Colonel Stephens immediately had me and the Salzburgers taken care of there. Afterwards we learned that Pastor Israel Christian Gronau, of Ebenezer, was in Savannah and was going to preach to the German people the following day, Sunday. The worthy Mr. Gronau came to the inn and took us to a house which a patron of high standing had given to the Salzburg preachers as a hospice.

OCTOBER 4. Journeyed on ahead with Mr. Gronau in a small boat to Ebenezer, which lies thirty miles beyond Savannah, because I wanted to confer with Pastor Bolzius as soon as possible and not waste any time. About four o'clock we arrived at the plantations which the dear Salzburgers were building on the river. We landed at the plantations and viewed the flour mill which the Salzburgers had built with much labor, thus erecting the first water mill in Georgia. From the plantations we rode to the town of Ebenezer, which lies an hour distant.

OCTOBER 5. Today I viewed the Orphan House in Ebenezer, which is very well and comfortably laid out. In the evening went along to the new church in Ebenezer to attend prayer service. The church is very well built in the style of the country. The dear Salzburgers sing accurately and beautifully, conduct themselves reverently during the hearing of God's Word, and behave courteously toward one another.

NOVEMBER 1. Today I learned that a small sloop had arrived from Philadelphia and would return in a few days. An English merchant with whom I was acquainted sent the good news to me and reported at the same time that the captain had come from the Whitefield Orphans' Home in Georgia. I went to the merchant's where the captain from Georgia was lodging. Both of them, however, said that I ought not to take passage on the sloop to Philadelphia, for the thing was too small for this time of year (in winter) and the sea was very rough. Then I went to the Englishman who was going to Pennsylvania by land and who was an experienced seaman and asked him for advice about the sloop. He said, too, that I should not travel on it because the little ship was too small for safety from the Spaniards and the winter storms. I told him, however, that God was well able to preserve me on a little ship and, even if I were to swim there on a plank, his hand would not be shortened. Then I went back home again, considered the matter in prayer, pondered my call, and concluded that I was called, not to Charleston or Georgia, but to Pennsylvania. Afterwards I went to the captain of the Philadelphia sloop and asked him whether he would take me with him. He replied that his sloop was too small for passengers and that he had not the slightest conveniences. But since I urgently insisted, he said that it could be done if I was satisfied with things as they were. I had to pay him three guineas for passage alone, also two guineas for a bed and various necessary provisions and victuals. He did not intend, however, to sail until November 12.

NOVEMBER 12. Had my letters sent to London, said farewell to my kind host who had shown me so much kindness, and about ten o'clock sailed away from Charleston with the sloop, after having again spent three weeks and two days there amid many trials and under the patience of God. There were in all nine persons of all nationalities on our little sloop. Several had been prisoners of the Spaniards and were now returning to their homes in Philadelphia. We had no weapons whatsoever, not even a pistol. The wind was contrary today, so we got no farther than the citadel or fortress outside of Charleston, where we cast anchor.

NOVEMBER 13. Today we had contrary wind and with great difficulty reached open sea again. I had a severe attack of seasickness. These little ships or sloops toss up and down so terribly that one has to hold on securely or even tie oneself down. When the waves rise up, the little ship rises, too, and falls down again with them. Never have I experienced such a voyage!

NOVEMBER 14. The wind is very strong, contrary, and

bitterly cold. My sickness increases and makes me vomit day and night. Our ship's company curses to make one's hair stand on end. As long as I was able to speak, I admonished them, but to no avail, for it has already become second nature. To be among such people is a foretaste of hell.

NOVEMBER 15. Today the wind was still contrary and carried us out of our course into a dangerous region where the Spanish privateers have their rendezvous. Toward evening our crew saw a ship, but it did not come any nearer to us. My sickness continued and grew worse.

NOVEMBER 18. The wind became very favorable for us and so strong that we sailed nine English miles in one hour, but the waves are too great and come into our little ship in such quantity that they threaten to sink it. Since Friday evening I have not been able to eat or drink anything whatever, and now I have a high fever. I asked the captain whether it were not possible to put me ashore somewhere, but he said that he could not get ashore even if I were to give him £100 sterling.

NOVEMBER 19. During the past night the wind was so violent that we sailed more under the water than on it. The crew again lay all over us. My fever was not so high, however, that the crew could dry themselves with it. Oh, how long the minutes and quarter-hours were for me! Around me I had the soaked sailors and dreadful blasphemers, from above the rain fell on me, from below and from the sides the sea water came into my bed. In my stomach the fear of vomiting tormented; in my blood the fever raged; on my body preyed the vermin which were an accumulation of my own and those of the crew. Only one thing comforted and sustained me in patience, and that was the thought that if the ship cracked, it would go down and carry my wretched, sinful body down into the depths and let my soul come to my Redeemer. Today the wind abated and the sun shone several times. The captain thought, by his reckoning, that we must be near the cape of Pennsylvania, but we saw no land as yet, though we did see two ships in the distance. My stomach was swollen, but nevertheless I did have a little appetite.

NOVEMBER 20. Today we saw the cape of Pennsylvania and at evening we arrived in the haven by God's grace and cast anchor near Lewes.

NOVEMBER 25. In the morning, about eight o'clock, we arrived at Philadelphia. So far the Lord hath helped! I was a stranger in Philadelphia and at first did not know which way to turn. On the way I had heard by chance that Mr. Zwifler was still alive and living in Philadelphia. First I stopped off at an inn, and then sought out Mr. Zwifler. Mr. Zwifler received me kindly, and when I inquired about our German Lutherans, Mr. Zwifler said that most of them had gone over to Count Nicholas Zinzendorf; those, however, who did not adhere to Mr. Zinzendorf had accepted an old preacher named John Valentine Kraft, who had just recently come from Germany. I had already heard of this Valentine Kraft in Charleston, that he hailed from the duchy of Zweibruecken, and that he had been deposed there because of certain circumstances. Afterwards tried to rent a room for my sojourn but was unable to find a decent one. Finally I rented one from the Englishman in whose house Mr. Zwifler lived.

From Mr. Zwifler's I returned to the inn and inquired as to the location of New Hanover and Providence. The English innkeeper fetched a man who just happened to be in the city but lived in New Hanover. This resident of Hanover was an intelligent man named Philip Brandt. He narrated the state of affairs in New Hanover and said that the people there had hired a man as preacher whose profession was that of a quacksalver and whose name was N. Schmidt. The aforenamed Philip Brandt was starting out on his return journey to New Hanover that same evening. I was really exhausted and afraid of the wet weather and bad roads, yet I was loath to miss the opportunity because it seemed to have been put in my way by God. The man hired a horse for me and I busied myself to get my baggage transferred from the ship to my rented room. Toward evening rode silently out of the city with Philip Brandt and arrived in the night at a German inn ten miles from the city. There were some German men in this inn who were saying that old Mr. Valentine Kraft was to be Lutheran preacher in Philadelphia, Germantown, and Providence.

NOVEMBER 26. We rode on in the company of several German men. Toward evening we crossed over two streams, one called the Perkiomen and the other the Skippack. The streams had risen with the rains and become deep; my horse was too feeble and the current too strong, as a result of which I was half immersed in the water, and since we still had eight miles to ride I caught a chill. We arrived at Philip Brandt's dwelling at night, and there I was well cared for.

NOVEMBER 27. Early today rode farther up with Philip Brandt to a deacon of New Hanover and requested him to call together the other deacons and present elders of the Evangelical Lutheran congregations because I had something to report to them. In the afternoon four elders and two deacons met. I had the letter from the Rev. Court Preacher Frederick Michael Ziegenhagen read to them by Mr. Philip Brandt. Some of them said that it was true that they had renewed an agreement with the aforenamed Schmidt to preach, but they would also accept me and for their part respect the letter from the Rev. Court Preacher, if the congregation was satisfied.

NOVEMBER 28. About nine o'clock I rode with the deacon to the church, which is located almost in the center of New Hanover. The church is built of plain logs, erected about a year before but not yet finished on the inside. New Hanover *Town Ship* lies in a district covering about seven miles, so some have far to go to church. There is a plantation here, and another one or two miles away, and everything is woods. The women as well as the men come to church on horseback because during the winter the roads are bad and they must go through high water. Because of the inclement weather there were not so many people in the church today. The so-called preacher, Schmidt, came and sat down beside me on a chair. I told him that I intended to preach my inaugural sermon and relieve him. He behaved very politely and said that he did not want to be in my way. After the sermon I read to the congregation the letter from the Rev. Court Preacher Ziegenhagen, as the deacons and elders had requested. In the afternoon had a number of brief visits during which I was able to speak a few good words. Some were happy over the situation, hoping that in time order would be restored. Others who were attached to Schmidt were not fully satisfied and thought that their old preacher Schmidt ought not to be discharged, and that even though he was not ordained and often drank to excess, he did preach edifying sermons. They felt that he could remain at least as an assistant and preach when I was not there. Others, who had long been separated, said that they would not allow themselves to be deceived again. They had already been taken in so often, and who knew whether I had not written the letters myself? Finally some had also taken offense at the salary mentioned in the reading of the letter and said they would have nothing to do with the affair, for it might be that this would lay a burden upon them and their descendants which would not be so easy to throw off. The deacons and elders are unable to do anything about it, for in religious and church matters each has the right to do what he pleases. The government has nothing to do with it and will not concern itself with such matters. Everything depends on the vote of the majority. A preacher must fight his way through with the sword of the Spirit alone.

NOVEMBER 29. Today three of the elders traveled with me to Providence to confer with the deacons there. We stopped in at the home of the widow of a former deacon and had the oldest deacon summoned to come there. I showed him the letter from the Rev. Court Preacher Ziegenhagen. He recognized the signature and said that he was glad I had come, that they had lost hope and no longer expected anyone from the Rev. Court Preacher. Since they had received no answer to their last letter of 1739, they had petitioned the Darmstadt Consistory the year before for a preacher. Thereupon an old preacher, Valentine Kraft, had arrived a few weeks ago and said that he had been sent by the consistory, though Mr. Kraft had brought no testimonials and had arrived in a destitute and wretched state. He pretended, however, that his letter and testimonials would still come. Moreover, there were many people here who had known him as a pastor in Germany. It was the opinion of this old deacon, too, that I should have an understanding with Mr. Kraft and either remain with the two lower places or the two upper places. I let the matter rest for the present.

NOVEMBER 30. The oldest deacon of Providence journeyed with me to the younger deacons and then to Philadelphia, where we arrived about nine o'clock in the evening, fatigued. I had to stop off again at an English inn on account of the horse I had hired. The innkeeper took me into a room where were sitting a number of Englishmen who put on airs of being men of *condition.* As soon as I came in, they asked me whether I was a *Moravian,* a *Lutherien,* a *Calvinist,* or a *Churchman.* I gave them a reprimand and said they must learn better manners and not welcome strangers with such questions. They apologized. Afterwards went to my rented room.

DECEMBER 1. The deacon from Providence came to get me and took me to a German inn where I was to speak with Mr. Valentine Kraft. Mr. Kraft welcomed me and said in the presence of some German people that he would take care of me all right and put me in a place for which I would be best suited. I even received a polite reprimand for having left Philadelphia on the first day of my arrival and gone to the country without getting in touch with Mr. Kraft. I was already conscious of what a comedy this was to be, but *acquiesced* under God's *direction.* I learned forthwith that Mr. Kraft had traveled through the whole province of Pennsylvania, appointed deacons and elders here and there, and established a general presbytery in the whole country and a special presbytery, as he called it, in Philadelphia. And besides all this, he had organized a consistory of which he was the president and Mr. John Caspar Stoever, the *assessor.* The *assessor,* Stoever, is a bookbinder whom the scoundrelly collector, Frederick Schultze, appointed a so-called Lutheran preacher here in a barn and thus conferred the dignity of ordination upon his

10

disreputable behavior. The purpose of the presbytery was to make it possible for Valentine Kraft and his *assessor* to travel around the country and carry on their trade with the holy sacraments. The consistory served the purpose of letting him ordain a few more lazy and drunken schoolmasters and place them as preachers in vacant places. He enjoys great respect because our poor, ignorant Lutherans are pushed into the corner by the Moravians on the one hand, and on the other are duped by his windy boasting.

DECEMBER 8. Today there came to me a man named Peter Boehler, who had been sent by Count Zinzendorf. He made inquiries about my call and my circumstances, and in kindness I gave him the information I thought necessary. I asked him about several things I had heard concerning him in Georgia and concluded with a conversation on the Moravian church.

DECEMBER 14. The elders accepted me and took me to a fine man who had a small room, where I was to live. The people here in the country have only one room in their houses, which is occupied by the whole family, so this proffered opportunity was all the more desirable to me because I could occupy the room alone. The congregation had conceived a suspicion that Mr. Kraft wanted to abduct me. They therefore urgently pressed me to remain with them and let Philadelphia go because it was too far away and Mr. Kraft could very well look after it. There was still another circumstance which made it necessary for me to stay up in New Hanover a while longer. Because I had been absent from New Hanover for two Sundays since my first sermon, the one party had demanded that their old preacher, the empiric Schmidt, should preach to them. He had declined, however, and said that he would preach if they brought him a written permission from me. So since Schmidt had withdrawn himself in this way, I looked upon it as a *direction* of God and promised to remain there for a time. I could not forsake Philadelphia, however, until they themselves discharged me or until I had been released by my superiors.

The Year 1743

JANUARY 2. In the forenoon I learned that Count Zinzendorf left the city the night before, about nine o'clock, with a train of his followers. He is going to New York and from there to London. I preached to our congregation in the Swedish church in the morning and installed the deacons and elders. I said to the congregation that exception might be taken to them, but that after all they were a fair representation, for as was the congregation, so also were the deacons and elders, and as were the deacons and elders, so was the congregation; they must all be improved together. I set forth to the congregation its obligations, and to the deacons their duties, and had the members of the congregation come forward and give their hands to their deacons.

JANUARY 4. Our deacons gave me a horse and accompanied me up to Providence. Mr. Kraft now took off his hypocritical mask because it no longer yielded any returns in Philadelphia. He became the boon companion of some worthless, drunken schoolmasters who wander about the country as preachers and make money with the Lord's Supper, baptism, and weddings. He got drunk with these fellows and carried on high.

JANUARY 5. We celebrated the festival of the Epiphany in Providence and I preached to the congregation again in the barn. The people in this congregation are eager and attentive to hear the Word. The dear deacons of this congregation are determined to begin the building of the church in God's name. I have already announced it twice to the congregation and encouraged them to pray and trust in God. A church is extremely necessary to us. With this end in view, I have written a letter and have had it circulated among the congregation by the deacons for subscriptions as to what each member will contribute as a freewill offering. We have no lack of food here, God be thanked, but

12

money is rare, since the country people must carry their produce to the city and receive very little for it.

It is not a good thing to build of wood here because it decays quickly, and it is expensive to build of stone. It is estimated that a stone church will cost all of £200 sterling. God has been guiding the people's hearts aright and made them eager to build, for after we visited the entire congregation, almost £100 current money has been subscribed. One pound sterling equals one and a half pounds current money. The congregation has taken hold with utter earnestness, as everyone acknowledges. We hope to devote to this purpose the third portion of the rest of the collection monies which are deposited with His Reverence [in Halle]. But where is the rest to come from? May the merciful God awaken hearts in Europe to come to our aid! The members of the congregation are so united that they are already hauling stones to the site, which makes me very happy.

JANUARY 9. I preached at New Hanover to a large assembly; after the sermon had also to baptize before the congregation. Because the schoolmasters, already described, intended to establish opposition congregations in various places and thus vex me, I made two announcements to the congregation: (1) They were not to pay anything when they had their children baptized, and also (2) at the Lord's Supper there was to be no offering of money at the altar for the pastor. Since those vagabonds are concerned only to get a few shillings for a baptism and the offerings at the Lord's Supper and thus produce much strife, thereby giving the sects good cause for slander, I have abolished the abominable custom, considering that there is no need to pay the pastor his salary just at the occasion of the sacred services. Anyone who desires to give toward the necessary support of the pastor can easily find a more suitable time and occasion.

Since there is also great ignorance among the youth in this country and good schoolmasters are rare, I was forced to take a hand in this myself. Those who might possibly be able to teach the children a little reading are lazy and given to drink. They patch together a sermon out of all sorts of books, wander around, preach, and administer the communion for cash in hand. It is a shocking pity and shame! I announced to the congregation that they should send to me their older children for school, because I intended to remain in each congregation for a week successively.

JANUARY 10. Some of the parents brought their children to me. Things look pretty bad when children seventeen, eighteen, nineteen, and twenty years old come with their A-B-C books. Yet I am happy that the children have such great eagerness to learn something.

JANUARY 15. Today I closed my school for this time. The children give me joy and good hope. In the forenoon I had to give holy communion to an old woman of the congregation ninety years of age; the woman delighted me with her believing conversation. In the afternoon was summoned to the other congregation in Providence. Last Sunday I also set forth the great need for a school building to the congregation in New Hanover. The wooden church has not been finished on the inside, it is true, but we can make it do if necessary. A few members of the congregation remained in the church after the service and indicated by subscription what they would give toward a school building. The total of what a few members are willing to give toward the building of a school was near £17 current money, which is a good beginning, it is true, but by far not enough.

JANUARY 18. A strong, cold, and stormy wind and frost set in. We were obliged to run to keep warm and get through, arriving safely in the city of Philadelphia in the evening.

The Anglicans in Philadelphia have their fine church; the Swedes, too; the Quakers have their *meetings;* the *Moravians* have a church house; the Catholics have their church buildings and are growing apace. Almost all the sects have their church buildings and *meetings;* the Germans alone have nothing in such a large city.

Twenty or thirty years ago one could have obtained a place for a church and cemetery in the city for very little money. Now there is scarcely a place in the city to be bought, or if there is one for sale as large as a small acre, they can demand £400, £500, or £600, depending on its location in the city. True, it is easier to get a place for ground rent, but they demand two and a half, three, and even four shillings per foot annually. At this rate one would have to pay ten, twelve, or more pounds sterling ground rent for a poor place for a church. Nevertheless, the places for sale as well as for ground rent grow dearer every day, and the Lutherans are increasing every year. The longer the matter of building a church is left standing, the more difficult and impossible it becomes. We decided, therefore, to present these circumstances to the congregation. I wrote out a number of points concerning the matter.

JANUARY 25. The deacons had made an appointment with a master mason in order to come to an agreement with regard to the church building. We were unable to agree, however, because what he asked was far too high and dear. Craftsmen here are very expensive. Our poor members are doing what they can and have already, to make a beginning, hauled to the site several hundred loads of stone which is being quarried elsewhere. This will not go far, however, and we must do still better.

FEBRUARY 14. Our elders and deacons have exerted themselves to the utmost for a church site, but many obstacles have been encountered. The Quakers are the owners of most of the sites here, and as such they have the upper hand and will not sell even a foot of it. Indeed, they even refuse to release any for ground rent when they hear that a church is to be built on it.

I have no lack of things to eat and drink, God be praised, and my clothes are still holding out, though they are subject to much wear on account of much traveling back and forth. Also I have to keep house in three places, that is to say, one in each congregation. But if I seek first the kingdom of God, the rest will be added unto me, for one man brings me a sausage, another a piece of meat, a third a chicken, a fourth a loaf of bread, a fifth some pigeons, a sixth rabbits, a seventh eggs, an eighth some tea and sugar, a ninth some honey, a tenth some apples, and eleventh partridges, and so forth. The parents, especially of the

15

children I instruct, when they have anything which they think particularly good, bring it to the pastor.

MARCH-APRIL.   In the week before Easter the gracious God gave us a lot for the church in the center of the city. It is an excellent piece of ground, and has room also for a graveyard. It cost somewhat more than £100 sterling; and if we were to sell it now, we could get £20 sterling more than we paid for it. The necessity of our undertaking, with the help of God, to build a church in Philadelphia, is continually growing more and more apparent. If it is not done, the time would soon come when there would be no hope at all for our little Lutheran group. On April 5 we laid the cornerstone of the first German Lutheran church in Philadelphia. The Swedish pastor from another place, who occasionally conducts services in the Swedish church which is now vacant, was present. The English pastor also had intended to be there, but an urgent call made it necessary for him to take a trip into the country. There was an immense crowd of people in attendance, foes as well as friends.

Muhlenberg's Journals for the years 1744 and 1745 have been lost, and only a few 1746 entries survive. During this time the St. Michael's church building was completed in Philadelphia and the still-existing church at Providence was built. In 1745 Muhlenberg married Anna Maria Weiser, daughter of a notable frontiersman, Conrad Weiser, whose skillful and friendly negotiations with the Indians of the Six Nations were important in the history of the American colonies. The Muhlenbergs built a house near the church in Providence where they lived until 1761. Here most of the eleven Muhlenberg children were born; the first, John Peter Gabriel, was born October 1, 1746.

The Year 1747

In Providence a Reformed neighbor married his daughter to a man of our congregation. I had to perform the ceremony and hence was invited to be present at the wedding festivities. As it is the custom in this country for a number of friends to be present, be they of the same religion or none at all, so on this occasion, too, there were some present who scoff at churches and preachers. It is for this reason that I would sometimes rather be in a foul-smelling prison than in such company. On this occasion there was a mixed company present, chiefly of uninvited guests. The bride's parents placed me, together with a number of our Lutheran and Reformed people, in a room by ourselves and left the young people and the others in an adjoining room.

We sought edification among ourselves and also sang some hymns. The scoffers in the next room began to act as if mad, disturbing me and giving no little offense to some of our young people. This grieved me and, after admonishing them several times in vain, I went home, and others with me. After I had gone, the unruly people did not rest until they had seduced the young people into dancing. Some of the young people whom I had prepared for the Lord's Supper withdrew and would have nothing to do with the frivolity. Several, however, did join in and take part in it, and the others told me about it. The parents of the bride apologized and said that they had been unable to do anything to stop it because the shameless people, fearing neither God nor man, would pay no attention to them, and besides they had not invited them to the wedding; they had come of their own accord.

There is a reason why such people are tolerated to some extent and why there is some hesitation to offend them. The country people are isolated and do not live near one another.

Their entire wealth consists of cattle and grain. The grain is stored either in barns or stacked in open fields. If the head of a house should give offense to some insolent Irishman or brutal German, he may very likely find that some harm has been done to his cattle or crops during the night, since everything stands out in the open, exposed to the revenge and spite of such callous people. Even before a man looks out of his house at night his barn and all his possessions may be completely burned, and before he is able to summon the aid of a neighbor or the justice of the peace, the enemy may already have perpetrated the utmost damage and fled several miles away into the forest.

MONTH OF MARCH. I had on several occasions been urged to visit a number of Lutherans who live in the northwestern mountains forty-six miles from my home. I made the journey because a number of the poor members of our congregation in New Hanover had moved there and, thinking back on the services they used to have, invited me to pay them a visit. The people there are making a poor and precarious living and lack both bodily and spiritual nourishment. Some of them are growing up wild and have no further interest in churches and schools.

The reasons why I am invited to come to these various distant places are the following: Our German Evangelical settlers in Pennsylvania are, for the most part, the most recent immigrants to this province. The English and German Quakers, Inspired, Mennonites, Separatists, and the like small denominations came to this country in the earlier, good times when land was still very cheap. These people selected the best and most fertile regions and so enriched themselves that they and their heirs now have firmly established homes and estates. In later years, however, when the poor Evangelicals also found the way and came to this country in great numbers, some of them, it is true, who had paid their passage and been shrewd in business, were able to snatch up some of the rich land here and there, but most of them had to be slaves for several years to repay their passage and then make shift with the poorer lands and struggle to make a living by the sweat of their brows. But finally, even poor land was no longer to be had, so great numbers of the poor rented the surplus land of those who had been here first. The rich, however, are raising their rents so high that the poor are unable to hold out. Hence they are moving farther and farther into the wilderness. Those who possess land have acquired large families which have also been obliged to move on.

So now these people, who were under our spiritual care for a time and were forced by necessity to go to the still uncultivated wilderness regions, write the most affecting letters from time to time, lamenting their hunger for the Word of God. They also tell their neighbors how good they once had it and how they wish they could hear the Word of Life again in the desert where there is no water. I have noticed that within the five years of my being here scarcely half of the original members of the country congregations are left. Some of the other half departed into eternity, but most of them have gone to distant parts, forty, fifty, sixty, seventy, eighty, ninety miles, one, two, and three hundred miles away to the borders of Pennsylvania and to Maryland and Virginia. Meanwhile, the congregations have not decreased, but rather have increased every year, because every year more and more Germans come in and those remaining settle their children around them as far as they are still able to find room and sustenance. It is perhaps also true that some move away from our regions who have an antipathy and repugnance to churches and schools and prefer to dwell in darkness where their works will not be exposed to the light. Consequently we, here and in distant parts, must pass through honor and dishonor, through evil report and good report, but we rejoice that the Gospel is being spread abroad in the wilderness and the name of Jesus is being made known.

JUNE 10. I set out from New Hanover with the schoolmaster, Jacob Loeser. Eight miles from New Hanover we stopped in at the home of an old man, one of the sect called Newborn, who had married Kaesebier's widow some twenty years ago, and begotten with her five children, whom I had instructed and baptized at the mother's request without the father's consent.

The old man had been a little awakened many years ago in the Palatinate. The awakening, however, went no further than that he separated from the Reformed church and the Lord's Supper and refused to give the oath of loyalty to the then ruling elector, for which he was examined by the consistory and imprisoned. According to his opinion he had been persecuted and expelled for the sake of Christ and the truth, but as a matter of fact he was only confirmed in his stubbornness.

When he came to this country, he joined the turbulent sect of people who call themselves the Newborn. This sect claims the new birth, which they receive suddenly through immediate inspiration and heavenly visions, through dreams and the like. When they receive the new birth in this way, they are God and Christ himself, can no longer sin, and are infallible. They therefore use nothing from God's Word except those passages which, taken out of their context, appear to favor their false tenets. The holy sacraments are to them ridiculous, and their expressions concerning them are extremely offensive.

JUNE 11. We rode eight miles farther to a place where the Lutherans and the Reformed had built a church together and where they were in controversy with one another. The members of both faiths are so intermarried in this country that here you will find a Lutheran husband with a Reformed wife and there a Reformed husband with a Lutheran wife. So occasionally the two parties have made trial of building a common church. They are so distantly situated that they cannot very well be looked after by us, as far as the interests of our people are concerned. Nor are they able to support a regular pastor; the consequence is that our people elect as pastors the schoolmasters who have come of their own accord, and the Reformed do the same thing. This is what they did at this place, saying they would rather have something than nothing at all, otherwise the people would have scattered among the sects. In general, such preachers are not only ignorant but unconverted besides. They do not know the fundamental truths of religion, but they affect only the outward forms and dispute about such matters as altar and table, the bread and the host, the preacher's robe and vestments, about whether to say *Vater Unser* or *Unser Vater*. This gives rise to heated religious disputes and disgraceful word battles among the common people—between husbands and wives, among neighbors, parents, children, relatives, and friends. The other sects turn this to their advantage and run down the whole on the basis of such individual cases.

This little church had begun and ended in strife, and no disposition had yet been made either of the church's ground or the building. And now since both parties asked me to make a transfer of the land and the deeds of the church, I thought of the future, when a regular pastor might be put there, and transferred and settled the affair in accord with the current English laws of the land, admonishing both sides to true repentance, faith, and godly harmony until such time as God would grant further opportunity to aid them. Their preachers, however, continued the quarrel in opposition to the deed, the Reformed preacher being the worst offender, until the party was obliged by law to lose its rights, take back what had been contributed to the cost, and leave the church to the Lutherans alone. The Lutherans thereupon discharged their preacher, Streiter, and have now taken as their preacher Magister Tobias Wagner, who lives near by.

In the afternoon we rode sixteen miles farther up, and at evening arrived in Tulpehocken at the home of my father-in-law, Conrad Weiser.

JUNE 19. We journeyed from Tulpehocken to the new city of Lancaster, which is thirty miles away by road, and arrived toward evening. On the way a man, at whose place we stopped, told us that several days previously Mr. Laurentius Nyberg's proselytes, whom he had gained in and around the city for the Moravians, had journeyed to Bethlehem to attend a celebration.

JUNE 21. In the afternoon had to ride twenty-two miles farther because I had promised to preach in Maryland on June 24. Ten miles beyond Lancaster we came to the broad river called the Susquehanna. This river, which is one and a half miles

21

broad, we safely crossed before nightfall, although we had storm and heavy rain while on the water.

We rode twelve miles farther through the night and about twelve o'clock arrived in the new city called York. These dear people in the city (some of them even congregated in the middle of the night) were overjoyed at our arrival and expected that I would administer the Lord's Supper to them next Sunday, as had been previously announced by letters.

JUNE 22. We rode twenty-one miles farther to the extreme border of Pennsylvania, where again I found a congregation in like dissension. A few deacons and elders adhered to Mr. Nyberg, and the rest were against him and his hypocritical procedures. I sought to reconcile them in love and promised that they would be visited occasionally whenever one of us came to York and, if possible, I would assign to them a schoolmaster who would take charge of their poor children and read an edifying sermon for the adults on Sunday.

JUNE 23. Preached there in a large barn because many people had gathered from far and wide. I found a number of acquaintances there who had been members of my congregation down below during my first years.

About two o'clock in the afternoon we rode away from this place with two men who had come to meet us from Monocacy in Maryland. We rode nearly eighteen miles before we even saw a house and were forced to continue through heavy rain and muddy roads because night was coming on. Finally the roads became so deep with water that the horses had to wade through it almost up to their knees, and the rain poured down so copiously that we could scarcely see one another. About twelve o'clock midnight we arrived at our lodging half-dead, completely tired out, wet, and ill, having covered thirty-six miles within ten hours in a continuous downpour of rain.

JUNE 24. The heavy rain continued. We went to the church where most of our people and also a few of those who were Zinzendorf-minded were present. Before we began divine service, I had them give me the church book and I wrote in it in English would have to go among them and master their language, adopt as much of their custom, dress, and manner of life as could be done without sin, and for the rest rebuke their national vice by a holy life. (2) They would have to translate our revealed historical and dogmatic truths into their language and make these matters as clear as possible. (3) They would have to learn the Indian melodies and tones and propagate the Law and the Gospel with these tones so that it would make an impression, and then with God's blessing and help await the fruitage, etc.

JULY 6-7. Journeyed home to Providence with my companion and found my colleague Mr. Peter Brunnholtz and Pastor John Christopher Hartwick on a visit at my house. After a few days colleague Brunnholtz complained of pulsation and fermentation of the blood. Because I had no more of the blessed medicine from Halle, because the illness grew increasingly worse, and because genuine *doctores medicinae* are rare in this country, I had to muddle through as best I could. I cleansed the *primae viae,* used a mild sudorific made of local roots, and thus helped nature so that on the third and fourth day the malignancy broke out and the patient became completely covered with measles. I kept him in a constant, steady sweat, so that the measles would gradually become ripe and would not be driven in; nor did we cease to pray publicly and in private for his recovery. I also took a small glassful of bezoar powder, which did a great deal of good. While nature was busy bringing the measles to maturity, we kept the bowels closed until the *materia peccans* had lost its power. Then we opened the bowels again and purged off the residuum with a mild laxative. The dear God granted his blessing, and Mr. Brunnholtz was soon on his feet again. He was very sick and delirious until the measles came to maturity. Not many young and strong people have died of this disease.

several brief articles to the effect that in this country the subjects of His Majesty King George enjoy the free exercise of religion; that the Lutherans adhere to the Holy Word of the prophets and apostles, to the Unaltered Augsburg Confession and the rest of the symbolical documents, and have the sacraments administered to them in a regular manner by regularly called and ordained preachers in accord with the Word and the Confessions; that they will not suffer open, gross, willful sinners against the holy Ten Commandments of God and the laws of the government to be considered among them as true members, and so on. I read this publicly to the congregation and explained it to them in the German language.

JUNE 25. We rode several miles farther to a newly founded town, where lived a number of Lutherans who belonged to the congregation but were unable to be present on the previous day on account of the heavy rain. Most of them signed their names to the articles in the church book and they also elected several from their midst as deacons and elders. The remaining two or three have joined with my former predecessor in New Hanover, the empiric Schmidt, who had been in Virginia for a period and had now returned. A large gathering of German and also English people was present. After much supplication, prayer, and preparation, I administered communion to a few Lutherans, baptized children, and married two couples. Both groups, in the town and in the country, begged me to take to heart their grievous and scattered condition, their poverty and need for a teacher, and to help them if at all possible. They would abide by their articles as far as possible and firmly hope that we would not wholly forget them.

JUNE 26. We set out on the return journey.

JULY 4. Journeyed to one of the Tulpehocken congregations, called "on the Northkill," conducted preparatory and confessional service with some satisfaction because those present were very attentive and considerably moved. Back again in the evening.

JULY 5. In the forenoon preached in this congregation on

the Gospel concerning the lost sheep; baptized several children; and examined and confirmed the young people. I administered communion, which was attended by an unusual degree of awakening in the congregation, and afterwards hastened nine miles farther to the larger congregation, which had been appointed to meet about three o'clock in the afternoon; preached there and said farewell, because I now had to return to my regular congregations.

As we were riding home with my father-in-law after the service, we met on the road a *regulus* or Indian king or chief of a savage nation. He had with him a grown son and son-in-law on horseback and was desirous of conferring with Mr. Conrad Weiser concerning certain land and war affairs. When one looks at these poor people, one deplores their blindness and darkness; and when they look at us, they think we are to be deplored, which is true in so far as we have the light and for the most part do not walk in the light, but love darkness more than the light! A long time ago the French papist fathers from Canada made an attempt to convert these savage nations, but accomplished nothing among them because several of them transgressed the Sixth Commandment, the stories of which they still know how to tell.

According to Mr. Weiser's description, they are very wise and shrewd in natural things and, though they do not possess the art of writing, they have the faculty of knowing and remembering many events of the distant past because they have been diligently handed down and preserved by oral traditions. Toward the white people as a whole they have a deeply rooted prejudice and secret mistrust, and they believe that we grew out of the earth on the other side of the ocean and that they grew out of the earth on this side of the ocean. They say that the white people should have remained on their own ground and lived there and not have bothered them. We came over here with no other purpose than to take their land away from them, to decrease their catch of game, fish, and birds, to drive them farther into the wilderness, and to make their life more difficult. They also complain that

their nations have been depleted by diseases, drunkenness, orderliness, and suicide since they received from the white p the strong, fiery drinks.

When one tries to explain to them something out o revealed Word of God, in the first place, their language lac essential phrases and expressions with which to conve spiritual and heavenly truths and make them understand best one is able to express with their phrases a natural t and the historical truths of the Word of God. Mr. We occasionally endeavored to tell them something out of th of Moses.

But even if one is able in their language to quote and the historical truths in some fashion, they reply: "What has revealed to you on the other side of the ocean m true, but that has nothing to do with us; our God ha other things to us on this side. You abide by your affa will abide by ours." When the English and French at war, they are not anxious to join with either side; to be bribed and won over with enormous gifts. The remain neutral and accept gifts from both nations; that both white nations will only weaken each ot Indians will not finally be annihilated and extermina Yet they would much rather see the English vi remain on top because they get goods more cheapl than from the French. Their histories of times of w covenants and treaties are transmitted by certain wi who are no longer able to support themselves. The occasionally come together to have the history sun one of these old professors of history. They bri from the hunt and for it receive the tradition. Th tones and kinds of melodies. There are certain ton of the body according to whether the subject n sad, or indifferent.

It is the opinion of Mr. Weiser that if an a made toward their conversion, the following others, would have to be observed: (1) One or

The Year 1748

This year God is visiting upon our land an epidemic sickness called pleurisy, which at certain times quite suddenly snatches away many people. When the almighty and sovereign Ruler of the world desires to discipline and punish men, he uses his otherwise beneficent elements for chastisement. After an exceptionally hot summer, a warm autumn, and a mild winter here, the sickness usually breaks out violently in January, February, March, and part of April.

An English doctor in Virginia ascribes it to the following causes: (1) In our *climate* the air is very clear and thin and does not have power sufficiently to press the *globuli sanguinis* in the lungs and thereby keep them in a fluid state, which has its effect upon the whole *massa sanguinis* and causes it to become viscid. (2) The sudden and frequent changes in the weather (since frequently it is exceptionally hot during one half of the day and exceptionally cold the other half, owing to wind and rain) cause *obstructions in the viae secretionis* and increase the viscidity. (3) The inhabitants of this country subsist mostly on such foods as contain much viscous fluid and make the blood thick and cohesive. (4) In the middle of August the nights are cold; the days, however, ordinarily remain very hot until October. As long as the nights here remain warm and the days are warm, too, nature is able to expel the coarse material as well as the *subtile* material through the *pores;* but when the cold nights set in and the days continue hot, the *laxatio partium solidarum* and *tenacitas sanguinis* occasioned by the heat and the *constrictio pororum* occasioned by the cold cause the material of perspiration to be not sufficiently broken up and expelled through the *pori cuticulares.* The finest, volatile parts, it is true, go through the constricted passages, but the coarsest remain, etc. (5) Then when

27

a sharp, winter air comes, the blood gradually coagulates and causes stagnation in the arteries of the lungs and occasionally also in the *pleura,* mostly, however, in the lungs, which are spongy and soft, and the sharp air is more apt to hasten the coagulation in their vesicles and blood vessels. He recommends blood-letting after the first onset and the true symptoms appear, and a root, native to this country and used for poisonous snake-bite, which thins the blood within twenty-four hours and which has helped to alleviate this condition in many persons.

God has very graciously spared our country congregations, while all around us many have been carried off. In one district, covering sixteen miles on the other side of the Schuylkill, about fifty women were widowed. In several instances every member of the home and family died, especially among the English. This chastisement fills many with terror and is teaching them to give heed to the Word, whereas before they simply went on living in security, thinking of nothing but their bellies.

In February I made another trip to the little congregation in Upper Milford and Saucon. We had about two and a half feet of snow. I thought the road would be open, but was unable to find the road except for nine or ten miles, and then it was so bad that I had to ride on into the night to cover the ten miles. It was night when I got between the mountains into an unusually deep valley where there are deep swamps and holes and the snow lay very deep. I could not very well go back, and it was still six miles farther to my quarters; there was no road and I could not see the snow-covered holes. First I rode two miles in the wrong direction toward the left and had to work my way laboriously back again. After that I kept to the road pretty well, but several times I fell suddenly with the poor horse through the snow and soft ice into the swamp and had to work my way out again with God's help. The horse became weary and reluctant to go through the unbeaten tracks of deep snow, so I was obliged to walk ahead on foot and make a track for the horse, which exhausted me greatly, and I still had three miles to go. I would have been glad to sit down in sheer weariness, but it was so bitterly cold and I was perspiring so profusely that I did not dare to rest and risk a sleep of death. I once more summoned up my remaining energies in the name of the Lord and finally reached my lodgings safely that same night. Had I remained on the road, my enemies would probably have jeered and said that I had died drunk, since I had no witnesses with me.

I was unusually encouraged on this trip to the congregations because I perceived a number of beneficent stirrings of the Spirit of God. Sometimes one would rather stay home when the bad roads and weather set in; but since one's coming must usually be announced several weeks in advance and the people must gather from considerable distances, the sectarian people profit by it if one fails to come. They say to our people, "That's the way your parsons are; they promise much, but keep little."

APRIL 28. We consulted together in Providence with regard to a suitable liturgy which we could introduce for use in our congregations. True, we had been using a small formulary heretofore, but had nothing definite and harmonious in all its parts, since we had thought it best to wait for the arrival of more laborers and also until we had acquired a better knowledge of conditions in this country.

To adopt the Swedish liturgy did not appear either suitable or necessary since most of our congregations came from the districts on the Rhine and the Main and considered the singing of collects to be papistical. Nor could we select a liturgy with regard to every individual's accustomed use since almost every town and village has its own. We therefore took the liturgy of the Savoy Church in London as the basis, cut out parts and added to it according to what seemed to us profitable and edifying in these circumstances. This we adopted tentatively, until we had a better understanding of the matter, in order that the same ceremonies, forms, and words might be used in all our congregations.

We thought of using at the distribution of the consecrated bread and wine the words of the Lord Jesus: "Take and eat, this is the body of Jesus Christ." etc. At the baptism of children we intended to ask the sponsors or godparents: "Do you in the name of this child renounce?" etc. On these points our opponents tried to stir up agitation even before we had finished our work. We consequently made the changes at once and put in the words which the troubled consciences wanted, saying, "This is the true body," etc.

NOVEMBER 5. In this past sixth year of my Pennsylvania pilgrimage I administered the Lord's Supper twice in each of my regular congregations and outparishes, omitting only two Sundays when I had to be absent and when the congregations were served by my fellow ministers. I baptized about one hundred and thirteen; confirmed thirty-eight young people; and buried about twenty-nine persons.

I am worn out from much riding; I am incapacitated for study; I cannot even manage my own household because I must be away most of the time. The Reverend Fathers called me for only three years on trial, but the dear God has doubled the three years and upheld me all this time with forbearance. I write this not out of any discontent or slothfulness, but out of the feeling of spiritual and physical incapacity and a yearning desire to achieve a little more quietude where I could gather my thoughts better, spend more time with my wife and children, and bring them up in the nurture and admonition of the Lord.

During this year a great deal has been conjectured and said about a hostile attack by the Spanish and French. Consequently there are two chief parties here among the English and they have entered into a violent newspaper war before the Spaniards and the French have come. The Quakers, who are the foremost party in this province, have on their side the German book publisher Christopher Sauer, who controls the Mennonites, Separatists, Anabaptists, and the like with his printed works and lines them up with the Quakers. All of these speak and write against the war and reject even the slightest defense as ungodly and contrary to the command of Jesus Christ.

The church party has the English book publishers on its side and they maintain in speech and printed word that defense is not contrary to God's command, but right and necessary and in accord with the laws of nature. This party makes use of the preachers of the Episcopal and Presbyterian churches on its side. The latter party held several lotteries and used the proceeds to build a fortification on the coast; they have organized for defense, dividing up into companies and regiments which drill at regular times.

Our pastors' association has been sharply watched to see which side we would turn to. We said, however, that we had been sent to preach to our people repentance to God and faith in the Lord Jesus, and hence we could not mix in political affairs unless we had express orders from our highest or provincial government; accordingly we remained silent. Graciously give us peace, Lord God, in our time. Amen.

The little group of Lutheran preachers in America was slowly strengthened by recruits from Germany; three came in 1745, one in 1748. They organized a ministerium in 1748, with Muhlenberg acknowledged as the leader to exercise supervision among the pastors and congregations. In 1749 Muhlenberg continued his parish labors and pastoral oversight.

The Year 1750

In the month of July my father-in-law, Mr. Weiser, was commissioned by the royal government of Virginia to undertake a mission to the savage nations dwelling on the borders of Canada. In order to reach there, he had to travel more than three hundred miles through the provinces of Jersey and New York. Since his journey would take him near the place where Pastor Hartwick is stationed and since we owed Pastor Hartwick and his congregations a visit, Mr. Weiser offered to take one of us along without expense. Pastor Hartwick had entered into our fellowship and had visited us several times at his own expense. On this account he had been slandered and called a Herrnhuter [or Moravian] by the New York preachers and various malcontents in his congregations to the detriment of his office. He had always encouraged his congregation by saying that one of us would pay a return visit. Now that this visit had never taken place, the slander began to grow and spread and even the well-disposed members of his congregations began to think that perhaps he had not visited us at all, but rather the Herrnhuters in Pennsylvania.

In short, it was hypothetically necessary that one of us should make the journey. I therefore conferred with my colleagues and would have been glad to see one of them accept the task, but they were all kind enough to push it off on me. Mr. Hartwick had made his journeys by water, but I was necessitated to go by land with my traveling companions and cover a distance of about 210 miles from my house to Pastor Hartwick's. I still had my old, stiff horse which had stuck fast in the ice the preceding year, but I started out on the journey with it in God's name.

AUGUST 16.   Rode thirty miles to Mr. Ludolph Schrenck's, whom I found well and cheerful at his post in Saucon.

AUGUST 17.   Traveled six miles farther with Mr. Schrenck to

Bethlehem, where Mr. Weiser had already arrived and was waiting for me with his companions, having been invited to drink coffee with the Zinzendorfer Bishop J. C. F. Cammerhof. We were taken into the bishop's house, courteously treated, and entertained with a little political conversation, as the time was too short to enter any sort of dispute concerning the *plans*. They have erected several large, massive buildings for use as churches and common houses and they have a considerable number of people there, especially children. The surrounding country is very pleasant to the natural eye, as a broad river, called the Lehigh, flows on one side and on the other the land rises gradually to high mountains.

In the afternoon Mr. Schrenck returned and we left Bethlehem. We traveled ten miles farther over a beautiful level road to Nazareth, the other famous dwelling place of the Zinzendorfers, which, however, is to be looked upon as only a sort of farmstead, in comparison with Bethlehem, and is inhabited by farmers and the like. Bishop Cammerhof told Mr. Weiser that several weeks before he had been among the same savages whom he was going to visit and expressed some doubt concerning his mission to them. From Nazareth we traveled five miles farther to an inn, where we lodged for the night. I was afflicted with such a severe *catarrhal* fever that I was scarcely able to utter a sound, which made the journey very difficult for me. Several days before my departure it had been unusually hot weather and I had had to do some riding at nights, which in August are already cold and damp and very apt to cause illnesses. My wife had let blood from my hand and pierced it a little too deep, so I had to travel with a swollen hand. All in all, a speechless rider with a swollen hand on an old stiff horse, I presented a rather sorry figure.

AUGUST 18. We started out early, ascended a high mountain, and had to lead our horses for several miles between rocks and stones. We covered about thirty-six miles on this day and at evening stopped in at the place of a Dutchman of rank who knew Mr. Weiser and insisted upon inviting him and the whole company to stay with him. This man lives on the border of

Pennsylvania, appears to be from the old nobility, and for some years had been a justice of the peace. However, he had not been very well versed in English law, and besides he lived rather remote from the higher and more learned authorities. Hence, when a quarrel was brought before him, he was not always able to help, and at times he could do nothing but advise both parties to go out in the courtyard and settle the matter with their fists. Whenever this happened, they had to become reconciled and go home in peace. This finally led to his resigning his office, and he withdrew from the world and its turmoil and went into retirement. He was now very old. He spoke in a very Christian and edifying manner and he prayed before and after meals and also before going to sleep, so devoutly and impressively that we were struck with admiration and our hearts were filled with joy.

AUGUST 19. We left Pennsylvania and passed over the broad River Delaware into the province of Jersey. We traveled about thirty-two miles on this day. In the evening we visited a Dutch Reformed preacher and discussed various edifying subjects so far as the occasion would allow. My *catarrh* grew worse and caused me great embarrassment, for when a preacher cannot speak he is the poorest creature, etc.

AUGUST 20. We covered about forty miles, the first part along the Delaware River near the border of Pennsylvania, and the latter part of the journey through wild, uncultivated country in the province of New York. We had our noon meal at the home of a prominent Dutch justice of the peace and major of the militia of the province. He was an old acquaintance of Mr. Weiser and had a great deal to talk about. He treated us to bear meat. At evening we were right in the thick of the forest; we saw a bear, which took flight from us, and also met several wild Indians with whom Mr. Weiser spoke. We had to take quarters for the night with a man who was called a Spaniard because his father had come into this country as a Spanish prisoner, married a Dutch woman, and begot this son. Spanish pompousness and Dutch rudeness had combined in this man. He refused to give us any supper and very haughtily told us to make our beds on the

34

straw. He sat in his armchair with great gravity, his six grown sons sitting around him, all of them smoking tobacco with the father and looking like chips off the old block. Weiser's name was held in great esteem wherever we went on this whole journey, but this Spaniard depended only on the wilderness where he lived and cared for no man but himself.

AUGUST 21. We started out early and rode the whole day. At an inn we were fed on *raccoons,* the American fox or badger, and pumpkins. After traveling forty-one miles we came to the town called Kingston on the Hudson River. We had now traveled two hundred miles from our home in five days and, though we were fatigued, through God's help we suffered no harm in body or limb.

AUGUST 22. On this day we stopped to rest and recover our strength, though we could not very well have gone on anyhow, since it was raining violently. Mr. Weiser could at this point have continued his journey on this side of the Hudson River, but he, too, desired very much to visit Pastor Hartwick and see once more his former place of residence and his old friends in the place where he lived with his parents when they first arrived in this country.

AUGUST 23. We rode a few miles from Kingston to the Hudson River, had ourselves and our horses ferried over in a boat, and rode from there to Rhinebeck, where Mr. Hartwick lived. There we made known our arrival to the joy of all who still remembered Mr. Weiser and who entertained a good opinion of the Pennsylvania preachers. A great many people gathered at Pastor Hartwick's home, desiring to converse with the long-awaited preacher, and all of them had a great deal to tell him. I had not yet recovered my speech, however, and was still suffering from the *catarrh.* This was a bitter annoyance to me because the people were unrelenting and they are accustomed to judge a strange preacher by his physical health and strength; they insisted upon hearing some conversation and answers to their questions, etc.

AUGUST 24. Mr. Weiser set out from Rhinebeck, and both

of us preachers accompanied him for twenty miles to a place beyond Camp to the home of a distinguished English gentleman who owns a part of the land upon which our Germans live. We were well received and were informed that the French of Canada had won over to their side most of the savage nations to whom Mr. Weiser was going and who had formerly been in alliance with England. This news sounds very ominous, if true. In the evening we said farewell to Mr. Weiser, left him with the English gentleman, Livingston, and rode back five miles to Camp.

During this week we visited an outparish, called Tar Bush, about six or seven miles from Camp. This region is called Tar Bush because the Germans, whom Queen Anne had sent to the province of New York in 1709 and 1710, were required to make tar or pitch there for a time. Camp is the tract of land on the Hudson River where these same Germans first established their encampment and called it the Camp. Only a few people assembled in Tar Bush, as most of them adhered to the Rev. William C. Berkenmeyer and the whole group had been not a little distracted by Carl Rudolph.

After we had returned to Camp I took a strong vomitory in order to break up by force the viscidity of the blood and humors, facilitate the circulation of the blood, and restore my speech. This began to work and brought about the desired effect, though it is not any too good for the lungs, where nature seems to deposit almost all the *materia peccans* from my whole body, and one of these days it will cause a *lesion*.

During the last days of the week we traveled back again the fifteen miles to Rhinebeck, where we had numerous visits from the well-disposed members of the congregations. We also made several visits.

In the *province* of New York the *Ecclesia Calviniana* is predominant. Most of the marriages are mixed, so that one is a Lutheran and the other a Calvinist. Mr. Hartwick, as they said, had several times preached against this practice. He had wanted to be too strict in adhering to the church order and had ruled that no Reformed person could act as the only sponsor for a

Lutheran child but must have with him a Lutheran godparent. He would not indiscriminately permit grandparents to act as sponsors, out of concern lest they would not live long enough, etc. He made too many journeys to Pennsylvania without the consent of his congregations, etc. He had not been simple enough in teaching the Catechism to the young people in preparation for confirmation. He is too *austere* in his manner and often does not speak to the people. He maintains no regularity at divine service, begins one or two hours late, makes the people sing long hymns, and preaches so long that the people who live far away have to ride home late at night and thus neglect their cattle. He is headstrong and stubborn and will let no one say anything to him or give him advice, saying that he had not come here to learn from them but to teach them. He did not maintain friendly relations with old Father Berkenmeyer, whereas after all the clergy ought to set a good example. These and the like were the complaints that the opponents brought in, although several of his friends also complained of several of the points mentioned and wished that we would speak to him about them. For the pastoral office in this country, and to get along with these people without sacrificing either love or the truth, one needs not only a certain measure of grace and talent, but also an unusually sanctified temperament.

SEPTEMBER 9. I preached in another outparish called Ancrum, situated in the mountains about eighteen miles from Rhinebeck. The service was held in a barn, German in the forenoon, English in the afternoon.

SEPTEMBER 18. We had our baggage transported to the house of a member of the congregation situated on the Hudson River, there to wait for a boat to take us to New York. My old, faithful horse, which had carried me for seven years over mountains and valleys, through thorns and thickets, I could not take back with me, for the road by land was unknown to me and it is impossible to take a horse by water. Consequently I was obliged to sell the saddle and bridle for traveling expenses and to make a present of the horse to a poor man. During my absence I had the misfortune at home of losing, through neglect, £10 worth of cattle, so this journey turned out to be so expensive that in future I must refrain from these all too distant friendships.

SEPTEMBER 26.   We journeyed from New York on the East River seventeen miles to a place called Flushing to visit a *gentleman* with whom we were acquainted, a man of our religion named Melchior Joachim Magens. This gentleman had studied law in Denmark. His father had been the Danish preacher in St. Thomas and had left his son a considerable *estate.* Because he thought that the climate and other conditions in New York would be more suitable to his health and that of his family, he purchased an estate there. He understands all the European languages and is especially well versed in theology. Up to this time he had held firmly to the Evangelical Lutheran religion and is also concerned to rear his children in the same. He had heard that Pastor Hartwick had been persecuted on account of his zeal in promoting the power of godliness and had written to him on two occasions, inviting him to become his domestic preacher. Mr. Hartwick, however, was unable to accept. He received us kindly, edified himself with us in conversations, and each evening had Pastor Hartwick conduct an English devotional service.

OCTOBER 1.   We said our farewells in New York and, going by water, arrived in the city of New Brunswick on the evening of October 2. We were unable to find a room or night's lodging in the inn because a festival gathering of Freemasons or some such people was being held there at the time. We therefore lodged with an English Presbyterian preacher, Mr. Arthur, who received us in a very friendly manner and kindly entertained us. He engaged in edifying conversation with us concerning the kingdom of God, gathered his household together, and offered a noble, spiritual, and edifying prayer for all conditions of men in all Christendom. This upright, faithful servant of God died soon after in his best years, to the great sorrow of his congregation and all other servants of God.

OCTOBER 3.   Pastor Hartwick continued his journey to Philadelphia, but I turned aside toward the Raritan *district* to visit Mr. John Albert Weygand. I met him on October 4, finding him in good health. I stayed with him one night, edifying myself with him and his father-in-law, Mr. van Doeren, in prayer.

On the following day I continued my journey by land, lodged with an awakened Dutch widow, and finally arrived home safely on October 6.

During this past fall many ships have again arrived with German people who spread out in crowds scattered throughout the country. It is almost impossible to describe how few good and how many exceptionally godless, wicked people have come into this country every year. The whole country is being flooded with ordinary, extraordinary, and unprecedented wickedness and crimes. Surely the rod of God cannot be spared much longer. Our old residents are mere stupid children in sin when compared with the new arrivals! Oh, what a fearful thing it is to have so many thousands of unruly and brazen sinners come into this free air and unfenced country!

IN DECEMBER I unexpectedly received a letter in the Dutch language, dated in November, from the elders in the congregation in New York, in which they called me to be their preacher and in which they set forth at length that their congregation, which was already divided, and disorganized, was in danger of falling into total ruin. In case I should not be able or willing to accept permanently, they requested that I should accept the office of teacher among them at least for one, two, or three years.

I did not wish to be hasty, but on the other hand I did not want to be negligent, for the Reverend Fathers [in Halle] do not restrict their care of souls and benevolence to Pennsylvania alone. I cannot see that I am bound to keep on pulling here until I die just like an old horse, especially when a younger, more energetic man should step into my place.

I replied that the circumstances would require some time for preparation and further inquiry into the will of the Lord. I would meanwhile leave it to their choice as to whether they would look around for a better man, or send me a regular call for a two-year trial.

The Year 1751

The school in New Hanover is still being continued, to our great pleasure, by Michael Walter. In Providence, however, we are having trouble with the schoolmaster because he has a bad wife who curses and indulges in shameful talk in the presence of the children and refuses to heed any admonition or warning against it. The man himself associates with people who are enemies of our church and its services. He is also unable to maintain discipline among the children. We have given him notice that he is to be relieved of his position as schoolmaster, but we have given him time to seek another opening. He boasts of his friends, our enemies, and places great reliance upon them. He wrote me an insulting letter in which he asserted that he would not vacate the schoolhouse and that if we throw him out his party will reinstate him by force.

His party consists of a few ignorant, cantankerous Reformed people and unbaptized Pennsylvanians who live hereabouts and who contributed a small amount toward the first schoolhouse which was built at the beginning. The new schoolhouse which we built last year, however, was completed without their help, with funds from collections and the alms treasury; consequently, they have nothing to say about it. Eight of these men came to my house and spoke in a rather rough manner. I firmly dismissed them because I was unable to speak sensibly with them since they had just come from the tavern where they had held their conference. We thereupon decided in the church council that the schoolmaster might remain until spring because he would have no place to go in winter. We were anxious to bring Mr. John Frederick Vigera up here to conduct the school since his school in Philadelphia is decreasing rapidly, but he declined.

At the outparish across the Schuylkill things have progressed to the point where, with God's help, the Lutherans and Reformed, together, have built their first joint schoolhouse and secured a competent schoolmaster, because our little group was too weak either to build it alone or to support the schoolmaster alone. And, besides, the Lutherans and Reformed are intermingled by marriage. I was rewarded with a great deal of trouble, vexation, and insults by several coarse fellows who have no regard for our religion, yet the school is making good progress and the schoolhouse is used for divine services both by us and by the Reformed.

Last year I redeemed a house servant from a ship on which he had just come into this country with German Lutheran immigrants. In return for the £15 which I paid, he was to serve me for several years. The man was very weak and infirm. At first he was very happy because he received good food, drink, and clothing in my house and had no hard work to do. He had hardly been with me for nine months, however, being hindered in his movements outside the house and being required to attend morning and evening prayers when I was at home, when he could no longer endure his good fortune and became surly and unruly. He permitted himself to be suborned by malicious people, gave me a great deal of heartache, and demanded either his freedom or another master. My jealous neighbors freed him by paying £11 10s., and in addition I presented him with brand new clothing at a cost of £5, so that everyone could see that I gave him more than he deserved. But I got no thanks for it, for those who had instigated him told him that he ought to throw the clothes at my feet because the jacket was not the same color as the coat. He was insolent to me and uttered some rough words, but he later came to get the clothes and went away to his own kind.

AUGUST 11. It was at this time that I heard of a sad case. A respected Dutch Reformed man, whose wife is a member of our church, had in the previous year bought from a ship a single German woman and a man and wife on condition that they were to serve him for several years on an estate which he owned near the city. This man gave these and his other German servants too much good food and drink and clothing and too little work. The women servants were members of Mr. J. F. Riess's party. Mr. Riess and his deacons were angry with this man because he had on several occasions spoken against them and their separation from the church. All of a sudden the two women came to the city and sought the advice of Mr. Riess, who sent them with his deacons to the mayor of the city, to whom they declared that their master had attempted to assault them. They declared themselves willing to swear to this on oath. Since there is a statute in English law which permits this, many a man has suffered innocently. Nevertheless, such an oath is not accepted indiscriminately when the women involved do not have a good character. I know that such wicked actions have actually been committed in Pennsylvania by unscrupulous strumpets who thought they could gain freedom from their masters in this way. Everybody in the party joined in the hue and cry, saying that the man should not get off without paying many hundreds of pounds, which would be a great help toward paying for their meeting-house and continuing their services.

The mayor of the city, however, was not disposed to accept the oath out of hand, but instead sent the women to jail. The accused man found an unexpected witness in the Newlander of this party, who had told some other men, when these women came with him to this country, that the women had already committed gross sins against the Sixth Commandment back in Germany. Mr. Riess's party thereupon drew up a petition and submitted it to the supreme court. The court, however, refused to accept the case and commanded the persons to go home and continue their service. The man told the unmarried woman to return to him the money he had paid for her and to go wherever she pleased; the married man and his wife he ordered to return to work on shorter rations and work off their sensual itch. After the maid had borrowed from her party the passage money, paid it back, and gained her freedom, she fell down on her knees before her master and mistress, begged their forgiveness, and admitted that she had been suborned. God shall bring every work into judgment, with every secret thing, and shall reward every man according to his works.

Another German *servant* ran away from his English master because he thought he ought to have meat every day. Two others were sitting in jail, having falsely accused their master of making them eat rotten meat. When the authorities investigated the matter, however, it was found that they had carried a piece of meat in a sack for a long time until it putrefied in order to use it as evidence. In the beginning the Germans had an excellent name and repute in these provinces, but now so many rotten people are coming into the country and acting so wickedly that the name has begun to stink.

Because Pennsylvanians protested vigorously against Muhlenberg's proposal to leave them, he spent only a part of the summer of 1751 in New York, and went there again for several months in 1752. Travel from Philadelphia to New York took three days. In 1752 Muhlenberg sailed by packet boat to Bordentown, New Jersey, rode in a stagecoach to Amboy, and went on to New York by boat. In the church in New York (which had no pastor at that time) and in communities across the river in New Jersey, Muhlenberg preached in German, Dutch, and English, and visited many homes.

The Year 1753

I was obliged to make a trip to Raritan, in Jersey, and look into the confused conditions there.

JULY 12. A deacon from Raritan, named John Leonard Streit, came in the evening to take me up. He lamented the present disturbed conditions in the congregations and gave me a one-sided account of the same from his point of view. Without adequate consideration I had made the appointment for this visit at an inconvenient time, for the people were just then very busy with the harvest.

JULY 13. I journeyed from my home with the deacon to the home of an elder in Indianfield, where Mr. Frederick Schultze is filling the office of preacher. The distance is only twelve miles, but we went astray and had to ride fifteen. The elder in Indianfield refreshed us with the necessary food and drink and spoke with me concerning the affairs of the congregation.

About two o'clock in the afternoon we rode three miles farther and stopped in to see another elder of the Indianfield congregation. He showed great pleasure at our visiting him. I conversed a little with his wife and children and inquired into their spiritual condition. The woman praised Mr. Schultze's sermons and wished that she and all others could live godly lives like children of God in accord with them.

From there we rode five miles farther to a neighborhood where English and Scotch-Irish people of all denominations live. My traveling companion said that there were also several German families there. However, the people were out in the fields, with the exception of a lame woman, whom I examined briefly as to her spiritual condition. She wept and lamented that in Germany she had had a wealth of spiritual nourishment and now she had to starve here in this country. She blamed the Newlanders for enticing the people away from Germany and bringing them here to a wilderness, etc. I gave her the appropriate counsel, instruction, and admonition, etc. The poor people, of course, hoped to better their material circumstances because, in various places in the Old World, they were so harshly treated that they could neither live nor die, etc. But the New World did not always fulfill the dreams they had concerning it while they were still in the Old World.

From there we rode thirteen miles farther to a ferryhouse on the River Delaware where one is taken across by ferryboat. This place is called Rose's Ferry, is situated about seven or eight miles farther toward the northwest, and is closer to Readingtown on the Raritan than Well's Ferry. This ferry had been owned in recent years by John Rose, a German of the Evangelical religion and a cousin of my wife. After the man died it remained in the possession of his widow and oldest son. The widow received us kindly and complained to me with tears that they lived among all kinds of people and strange sectarians, that they had little opportunity to hear God's Word and receive the holy sacraments, and that her only son had in his second marriage taken to wife a Philistine, the daughter of English parents who had not been baptized. She said that the father would turn over in his grave if he knew or could know of it, especially since she had already seen several cases where heathen or unbaptized wives had led their husbands, along with their children, astray into heathenism. I spoke with the son in private and asked about the circumstances. He said that his wife had promised him before the marriage that she would be baptized and that, with that in view, she had learned the Catechism, diligently read the Bible, and up to this time led a quiet and blameless life. He asked me to examine and baptize her on my return journey, etc. In the evening we had an edifying conversation and we lifted up our hearts in prayer and song, which was a great refreshment to me after the wearisome journey of the day in the hot sun.

JULY 14. We were ferried over the Delaware River early in the morning, and on this day we rode twenty-seven miles in the almost unbearable heat of the sun to the home of an upright elder of the Raritan congregation.

JULY 15. I rode five miles from Elder Rudolfson's house to the church and found many people assembled at the church. After having spoken with the elders and deacons who were present and with other old acquaintances, I opened the service and preached on Luke 15, concerning the lost sheep and the lost coin.

In the afternoon I was obliged to hold an English service because a great many English and Dutch people had assembled. By God's grace I laid the emphasis on true repentance, living faith, and godliness. I said in conclusion that these three points, together with the two sacraments, were the chief content of Evangelical Lutheran doctrine. I made special mention of this because a false saying has been circulating among the English to the effect that the Lutherans are secret papists. The English people were very attentive and expressed a desire to be the kind of Christians which this doctrine set forth. In the evening I had an edifying conversation with a number of members of the congregation who gathered together.

JULY 17. In the afternoon, accompanied by my host, I visited the English justice of the peace because he desired to speak with me concerning the church's land. Several years before, the elders and deacons had been seeking a place for their church which could be reached with equal ease by all four congregations. Since the English justice of the peace, Ralph Smith, lived in the same locality, they came to an agreement with him on four acres of his land, which he owned subject to a nominal annual ground rent to be paid to a prominent land-owner. The justice of the peace had measured off the four acres himself. Afterwards he drafted a deed of conveyance in which he set forth the boundaries and described the four acres, adding that they might be more or less than four acres. Since the justice of the peace, who is a member of the Presbyterian Church, shares the secret prejudice of his fellow Presbyterians that the German Lutherans retain too much of the papistical leaven, he wrote into the deed of conveyance a derogatory clause, stating that the church site is to remain the property of the Lutherans only until a further reformation takes place in our church and in the English High Church, etc. In this way the church and its land might perhaps fall under Presbyterian jurisdiction since the Presbyterians claim to be more reformed than the High Church and the Lutheran Church. Most of the elders and deacons are inexperienced in the complications of English law. At the same time they are very cautious and desire to prevent the preacher from having a hand in, or any claim upon, the land of the church. Meanwhile, the English are very cunning in their ways. The consequence is that occasionally a mistake occurs which afterwards the preachers have to set to rights.

After the deed of conveyance had been drafted, signed, sealed, and witnessed, Balthasar Pickel and others showed it to us and expressed the opinion that we might be able to obtain from the real owner of the land a better title, namely, a fee simple. This is impossible, however, because when an owner alienates a parcel of land subject to a ground rent, he cannot afterwards reconvey it to another in fee simple. We preachers do not have the time or the opportunity to study the English laws, and English lawyers will give no advice unless they are paid in cash. Consequently we did not know what to do with the deed of conveyance. Finally Pastor Hartwick came and, seeing the prejudicial clause, crossed it out with pen and ink. The matter hung fire in this way and the elders laid out the church land in lots and rented them to various persons for an annual rent. These persons built houses on the lots and sought to make their living near the church. After the justice of the peace saw that the church was deriving a few pounds annually from the rented lots, he surveyed the church land once more and said that he had made an error in the first survey, that there were seven acres of land instead of four, and that he wanted three acres back again. The elders cited the deed of conveyance, particularly the words stating that it might be more or less than four acres. But the justice of the peace, when he saw the deed of conveyance, said that it was null and void because one article in it had been crossed out.

It was on account of this land that the justice of the peace wished to see me. Having taken with me an elder, I spoke to him about the affair. He said: (1) The clause in the deed of conveyance which seems detrimental to us was read in the hearing of the elders and they had made no objection to it; on the contrary, they had put their hand and seal to it and thereby confirmed the correctness of the deed of conveyance. (2) He learned, however, that an ignorant preacher crossed out a part of the deed, and this invalidated the whole deed of conveyance. According to the law he could now dispossess the people who are living on the so-called church land. (3) He could have the person who crossed out a portion of the deed cited to appear in court. As he read it to me from a book of English law, the nose and ears of any person who erases anything from a signed and sealed contract must be cut off, etc., because it falls under the head of *forgery*, etc. (4) For the sake of peace, however, he is willing to demand only the land in excess of the stated four acres. If the congregation amicably agrees to this, he will give it a new deed of conveyance, omitting the seemingly derogatory clause.

I said the following to the justice of the peace: (1) Regardless of whether there was a deed of conveyance or not, there were at hand living witnesses who could testify that he himself had surveyed and sold the parcel of land upon which the church and houses stood for the use of an Evangelical Lutheran congregation and that he had stated that it might be more or less than four acres. (2) He had had no right to put such a derogatory clause in the deed of conveyance; consequently, no essential part of the deed had been crossed out. (3) The congregation could not be responsible for the erasure; it must rather be considered an accident. (4) And in view of the fact that, as I had been told, he had been willing several months previous to accept a payment of £6 for the surplus acres, if he was now willing to stand by his word, accept the money, and give us a better deed of conveyance, the controversy would be closed.

He stuck to his view, however, and said that after a deed of conveyance had been signed, sealed, and witnessed by both parties, no *forgery* must occur. But since the *forgery* had occurred, he considered the deed null and void; nevertheless, he would abide by his promise, let the congregation have the four acres, and himself collect the annual rents from the two houses which stood on the remaining three acres, which amounted to about £3 *current* annually. I was unable to do anything further because the coat was spoiled in the cutting, etc. If they had shown the deed to me before it had been executed I might, with the advice of a lawyer, have been able to prevent the misfortune. The church, the schoolhouse, and two other ground rent houses stand on the four acres which the man does not contest. So whatever happens, the main thing remains, and the rest, together with the costs of a lawsuit if it should come to court, they will have to charge to experience. After this unpleasant conversation we were refreshed with tea, and the justice expressed his approbation of the English sermon of two days before. He also said that he had read the life of Dr. Luther and of his work in the Reformation.

In the evening I rode from there, with my host, seven miles farther into the mountains and lodged with Jacob Oof, having promised to preach there on the following day. The housewife is of Reformed parentage, awakened first by Mr. Nicholas Kurtz's edifying preaching, and that of others, and was confirmed with her husband last year. She appears to be a sincerely humble soul who is hungry for grace and lives in faith, of the type of Mary who was intent upon the one thing needful as she sat, full of devotion, at Jesus' feet. I met another English widow in this house who kept herself busy, like Martha, but she was also eager to listen to edifying conversation. This woman had a grown son who had been bound out, until he reached his majority, to a German shopkeeper, and she lamented in tears that this grown man had not yet been baptized. She had instructed him as well as she was able in the English Catechism, but his master took no interest in his spiritual welfare, etc.

JULY 20. Accompanied by an upright member of the congregation I set out on the return journey. In the afternoon we arrived safely at Rose's Ferry, where we learned that a number of people had gathered together, desiring to hear a word of admonition from me, but that they had dispersed again when my arrival was delayed. I asked young Mr. Rose whether his English wife was still willing and prepared to be examined and baptized. He was dismayed and said that her father, who is still living, had got word of our intention and used some hard words, saying that he would never again in all eternity recognize her as his child if she permitted herself to be baptized. The son-in-law and daughter, however, had replied that it was deplorable enough that the father continued to live as a heathen, etc. He, the son-in-law, was bound to take care of his wife's eternal welfare. And despite the fact that the father would refuse to recognize his daughter as his child on account of this good and necessary act, it should nevertheless be done and in this way they would receive a far better father in heaven. We spent the evening in good conversation, prayer, and the singing of hymns.

JULY 21. Early in the morning I examined Christopher Rose's wife. She had learned the chief parts of the Catechism and also had read God's Word diligently. She was able to give a fair reason for the faith that was in her, and she testified also that she had a desire to be received into the most blessed covenant of the triune God. I delivered to those who had assembled a brief address and admonition based on Acts 10, concerning the course of the conversion of Cornelius the centurion, and then after prayer administered baptism. All members of the family, especially the old mother, were very happy and embraced the new Christian with tears in their eyes.

About eleven o'clock I rode away from here, accompanied by Mr. Rose, and set out for Neshaminy because I had promised to preach to the Dutch and English people there on the following day. Mr. Rose told me that a German married couple lived on this road, in service with a Dutch Reformed man, and that these people had a child to be baptized. Several weeks before, they had walked ten miles to have their child baptized in Neshaminy because it was said that I was going to preach there. But since I had not come, they had asked the Dutch Reformed preacher to baptize their child; but he would not baptize it unless they promised to rear the child in the Reformed religion. And since they neither would nor could promise such a thing, they had returned without having gained their end. On the preceding day they had again come five miles with the child to Mr. Rose's house and turned back again with sad hearts and without success because I arrived too late. We journeyed to the house and found the parents at home. Since they were embarrassed for lack of a sponsor, Mr. Rose stepped in, and I baptized the child to the joy and comfort of the parents. I admonished them from God's Word to true concern for their immortal souls and to faithfulness in their earthly service.

Nine miles this side of Neshaminy we visited an old Dutch Lutheran, Isaac van Horn, who was delighted with my coming and continued the journey with us. Toward evening we arrived safely at the home of old Barnt van Horn in Neshaminy. They knew nothing of my coming because it had not been reported from Philadelphia, or else the letter had not been delivered. That evening, however, several messengers were sent out to invite those who lived nearby to come on the following day.

JULY 22. The few remnants of Dutch Lutheran and English church people assembled. In former times there had been a fine little group of Lutherans in this place, occasionally served by preachers and latterly by Mr. van Doeren. After the latter died, some of the older people occasionally came to our church in Philadelphia, but they had not been able to understand much of the German language. In recent years old Barnt van Horn had attended our annual synodical meetings and on each occasion fervently implored that one of us should visit and serve them. This was not done, however, because we did not know the language. Meanwhile, during these many years, the little group has decreased greatly, some of the older people having died and others having moved away, and the young people having gone over to other parties and persuasions, not only because of lack of instruction but also through marriage. The Dutch Reformed, the English Presbyterians, and the Quakers have churches, meeting houses, and preachers in the locality, but our own people have neither church nor preacher and are "as a lodge in a garden of cucumbers."

In the morning I preached in the Dutch language in the barn to about thirty persons, and in the afternoon in English to a somewhat larger number of people. I also baptized two children. The good people pressed me to come back again very soon, which I promised to do four weeks hence, God willing, if my brethren were able to take care of my services at home. They told me that they had a cemetery there which comprised an acre of land. They said that they might in time be able to build a schoolhouse and church on this land in case the congregation began to grow and increase again. This might very well occur if only one could find the time to make these visitations. After the service I engaged in good conversation with several who were present, and in the evening I catechized the children and Mr. van Horn's Negro slaves.

JULY 23. I continued my journey homewards, and since the road is very difficult to find, Mr. Abraham van Horn accompanied me for fifteen miles; the remaining fifteen miles I rode alone. The heat was well nigh intolerable, but I arrived safely to within two miles of my house when my horse fell with me. I rested at my neighbor's house until I had taken some medicine and was able to get up again. Neshaminy is situated about twenty-two miles from Philadelphia and thirty miles from my house. This traveling has become much more difficult and wearisome for me ever since I was obliged to leave my horse behind, three years ago, while on my tour to Rhinebeck and Camp in the province of New York. Since that time I have had to get along with poor animals which are unsuited for riding.

IN THE MONTH OF AUGUST a young man, whom I instructed and confirmed several years ago and who was a member of the congregation in New Providence, died. About two weeks before his end, he had a most terrifying dream. A messenger of death came to him (in the dream) and summoned him to appear at once for eternal judgment. He was so frightened by this that his whole body was quaking when he woke up, and he called upon his wife to pray with him. About ten days later he went to a public *auction* several miles from his home for the purpose of buying household goods for his inn. On such occasions, alas, it often happens here that willful sinners of every religious party and nationality, both young and old, indulge too freely in strong drinks and by their revelries betray from what spirit they are sprung. This time, too, after the auction was ended, a number of wicked English and German men decided to have a horse race on the public street and thus, by their wantonness, to abuse these poor creatures [the horses]. Together with other spectators, the above-mentioned young man stood alongside the street, where he thought he would be safe. But when the racers approached, goading on their frenzied steeds, an Englishman's horse got out of his rider's control and headed for the spectators. The young man was trampled under foot and his head was so severely battered that he remained speechless for three days and nights, was completely out of his mind, and finally died, widowing his wife and orphaning his children.

Until 1761 Muhlenberg went on with his work as a country pastor, living with his wife Anna Maria in the house at Providence where the family grew steadily. Eight children were born there, of whom two died in infancy. In 1761 the Muhlenbergs moved to Philadelphia where difficulties in St. Michael's Church required attention. During this period the colonists suffered hardships resulting from the French and Indian War. There were savage massacres along the frontier.

The Year 1762

JANUARY 25. [Philadelphia.] The wife of Jacob Koehler, the miller, came with a Reformed woman, Mrs. Iserloos, to report that her husband, Jacob Koehler, had deserted with another man's wife. She asked me for a marriage certificate, for she had been married to him in New Providence in June, 1757. Thereafter a woman from New York brought me a letter from Pastor Weygand, dated December 9, 1761. Then I went out and visited (a) Widow Bantleon, who was up again, (b) the bookbinder, George Otto, who was somewhat *light headed*. Nevertheless, I could speak to him a little about the condition of his soul and, when I had prayed with him, his mind became clear again. Also spoke to Mr. Andrew Bosshard, the elder, about congregational affairs as well as about the bookbinder. (c) From there to Apothecary Schneider's, whose wife was somewhat better; spoke with both of them about various things. (d) Then visited Mr. David Schaefer's aged mother-in-law; the children were not at home. (e) To Mr. Hillegas', where I encountered Mr. Henry William Stiegel.

Mr. Hopkinson urged me to go with them to Pool's Bridge, to Mr. Philip Feuerlin's, where I was to inspect a *clavicord* which Mr. Stiegel was having made. Feuerlin's brother, who lives downstairs in the house, said that he belonged to our congregation and was married to Mr. Jacob Beyerle's daughter. I had an opportunity while there to speak with Mr. Beyerle about former days, also went into his house and saw his wife, who was very pleased. From there went home, where *Madame* Jung, the *schoolmistress,* was waiting for me. To *Madame* Jung I paid the first quarter year's fee for the three girls, i.e., the amount due from November 2, 1761, to February 2, 1762, namely, £1 2s. 6d. In my absence Mr. Honig had been here with an Englishman who desired a remedy for epilepsy. Also a visit from Mrs. Gob.

JANUARY 26.   Had Mrs. Jacob Koehler write a letter to her fugitive husband. Also had visits from Mr. Jacobi and from a resident of New York, named Mr. Huth, who brought me a letter from Pastor Weygand, of New York, and said that Pastor Nicholas Kurtz had arrived in New York after a long journey and had preached in the Swamp church. Visits in the afternoon from the wives of Messrs. Dick and Fiedler, with whom I had an edifying discourse.

JANUARY 27.   I visited *the Revd.* Richard Peters, but he was soon summoned to the governor and consequently was unable to speak long. From there went to *the Revd.* Jacob Duché's, but did not find him at home. On my return, visited Dr. William Smith's wife, whom I found to be ill. Then to Mr. Brechel's; to the sick bookbinder's, Otto, where I encountered the apothecary's wife; to Mr. Caspar Graef's, where I had dinner; and on my way homeward I stopped in at Mr. Cover's, Mrs. Strauss's, and Jacob Schneck's. Had a visit in the evening from Henry Krebs, who told me about his laborious court cases and said, among other things, that godlessness, marked by gluttony, drunkenness, violence, and disputation, was gradually gaining the upper hand in New Hanover.

The son-in-law of Widow Kirchhof was here in the forenoon and requested me to go to Germantown next Friday to baptize his child, which I promised to do. Mr. Stiegel was at my home during my absence; in accordance with an earlier agreement he requested me to pay him a visit at his iron works, God willing, near the end of February.

FEBRUARY 1.   Was obliged to go to Germantown to baptize the child of John Geissel, son-in-law of the late Christopher Kirchhof. The road was cut exceedingly deep and it was dangerous because of the mud holes in it, but I got through safely with the help of God, baptized the child, and was asked by two neighbors if I would accept their four children for instruction looking toward confirmation next spring. Promised to do so. Toward evening rode back home; had to dismount from my horse several times and cross mud holes on foot, which undermined my health. His Reverence Dr. Charles M. Wrangel's servant brought us some garden vegetables. An old widow stopped in toward evening and asked for alms. In the evening no one came, except Mr. Epple, who reported the death of the baker, Lawrence Werthe, and requested me to preach the funeral sermon.

FEBRUARY 4. Was to go to Provost Wrangel's as guest, but could not. Sent my son Frederick to the provost's with a letter. Borrowed £10 to repay Mr. Truckenmueller, which I succeeded in doing. Later the provost sent some of the roast turkey by his servant. In the afternoon went to Mr. Andrew Bosshard's, spoke to him about a seating for Mrs. Weiss in his wife's pew. He said that there were only three seatings in his wife's pew, in which four persons were already enrolled; but he was of the opinion that there was still a vacant seating in Mrs. Schaefer's and the apothecary's wife's pew. For this reason I went to the apothecary's and inquired; his wife confirmed the opinion. Accordingly I returned to Mr. Bosshard's and requested him to consult Mr. Schaefer about this matter too. Also saw the sick man, Otto, and prayed with him. From there went to Mr. Leonard Melcher's, whose wife is a member of our congregation; there I found my wife, and later Mr. Jacobi and his wife also arrived from Germantown. From there we went to Mr. Fosseberg's and had edifying conversation and prayer there. His wife desired to be confirmed. At nine o'clock we went home again through deep mud. Elias Botener was waiting for us in order to get a prescription for a sick Englishman.

FEBRUARY 10. Received a letter from the assistant, Carl S. Friderici, of Smithfield, beyond the Blue Mountains. He reports that he is still serving the Saucon congregation every other week and that he must ride thirty miles over poor roads each time. He works very hard and has too little *subsistence*. About eleven o'clock in the morning went with my wife to Dr. William Smith's wife and, on the strength of an *order*, received £30 as a part of the £60 designated for several of our preachers.

From there we visited the youngest preacher of the High

Church, Mr. Jacob Duché, who was ill. He told us (1) about the intention of sending an English bishop to Canada, etc. because the see of the Catholic prelate is vacant, and (2) that he is planning to go to England and promised to take my two sons with him. Then we visited Provost de Wrangel, who treated us with the greatest affection and entertained us with edifying discourse. In the evening the doctor had an Englishman, Mr. Linck, summoned to the house. This man, together with his wife, had been awakened in the evening *lectures* by glorious expositions of Psalms 22 and 69 and had been converted from darkness to light. The man spoke very profoundly out of his experience, and the doctor gave him most excellent rules and counsels for the furtherance of the works of grace which had been begun in him. After we had an evening meal, we hastened homeward. The doctor, in his love, wished to keep us there. But it was a good thing that we hurried away, for a deep snow fell during the night and we should have had difficulty getting through the following morning.

FEBRUARY 11. Received from Pastor John Siegfried Gerock a letter with encouraging and *cordate* contents. About one o'clock united John Nicholas Hunter, widower, and Elizabeth, unmarried daughter of Adam Tatz, in marriage. The young man promised before the witnesses that he would send his wife for instruction and confirmation because she had been in the service of English Quakers, had forgotten the German language, and had not learned anything.

Later the wife of Riess, the tailor, came and requested that I reconcile her with her parents in the evening. Her father is Mr. Rohr, of Zwickau. Toward evening had a visit from an old man named Knecht who came from Hackensack and New York and requested alms. In the evening spent a couple of hours at Mr. Rohr's in an effort to reconcile Mrs. Riess with her parents, against whose wishes she had been married two years before. In the time which remained I wrote a letter to Pastor Gerock in Lancaster and reported my intention to journey to Tulpehocken, God willing, on February 15.

FEBRUARY 15. In the afternoon started the journey on bad roads with my wife and Peter, drank *tea* at John Bergenthaler's, lodged for the night at Siegel's.

FEBRUARY 16. At eleven o'clock reached Mr. John Schrack's, spent the night in our house in Providence with Dr. Martins.

FEBRUARY 17. We rode to Reading, arriving at Mother's about eight o'clock in the evening.

FEBRUARY 18 and 19. Remained in Reading, conferred with Mr. Bernard M. Hausile, etc.

FEBRUARY 20. Rode with Brother-in-law Frederick Weiser to his place in Heidelberg, and from there to Mrs. Kurtz's.

FEBRUARY 21. Preached on the passion of Christ (Luke 12:50) in the Tulpehocken church and baptized two children.

FEBRUARY 22. Visited the school near the old church, then rode to Brother-in-law Frederick's.

FEBRUARY 23. Rode to the Heidelberg church, preached on Exodus 12:26-27, and returned eight miles to Mrs. Kurtz's.

FEBRUARY 24. Rode to John Weiser's with Schoolmaster Zeits, had good *company,* etc.

FEBRUARY 25. Rode with John Weiser and the schoolmaster to Lebanon in dreadfully cold weather. Back from there to N. Ley's, whose child I baptized, and thence to Philip Breitenbach's, where I spent the night. Today Henry Krebs, Lawyer Ross's clerk, gave me a *fee,* three pieces of eight.

FEBRUARY 26. Baptized Andrew Kreutzer's child and prayed with his sick wife. Then to John Weiser's and finally to Mr. Nicholas Kurtz's dwelling place. About two o'clock in the afternoon rode eight miles with Mr. Breitenbach to George Schwingel's, where I spent the night.

FEBRUARY 27. Four miles farther to Mr. Henry William Stiegel's iron works. Preached there on Psalm 22:26, 27 and spent the night.

FEBRUARY 28. Rode seven miles with Mr. Stiegel to Ephrata, and then three miles more to the Conestoga church where I preached about the temptation of Jesus, Matthew 4:1ff.

Went home with George Yund and spent the night with him.

MARCH 1. Rode twenty-one miles from there to Reading, stayed there until March 3, and rode with my family to Providence, where I remained and preached on March 7 about the inner sufferings of our Mediator.

MARCH 8. We rode to Philadelphia in a heavy snowstorm and arrived safely, praise God.

MARCH 29. Two deputies came from New Providence with a written *recommendation* from the German justice of the peace in which the complaint is made that English neighbors, especially a Quaker, seized a fishing place in the Schuylkill which they have long had in their *possession,* and they requested me to intercede for the Germans with the government, etc. Since I could not go out I gave them an English petition addressed to the government, etc. Had a visit in the afternoon from the apothecary's wife, who complained that she was affronted in church yesterday afternoon in connection with her pew, etc. This trouble will constantly increase, for the church is too small for the large number of people. The Rev. Michael Schlatter stopped at our house in the evening to spend the night. Afterwards united Richard Jobs and Mary Ward in marriage for Provost de Wrangel; the witnesses were George Ham and John Jones.

MARCH 30. Talked with Pastor Schlatter in the morning. Then Peter Walter came to give me 7s. 6d. for services in connection with his wife's funeral last Saturday. In the afternoon gave instruction to the young people in the schoolhouse; Mr. John Frederick Handschuh had a funeral and consequently could not help. Afterwards visited Mr. Sauter. On my return home, found Messrs. Keppele, Saeckel, Bosshard, and Schaefer waiting for me, with whom I conferred (a) about holding a meeting of the church council, (b) about liquidating the debts, and (c) about the assignment of pews in the church. Mr. Schlatter took leave in order to go to New York. Instructed two adult journeymen in the evening. Also visits from Messrs. Fiedler, Kessler, and Enderle, who had much to say pro and con. Visit from

Peter Becker, of Providence, who wanted to buy my property. Finally from Jacob Timanus, of Upper Dublin, who requested me to visit the forsaken congregation there on Easter Monday, in the afternoon, after preaching in the morning at Barren Hill.

APRIL 1. I was given to understand that the *land tax* is £2 5s. In the morning instructed the young people from Germantown. At one o'clock had a visit from the Rev. Dr. de Wrangel, who gratified me with a report of his last journey in Jersey. At half past two o'clock went to the schoolhouse and instructed the confirmands until after five o'clock.

APRIL 2. Heavy, cold rain. Visit from Widow Duerr, who brought some fish. Received a letter from *Magister* Gerock in Lancaster. Also a letter from Mr. Friderici, adjunct in Saucon, through an elder of the Saucon congregation, in which he requests a *decision* in the case of Erdman's fourteen-year-old daughter. The girl is already confirmed, drank *spiritus vini* several times, and was punished by her stepmother. Later the horses' harness, saddle, woolens, and linens belonging to the parents were slashed to pieces, etc., so that neighbors kept watch, etc. in the house, and the counsel of *conjurors* was even sought. Finally it was discovered that it was the girl who had done this. She offered the excuse that Satan, in the form of a *gentleman*, had supplied her with a knife for this purpose and had *encouraged* her. I presumed, on the basis of the man's account, (a) that the girl's will was not broken in her youth, (b) that the strong drink and her mother's punishment conspired to the same end, and that, furthermore, the inscrutable malice of the natural heart could easily do such a thing under the influence of the evil spirit with a swiftness and cunning that might seem baffling. I advised that this malicious behavior ought to be punished in order to impress and improve the girl with the paternal rod of discipline; otherwise she will try something worse. Meanwhile, until she reforms, etc., she ought to be excluded from holy communion, but not from the church.

Mrs. Paris, a Reformed woman, registered her twenty-year-old maid for instruction and confirmation. Toward evening received a visit from Mr. Pawling, of Providence. A message arrived summoning me to Mr. Richard Peters' next Monday for a conference with Col. John Armstrong.

APRIL 3. Visits (a) from Provost de Wrangel's servant with instructions that the doctor will preach in Barren Hill on Good Friday, once in English and once in German, and that I should send out notice to this effect; (b) from a blind woman seeking money to pay the physician for her eyes; (c) from Mr. William Essig, of Germantown, on account of his children's confirmation; (d) from Adam Krebs's wife, who brought a quarter of sugar; (e) from a poor widow, who announced her intention to commune; (f) from two men who came from Germantown to complain about their distress over the congregation's controversy with Mr. Henry Rapp, etc., and to ask for advice. I could not say much to help them. Afterwards an unmarried woman, a native of Wuerttemberg who is in service at Dr. Kearsly's, announced her intention to commune; she has been in this country ten years but has not yet communed here; she is a constant reader of Arndt's *Wahres Christentum* and is conversant with practical truths.

APRIL 8. Dr. de Wrangel told me that the marriage of William Culin and Sarah Culin, performed last Monday, would become involved in unfortunate legal action because the bride was under age and the guardian, a Quaker, had not given his consent; he intends to take to the *law,* and in such cases the preacher must pay a fine of £50. The case grieved me deeply on account of the sad consequences, since Mr. Handschuh had approved these people for publication of banns without having fuller knowledge and, in addition, had forced the marriage upon me—perhaps even with the intention of ruining me and placing a stain on my office. Anyone who sides with the world and has money can get along, but a disciple of Christ does not fare better before the courts here than his Master did before the Sanhedrin. This matter has already given me a sorrowful night in anticipation.

About four o'clock this afternoon I had to go through the

mud and water to Mr. Richard Peters' in order to have a trouble-some conference with him and Colonel Armstrong about the *land affairs* which are *depending* between the proprietaries and the late Conrad Weiser. From this conference I concluded that self-interest is the only driving force in earthly-minded persons, from greatest to smallest.

MAY 27. The *fair* was held today, and there was worldly revelry in all parts of the city. Was in the schoolhouse in the morning to help receive announcements of intention to commune. Some people also came to my house to announce their intention. In the afternoon instructed the confirmands in the church on account of the intense heat. Wrote letters to Mr. James van Buskerk, to the elders of the Swamp church in New York, and to Mr. Weygand to invite them to the synod on June 27.

JUNE 8. Squire Jameson, whose daughter I married yesterday to John Edward, came and threatened me with a lawsuit. I had to give him a *species facti* setting forth the circumstances of the marriage, which grieved me very much. Mr. Caspar Graef measured me for a suit. I requested him to tell Apothecary Schneider that they should remain quiet because I hoped on my return from Jersey to effect a settlement with regard to the congregational constitution before the synod met.

About 10 A.M. I rode off toward Gloucester with my sons Peter and Frederick. On the way stopped in at Mr. Handschuh's and Jacob Walter's. About twelve o'clock we set out from Gloucester Ferry and crossed the Delaware safely. In Jersey the *court* was just in session, and consequently there were many people in the ferry house. Rode away with Mr. Jacob Fries at about 2 P.M. Philip Schmick also accompanied us with his wagon. I could not long endure riding in the penetrating heat, so I sat on the wagon and proceeded until ten o'clock in the evening. We covered some thirty miles and arrived, tired, at Jacob Fries's. On the way I had pleasant conversation with Philip Schmick, who had served in the Prussian army.

JUNE 9. Instructed seven young people morning and afternoon. After the instruction I rode with my host, Jacob Fries, and Schoolmaster Kuhleman to the home of an elder and founder of the church there, John Michael Mueller, *alias "Gross Hans."* He was very sick, a stroke having paralyzed his left side. He also had an opening in his arm through which sluggish nature was expelling all its superfluous *excrementa.* The man was charged by his neighbors with mercilessness, pride, and insolence toward the poor, and several are of the opinion that he was being punished by the same means by which he sinned. He wept and said that he was a poor and great sinner, etc. He declared that he was leaving £100 for a new church in his will, that he was derided on this account by his brother-in-law, who tried to make him retract, etc. The objection was raised that his bequest rested on a shaky foundation and that the church would probably not get anything out of it. I told him to think back over his earlier life and not act like the Pharisee, but rather like the penitent publican.

My host complained that they had not had rain for a long time and that all the crops in fields and gardens were withering, which was sufficiently clear to the eye. We said that it should not be surprising if God takes all his blessings from us because sins are heaped on sins, etc. No other remedy remains but to fall penitently into the outstretched arms and judgments of the righteous God and plead in the name of our Surety. During the following night the Lord God granted us a gracious and heavy rain which refreshed everything and revived what was dying.

JUNE 11. In the forenoon rode with my host and the schoolmaster to sick Michael Mueller's. Found him quiet and composed, examined him on the basis of the Ten Commandments, asked him not to imitate malefactors who appear before secular courts, but to *plead guilty,* acknowledge his responsibility for all sins, and appeal to the Surety in the court of God; thus the case will be shorter and will turn out to his advantage. He agreed, made his confession, heard his sentence from Isaiah 1:18, "Though your sins be as scarlet," etc., and received holy communion. Afterwards we visited Philip Schmick, my wagoner, whose family is Reformed. In the afternoon I instructed the young people and observed that some wholesome impressions were made on their hearts, which refreshed me.

JUNE 12. Had the young people again early in the morning. Then recorded ninety persons who appeared, in the course of time, to announce their intention to commune. In the afternoon I conducted preparatory service and confession in the church for those who were present, examined the nine confirmands in the five parts of our Catechism, and thereupon had them renew their baptismal covenant, those present being deeply moved. After the service two Lutheran men brought their awakened English wives to the house where I was staying and asked me to instruct them in English and receive them and the others for confirmation. I found that they had an understanding of the principal truths of our Evangelical religion, prayed with them, and promised to receive them tomorrow, God willing, with the others. The most gracious God granted us another agreeable rain during the night.

JUNE 13. Several more fellow-believers came from a distance, early, to announce their intention to commune, and I had various matters to discuss with them. At eleven o'clock we went to church. On our arrival the large assembly was somewhat disorderly. (a) Baptized six children. (b) Preached on Revelation 3:11, "Behold, I come quickly," etc. (c) Examined eleven persons, statement by statement, in the Order of Salvation, and then especially in the fifth part of the Catechism, concerning the Lord's Supper. I had them vow fidelity before God and the congregation and laid my hands on them. Those present shed many tears and were deeply affected. Then, *apart* from the others, I called on the two English women to confess the Creed and confirmed them. I administered holy communion to 125 persons in all.

After this had been done, two more children were brought for baptism. Then a Lutheran man and his English wife, who live far away and arrived too late, announced their intention to commune. He was well recommended by several people who knew him but had been among strange parties and had not received holy communion for eight years. Since the couple understood English better than German, I examined them in English and discovered that they possessed a good and adequate knowledge. I held confession and administered holy communion to them. After six o'clock in the evening we were finished.

Later the people took leave in a loving and affected fashion and they asked me to be sure to come again soon, for they had had no visit from Philadelphia in two years and were like scattered sheep without a shepherd. There are only a few settled families who have land of their own. Most of them are scattered among all kinds of English sects and support themselves by manual labor. To be sure, they have a wooden church, built twenty-two years ago, but it is dilapidated and much too small. They also have a schoolhouse and a schoolmaster, but the schoolmaster cannot make his living from the school and accordingly tries to supplement his income by bloodletting, cupping, etc.; moreover, he reads sermons on Sundays to the members who live nearby. Of their own accord and out of love, the poor people laid together their mites and offered them to me for my traveling expenses. I returned 30s. to the church and gave 20s. to the schoolmaster because he complained of his penury.

JUNE 14. In the forenoon united John George Maeglin, unmarried, and Anna Maria Uhl in marriage. Their banns were properly published, partly in the English church and partly in ours. Afterwards took leave and in the afternoon, accompanied by the schoolmaster, Mr. Fries took me by horse eighteen miles farther to a Swedish church located on *Raccoon Crick*. Some time ago Dr. de Wrangel preached several times in German and administered holy communion to the scattered Germans living thereabouts, and he told them that I would also visit them and conduct divine service in their church. We were strangers there and took quarters in an English inn where tipplers were having quite a high time and where there was so much disorder that we had to bolt up our room.

JUNE 15. Quite a number of Germans assembled at the

church between ten and eleven o'clock in the morning. After the service I dined in the inn. The Germans collected 15*s.* for traveling expenses. I gave half of it to the schoolmaster and the other half I paid out to my traveling companion, Martin Becker, who lent me a horse and accompanied me to Gloucester. We reached Gloucester toward eight o'clock this evening. Mr. Arndt Hassert was there with his family, and also Captain Seward with his family. They took me along in their *boat* up to their ship, opposite the drawbridge. From there I went with a boatman who carried my portmanteau to the shore in the city, whence it was a couple of miles through the city to my house. I gave the boatman 5*s.* for his pains. The walking made me very warm.

JULY 1. A recently founded, poor congregation in Winchester, in the province of Virginia, consisting of Evangelicals from Germany and some young people whose parents live among us, was given permission, in response to its urgent pleading, to collect contributions in our United Congregations toward the building of a church. They also requested the Ministerium to examine their somewhat educated schoolmaster in order that he might be allowed to administer the sacraments in case of emergency. It is exceedingly difficult to say yes or no in such circumstances. Ordained preachers live far away and are hardly able to visit such remote groups. The people would like to cling to the religion and practice of their ancestors. A number of preachers who were ordained and then dismissed on account of depravity in Germany wander about in America and serve in such forsaken congregations until their sinful life becomes too manifest. Many others set themselves up as preachers and exercise the office without any ordination or examination whatsoever, if they have some gift of speech. If these people who live far away have nothing at all, they and their children either relapse into paganism or are dispersed among all kinds of peculiar sects, etc. This raises the question: What is the best thing to do, or which is the least among many evils?

The agreeable and kind bequest of a noble lady, which was

conveyed by General Superintendent Roth, of Stettin, to Court Preacher Ziegenhagen in London and by the latter through exchange to me, was duly received by me on January 1, 1761. The prominent, charitable benefactress expressly stipulated that the said bequest, which amounted to £63 15s. sterling in London and £100 current according to exchange here, should either be put out at interest or applied to the purchase of some good land, and that the interest or income should be given as gifts to such preachers as visit congregations which have no preachers and minister to them with the means of grace. Since, in these times of extensive war, the price of land is much higher than it is worth and practically none is obtainable, I put the said Christian bequest out at interest. I did this on May 1, 1761, four months after I received it, because the purchase of land was not feasible and I did not wish to have the money lie idle any longer. The said £100 yields £6 interest annually. Inasmuch as two years will have passed in a few days and £12 have accordingly accumulated in interest, I divided the said £12 between two pious, Jesus-loving, poor preachers because they have already visited divers poor, shepherdless congregations on the frontiers between Christians and pagans and intend to visit them again, now that, through the benefactions received, they are supplied with traveling expenses. I have taken a *quittance* from both preachers and asked them to prepare diaries, which I shall send separately every year, as long as God prolongs my life, in order that the noble benefactress might condescend to see what is being done with her bequest.

OCTOBER 20. Visit from Christopher Raben and Schoolmaster Selig. My wife took a *lottery ticket* from them. Visit from Matthias Hollebach, who inquired about my place in New Hanover, etc. He also said that things were going badly and that much murmuring had arisen. My neighbor, Mr. Kuemle, sent a bottle of Rhine wine and plums. Mr. Treichel, at Mr. Hoffman's, sent six bottles of Rhine wine and a dozen *herrings* as a present. About two o'clock I had a visit from Mr. Kreuter, of Germantown. At four o'clock I buried the two children of

Mr. Trautwein and Andrew Pertsch. Text, Isaiah 26:20. Henry Rohn reported that his child, the one who received emergency baptism last night, had died. Paid to Mr. Balthasar Fleischer for shoes *in full,* £2 9s. 6d.

NOVEMBER 21.   About ten o'clock I was wakened and summoned to a young Englishman who had been stabbed in the body with a knife in a fight during the evening. When I arrived the house was full of people, and two English doctors also came to bind up the wounds. The *omentum* was cut and the intestines out. They could not get them back in again, so they cut off some of the *omentum* and with great difficulty put the intestines in, sewed up the opening, and opened a vein in the arm. When they were through, the *constables* and a magistrate came, bringing about eight or nine fellows whom they had arrested. They confronted the patient with them to see whether he recognized the culprit among them. There was a Portuguese sailor among them and he pointed to him. The Portuguese defended himself and said that he had been in the Roman chapel at the time. The English Dr. B. said to the patient that he was near eternity and should take good care that he did not denounce an innocent man, etc.

The doctor asked whether I had not observed that the Portuguese had betrayed no emotion and whether this was not an evidence of innocence. I answered that this was not to be taken as an infallible evidence, since bandits might kill any number in one evening and, by dint of a blasted conscience, betray no emotion, etc. It therefore could even be, in certain circumstances and to some extent, a *probable* sign. The patient said that he could not assert it with entire certainty, but he nevertheless believed that the Portuguese was the culprit. A young German fellow was also wounded at the same time, though not so gravely.

These are the fruits when untrammeled young people rove around this way on a Sunday night. When all the outward turmoil had subsided, I sought to examine the patient a little with regard to the state of his soul but found him quite ignorant and muddled. I said a prayer of penitence for him to say after me, which he did at first, but could not continue because of pain. About one o'clock returned home.

NOVEMBER 23. In the evening I had a visit from a scholar from New England, Mr. Webster, who was desirous of speaking with me concerning the doctrine and discipline of the Lutheran church. So far as time would allow, I answered his questions concerning our doctrine of baptism, Lord's Supper, predestination, divine providence. Afterwards he was anxious to know the specific differences between us and the Calvinists, Papists, and Arminians, and also our church government and discipline. Finally I asked him whether and when God had begun his work of grace, repentance, and conversion in him. He gave a good account thereof and finally asked me to read some Latin and Greek to him because he wanted to hear the *pronunciation* and *accentuation,* etc. Afterwards I was summoned to the wounded patient, but when I arrived he had just died. Visit from Mr. Heidt, who said that he intended to set out on his journey to Germany in about ten days.

DECEMBER 28. I received a recipe for ink powder. For a quantity of good ink:

1) 8 *loth* strong black gallic
2) 4 *loth* copperas
3) 2 *loth* alum
4) 1½ *loth* gum

This is all mixed together and put in a clean pot. Over it is poured a glassful of wine vinegar, and a small handful of salt is thrown in. Next, a glassful of boiling water is added, stirred well, and after twenty-four hours another quantity of boiling water is poured over it; for several days stirred frequently, will become good and black.

DECEMBER 31. Heavy rain. Corrected the verse for the New Year; stayed up; was annoyed by much foolish shooting. At twelve midnight I received a serenade from Mr. Hafner, etc., and heard the ringing of the bells.

"Praise God! One step toward eternity," etc.

The Year 1763

MARCH 6. The weather was damp, unhealthy, and thawing. Went to church. Baptized three children and preached on the first two words of Christ from the cross. Arranged privately for a meeting of the *trustees* next Thursday. Came home at 12:30 P.M.

I borrowed Mr. Keppele's horse and rode to the Schuylkill through deep roads with my son Frederick. Arrived about three o'clock at the schoolhouse in Kingsessing, where I found the congregation assembled. We sang a portion of Psalm 22 and Psalm 32, and I delivered a didactic sermon in English on the first two words of Christ on the cross. The people were very attentive. According to the order of the provost I made an appointment with the young people for tomorrow forenoon, at ten o'clock, to be catechized by the schoolmaster.

After church we had cold rain. First I rode to see an old German Evangelical couple, born in Alsace, about whom His Reverence the Doctor had mentioned that they desired communion. However, they begged off until another time because some of those belonging to the family were not present. They spoke proudly of the fact that the provost had visited them several times and edified them with God's Word, of which they had had little since Mr. Brunnholtz's death since they were too old and feeble to come to Philadelphia to church.

From there I rode to the home of Captain Coultas, an Englishman greatly respected in the whole country who fills the office of *sherif* and is also justice of the peace. In the evening he told me how he had been awakened and led to Christ by His Reverence Dr. de Wrangel's teaching and life and how he had become a communing member of the Evangelical Lutheran Church, which caused some respected friends in the English High Church to show their astonishment and secret ill-will toward him.

To these people he had replied that he had found too much politics and party feeling in the Philadelphia High Church, and his soul had no pleasure in such things but took pleasure rather in the essence and practice of the Christian religion. And since he had found in His Reverence Dr. de Wrangel the purest motives and endeavors toward the true, upright essence of the kingdom of Jesus Christ, he had with full conviction joined his congregation and church and up to now had received satisfaction and edification for his soul. He could say with truth and joy that Dr. de Wrangel had gathered a congregation in this vicinity where, before, everything was dead and scattered, and had led to Christ, through the means of grace, more than twenty persons who formerly neither knew nor believed anything at all. He said that he would rather sit on the lowest benches with such souls than with those who sit in the church pews in great outward pomp but have no experience of real Christianity, etc. He is a gentleman who is active day and night doing good for his fellow creatures, but especially for his brethren in the faith. And now that grace and faith have taken root in him, his works of love that grow out of his faith are truly sanctified and very considerable.

An English *Baptist* preacher was also lodging there the same night; lives a hundred miles away and discoursed very powerfully and edifyingly on the article of justification. He had been unfortunate a few days before, having been robbed of £120 by Irish Roman people. Some of them have already been put in prison.

MARCH 7. Squire Coultas and the *Baptist* preacher, Mr. Marsh, rode early to the city. I rode to the schoolhouse about ten o'clock. Although it was raining and the roads were very deep, I found more than thirty young people and children, and also a few adults present. First I had a brief prayer; afterwards the schoolmaster sang a Psalm with the children. The young people had their notes before them, from which they sang. Then the schoolmaster questioned them on the five chief parts of Luther's Small Catechism, which the children had learned by heart and recited well. Then they were catechized on the Order of Salvation, which is appended to the Catechism, and also gave the *dicta probantia.*

After this the schoolmaster catechized them on a number of important points of doctrine on which he had written out exegetical remarks gathered from the catechizations of His Reverence the Provost. For example, on the moral law and its bindingness; how far it extends; on the Gospel; on the Sabbath of the New Testament; and so on. It is extremely necessary to inculcate these matters among the youth of these parts because they are being contradicted. After the young people had also given a good conduct of themselves in this respect, they sang a song from Dr. Isaac Watts' *Spiritual Poesy.* Finally I made a further simple little experiment and asked a few practical questions about the Ten Commandments, the creation of men, and their fall and redemption, to which they gave full and satisfactory answers according to the capacity of their power of judgment. Finally they promised to memorize the *protevangelium,* Genesis 3:15.

I can well say that such a school for the youth as this is after all the most effective attack upon the enrooted kingdom of darkness and is the right mustard seed from which the kingdom of Christ must grow if it is continued by God's grace and help. Finally we sang Psalm 146 in fine harmony and closed with prayer. I told the children that I was delighted with their industry and that I was willing to send them something, either a little cake for each, or a little book; they should tell me what they wanted most. One of them replied that a book lasts longer and is more useful, and the rest concurred in this. Consequently I am a debtor and must keep the promise if I am not to lose my credit. About one o'clock I rode back to Philadelphia and arrived home about three o'clock, wet and bespattered.

About four o'clock I buried Jacob Frantz's little daughter, Dorothea, who died of purpura. The roads were extraordinarily deep and muddy, but still there was a large *suite*. Funeral text, Revelation 7:14, 16. Afterwards I was summoned to a young man who had shot off his thumb while shooting pigeons. When I got back home I found Messrs. Jacobi, Groothouse, and Gilbert, who had ridden in from Germantown with His Reverence Dr. de Wrangel almost at the risk of their lives because of the bottomless streets. They said that the provost was waiting for me to go with him to the king's *attorney*.

I waded out and found the Reverend Doctor already with the *attorney*, along with Messrs. Wighard Miller and Christian Lehman and Mr. Galloway, Esq. Jacobi, Groothouse, and Gilbert also came later. They held a long conference with regard to the church's suit. They also found a few errors in the procedure, which can easily happen when so many cooks do the cooking and are unfamiliar with the English language. They decided: (a) that Christian Lehman should act as witness concerning the *deeds,* etc.; (b) that Muhlenberg should give testimony before the court concerning the first *plan* of the United Congregations and because he is timid, His Reverence Dr. de Wrangel was requested also to give testimony with regard to the united *plan* because he had at various times attended the annual *synod* as provost of the first Swedish church. The *attorneys* finally said that it would be safer if they took up, first thing in the morning, the action concerning an illegal marriage which Henry Rapp had performed.

We broke up about nine o'clock, and since it was necessary to confer with Dr. de Wrangel further, I went with him in the dark to Wicaco, though we were both wet and muddy enough from the journey. We got stuck fast on the way, however, and had to borrow a lantern. We arrived at Wicaco about ten o'clock. The provost was more concerned about my welfare than his own.

I could sleep but little because the wind and rain stormed through the whole night and I always feel in such lawsuit *troubles* as if I am going to be hanged. Prayer and sighing do not always help and avail, and faith sees nothing; one's confidence is beset by the consciousness of one's many failures in office, one's constitution is enfeebled, and the spirit of life is dried up, and so one stands there before God, forsaken on every side, like a poor malefactor upon whom the judgment has been spoken, to enemies a hideous object, to the ignorant an object of all sorts of judgments and reflections. In these last years if, next to God almighty, I had not had the Rev. Provost de Wrangel for protection and help, I would have sunk. God the merciful Father in Christ will, some day, out of grace for Jesus Christ's sake, redeem me from all evil and bring peace; otherwise I see no help, for the *trouble* in my office and family is increasing daily and my powers of body and mind are steadily decreasing.

MARCH 8. The storm and rain still continue. The provost gave me a horse to ride home and promised to follow. About ten o'clock I went to Mr. Andrew Banckson's, a respected Swedish merchant and *trustee* of the church, where I found His Reverence Dr. de Wrangel already there. At 10:30 A.M. we went to the *courthouse,* which was already crowded with all sorts of people.

The *court* opened and dealt first with something concerning a road that had been laid out and other matters. Finally the name of Henry Rapp was called out and he was commanded to come forward. It was read out to him that he had been arrested three months ago on account of a marriage, since he had married a woman to an Irishman who was already married. He was then asked whether he pleaded guilty. He answered, "Not guilty!" He said he knew nothing whatever of having married such a couple, but that he was not ready for his defense. The king's *attorney* asked whether he would be ready on the morrow. Answer: He did not even know why he had been arrested and must have time until another *court*. Hereupon he thrust a few dollars at an advocate who stood up and spoke for him. After he had spoken for him and in favor of postponement of the matter, the king's *attorney* replied and insisted that it must be taken up now. Another advocate, Squire Joseph Galloway, also spoke, saying that it must be tried at this time. The *justices* of the peace, sixteen of whom were present, took a vote as to whether it should be dealt with now or in the next *court*. Twelve voted that it should be tried now and four desired to have it postponed, namely, Messrs. Stedman, Duché, Jones, etc. Squire Coultas directed the rest. Finally it was declared that the case should be taken up at three o'clock in the afternoon. The advocate who had spoken for Rapp whispered in my ear, *"Rapp will be tryed* P.M. *three o'clock he is a rogue, and may perhaps make away."*

The provost and I left the *court* since nothing was coming up with regard to the church affair. We had our noon meal with Mr. Banckson; received news that Rapp's *action* was to come up and the church's case would be turned over to the *Supream Court*. After three o'clock Dr. de Wrangel and Mr. Banckson went to the courthouse to listen to the *tryal*. I begged them to excuse me from going along since I felt ill. I went away and visited a sick person, and from there went home. How it turned out, I do not know.

MARCH 9. Mr. Zoe reported that Frederick Walter's little daughter had died and was to be buried tomorrow afternoon at four o'clock. Stephen Rigler paid for his little daughter's grave fee, 5s.; for my pains 7s. 6d. Visit from Christopher Raben and Schoolmaster Selig, who requested divine services at Barren Hill and also reported that yesterday Rapp's *action* had been postponed until the next *court*.

APRIL 9. I was very anxious and worried about the Germantown lawsuit, not knowing whether it would come up or not, or how it would turn out. It is not proper to set down here what I thought, said, and felt in secret prayer before the heart-searching Majesty. Wonderful is God's governance, unsearchable are his ways! About 10 A.M. I was unexpectedly summoned to the Supreme Court at the *State House*. I had to take an oath in public court that I would give testimony in a criminal investigation to the best of my knowledge and conscience. I was somewhat doubtful, because I feared it might be prejudicial to my office if I were to permit myself to be qualified by an oath, but it was explained that the English laws required it, regardless of one's station or office. It had to do with the murder which occurred on Sunday evening, November 21, 1762. After being qualified I had to go into a large private chamber where I found a number of justices of the peace, who examined me with reference to what I had heard from the mortally wounded Robert Willsby on the aforesaid night.

When it was over I went to Leonard Melcher's house and spoke with a woman from New Hanover concerning her sorry matrimonial dispute with her husband. From there I was again summoned to the Supreme Court and had to testify to the same facts respecting my knowledge of the affair in open court. The sentence finally turned out to be that it had not been an intentional but an accidental murder, which involved a sentence only of a brand on the hand, but not hanging.

In the evening I had a visit from my brother-in-law, Samuel Weiser, and Andrew Montour, an Indian agent. Late in the evening I meditated a little more and also recorded a number of children who had been announced for baptism tomorrow. I was summoned to the sick wife of George Beck, the confectioner.

APRIL 11. I went first to Squire Ross and inquired as to whether the Germantown suit would not come up in this session of the *Supream* Court. He was of the opinion that it was impossible, which disappointed me greatly and gave rise to much misgiving. I therefore resolved to look with utter calmness to the Supreme Ruler, who would accomplish it in accord with his all-gracious will, to his glory, and to the best interest of souls. From there I went to George Beck's sick wife, whom I found somewhat better. Afterwards I had a visit from Conrad Fleck, who wanted to be naturalized, but he arrived too late. He gave me 7s. 6d. *pro salario.*

Received a letter from Pastor Kurtz, of Tulpehocken, through Caspar Krueger and Liebegut, in which he inquired about Germantown. I wrote a reply to the effect that in the Germantown affair things looked blacker than ever. Visit from William Collins' wife, who wanted to buy our house. After we had informed ourselves concerning her circumstances, however, her character was described as bad. Mrs. Meyer, formerly Creutz, announced her daughter for instruction and confirmation.

In the evening I wrote a letter to Pastor Gerock, of Lancaster, informing him that Pastor John George Bager was still wanted in New York and that he should set out on his journey; that the outlook for the Germantown affair was very doubtful; that we must soon convoke a *committee* of the Ministerium and deal with common matters; finally, also concerning Pastor Andrew Borell in Wilmington.

APRIL 12. We had heavy snow and rain. First a man from Germantown came and wanted to compel me to bury his brother's child tomorrow in the disputed Lutheran cemetery and deliver an address in the church. Later two more came and said that since the lawsuit was not going to be settled in this *Supream Court,* the group was inclined to occupy the church next Sunday by force and throw out Pastor Henry Rapp, etc. I said that we preachers and elders would have nothing to do with such procedure, etc. Then three more came, namely, Mr. Gilbert, Mr. Kreuter, and his brother-in-law. They said that a great disaster would result if the affair was not settled in the *Supream Court.* I at once gave them a new *species facti,* and also another document, and said that they might go immediately to Squire William Allen, the chief judge, and to the King's agents, submit my documents, and set forth the danger by word of mouth. As far as the child's funeral was concerned, I told them that they must excuse me this time and rather take along a schoolmaster who would be able to take care of the funeral services.

In the afternoon Messrs. Gilbert, Metz, Nubel, etc. came and reported with great joy that the Supreme Court had ordered and decided that the opposite party should give the key to our people and grant them permission to hold divine service in our church every other Sunday, to wit, once in the forenoon, and on the alternate Sunday in the afternoon. Since I had promised to conduct divine service next Sunday morning in St. Peter's Church at Barren Hill, I arranged that I would, God willing, preach the first sermon in Germantown on the afternoon of the same day.

About two o'clock in the afternoon I went in a heavy rain to the schoolhouse, where all the young people who had announced themselves were to assemble for instruction. They were nearly seventy in number. Both of us preachers began to instruct them. Before this I married Jacob Ott, previously unmarried, and Catharine Reiss, unmarried, of Lower Dublin, the banns having been published thrice. In the evening I was summoned to Mr. Wildberger's to marry Philip Altimus, unmarried, and Catharine, daughter of the late Bauman, the banns having been published thrice. From there I stopped in for a little while to see Mr. Halling and his family.

APRIL 13. Today another messenger came from Germantown with the report that our people had demanded the key to the church and that Christian Schneider, as Rapp's elder, had replied that they would not open the church for a schoolmaster, but if they brought a preacher along, the church would be opened. And now our people thought that I must positively come out today in order to take *possession.*

In the meantime, however, I received news that Thomas Meyer, one of our first Lutheran deacons before my arrival, had fallen out of his shallop on Monday and drowned, and must be buried today. This Thomas Meyer was born in the Palatinate in 1709 and came to this country in 1732. Just before my arrival in 1742, he had journeyed by way of England to Germany and also had the honor of seeing His Reverence Court Preacher Ziegenhagen. He had the custody of the church's strong box, which we accepted during his absence. He returned in 1743, bringing with him his brother, Matthaeus Meyer. He was a well-to-do man so long as his first wife, Catharine Uterich, was living. Two children of this marriage are still living. In his second marriage—he married an English person, Adam Andree's widow—he was ruined completely, had difficulty in making ends meet, at times even suffering hunger and privation. On April 11, as he was on the water following his calling and was about to beach his shallop, he fell out and sank.

In the evening, about six o'clock, he was buried in our cemetery. I had intended to preach a funeral sermon on the texts, Hosea 13:9, "O Israel, thou hast destroyed thyself," etc., and Amos 3:6, "Shall there be evil in a city," etc., but it had grown dark. I read only his biography and discoursed on Psalm 71:17, 18, "O God, forsake me not." John Molidor's daughter, Barbara, seventeen years old, announced herself for instruction and confirmation.

APRIL 21.   About eight o'clock I went to *Chief Judge* Allen, Esq., said farewell to him, thanked him for his faithfulness and good will toward our German nation, and commended my three sons to his fatherly supervision and him to God's most gracious protection.[1] He was very friendly and said that he hoped, God willing, to return in fifteen months. From there I went up on the ship and spoke with Captain Budden. Thence to Mr. Groot's, who promised to write a letter to Mr. Copius concerning Mr. Justus Meyer's *affair.* I stopped in for a while at Mr. Keppele's.

In the evening I went to church. I found a large gathering present and I gave a meditation on Luke 24:34, "The Lord is risen indeed, and hath appeared to Simon." After church a Catholic man made a complaint that a Lutheran neighbor woman had ridiculed and defamed him because of his faith. I went with him to the woman and admonished both of them to repentance and conversion. Spent the evening writing.

APRIL 27.   About twelve noon His Reverence Dr. de Wrangel, who had just returned from Wilmington, visited us. At twelve o'clock I said farewell to my three children in the presence of the provost, commended them to the Lord God in prayer, and requested the provost also to give them a blessing, which he did. Also said farewell to Mr. Justus Frederick Meyer. We had our noon meal together and about one o'clock my wife went to the ship with the children. The provost remained with me and told how things had gone on his church visitation in Wilmington, how he had preached (1) Swedish, (2) English, and also (3) to the poor Germans scattered thereabouts. He also made some remarks as to how grace was beginning to work in the two preachers of the *English Episcopal* Church, the *Rev. Messrs.*

---

[1] *The three Muhlenberg sons, Peter (aged 16), Frederick (13), and Henry (9) went to Germany for education at Halle.*

Peters and Duché. Afterwards Mr. Nicholas Hornell, the adjunct, came also.

The ship departed about 4 P.M. under command of Captain Budden. The passengers were: Mr. William Allen, Esq., *chief judge;* Mr. Henry Groot's wife and her little son; Mr. Shady, a sugar refiner, and his wife; Hofman, a Newlander; Henry Keppele, Jr., Mr. Meyer, and my three children.

MAY 24. Visit from the late Pastor J. Conrad Steiner's widow; also from John Juerger, of New Hanover. From two-thirty to six o'clock in the afternoon I had the confirmands in the church. Toward evening a visit from John Juerger, his wife Sybilla, and the former's mother-in-law, who desired to be reconciled. Further, a visit from the wives of Caspar and Jacob Graef. My wife accompanied me to the *Presbyterian* Church because the ministers were holding synod and the *president* of Jersey College was preaching an evening sermon. Pastor Hornell was also present during the instruction of the confirmands.

MAY 25. In the forenoon I went to our school, examined several classes, and distributed trinkets among the children as rewards. About one o'clock I was summoned to Mr. Tauberman's sick wife, of the Reformed religion. The woman exhibited awakening and feeling for her moral depravity, and prayed for grace with Jesus.

When I got home about three o'clock I found Pastor Hornell and Apothecary Schneider, the latter having brought a dozen small Halle Bibles to be sent to New Hanover for sale. Mr. Hornell went with me to the funeral of John Jacob Binder's child, where I spoke on the words from Matthew 17:4, "Lord, it is good for us to be here." Mr. Hornell went home with me again, where we found Mrs. Robison, a Swedish widow, and her daughter Mrs. van der Spiegel on a visit. About seven o'clock I went with Mr. Hornell to the *Presbyterian* Church and heard the Rev. Mr. Smith preach very edifyingly on Luke 16:31, "If they hear not Moses and the prophets, neither will they," etc. When

I came home I found there the cabinet-maker, Philip Flag, unmarried. He stayed with me until after ten o'clock.

MAY 30. Mr. Rein gave 7*s*. 6*d*. for his daughter's confirmation. Susanna Barbara Pfeister gave 7*s*. 6*d*. Catherine Liebrich, working at Thomas Schoot's, gave 5*s*. for confirmation. Visit from Mr. Truckenmueller and from Apothecary Schneider. Paid 5*s*. to Maus, the stockinger, for stockings, in behalf of Dr. Martin. Wrote a brief letter to Mother-in-law Weiser to go with Elias Botener.

In the afternoon came news that our former servant girl, Maria Wintzenholter, had been put in *prison* under *suspicion* of theft at the market. She sent word to ask us to intercede for her. My wife went out on her account. Visit from the Rev. Mr. Schlatter. Later on, *Mistress* Halling also came. She gave me 10*s*. for the confirmation of her servant girl, Anna Maria Schoch. She remained in our company.

About 6 P.M. His Reverence Dr. de Wrangel came for a friendly visit. The Rev. Samuel Harker also stopped in later. He said that the *Reverend* Synod of the *Presbyterian* Church had expelled and condemned him without trial on account of his published writing, *De gratia universali*, in spite of his asking that they convince him with counter-arguments. Afterwards Mr. Billmeyer, of York, came and conferred a little with the provost with regard to placing Pastor Hornell in their vacant congregation. The provost, however, had to leave at once to go to the *hospital* to visit the sick. Mr. Billmeyer stayed on and said that the provost had very kindly promised that Pastor Hornell should come to York in four weeks.

In the meantime Mr. Hartwick also came and asked whether some men from Frederick, Maryland, had not been with me. Answer: No. He said that the congregation must be supplied. He asked whether I had appointed anybody to go there. Answer: I had left the matter in Mr. Gerock's hands, who had recommended Mr. Samuel Schwertfeger to the place. I asked whether he himself still wanted to go there. Answer: No, but he nevertheless wanted the place filled.

Also had a visit from two men who had been sent from Easton. They asked whether Pastor Bernard Hausile had written to me yet. Answer: No. They said that he would preach for them next Sunday and that he had promised to visit them four times a year. He had also promised them that he would urge at the next synod meeting that other preachers of ours should help in order that the congregation might have divine service every four weeks until they could be supplied with a qualified laborer. Visit from the awakened Frederick Dobelbauer. He gave 7s. 6d. on account of confirmation. The Rev. Mr. Harker left me a copy of his treatise, *De gratia universali.* I gave him a *douceur* for it. During the night I felt uneasy and oppressed.

MAY 31. Visit from Messrs. George Kuhntz and Bonner, of York. They delivered to me a communication concerning Pastor Hornell which the York church council had sent to Pastor Gerock and which he had sent to me with comments. Mr. Gerock requests a reply to his last letter of April. Visit from Widow Zimmermann. She gave 7s. 6d. on account of her daughter Maria Elisabeth's confirmation. The one faction of the German Reformed congregation which holds to Pastor Rothenbuehler has taken up a lot not far from my residence and is keenly bent on building a new church.

As we have already learned several times through the English newspapers, efforts are being made in England, under the auspices of His Royal Majesty, to establish eminent colleges in Philadelphia and New York for the propagation of the holy Gospel, according to the true church, among Christians and heathen. Visit from Pastor Schlatter. About six o'clock I was called to Freyburger's very sick wife to give her communion, which I did. Afterwards I had a visit from Mr. Conrad Grosch, an elder of the congregation at Frederick, Maryland.

Finally I rode out to Wicaco on a horse sent by His Reverence Dr. de Wrangel, where in the pleasant company of the Rev. Messrs. Duché, Harker, Dr. Clarkson, etc., we engaged in a discussion until nearly eleven o'clock concerning the religious controversy between Mr. Harker and the synod. Today our good friend Mr. John Nicholas Kurtz sent his eldest son as a messenger with a letter dated May 28, *a.c.,* recounting the obstacles and difficulties which had been laid in the way of his accepting the Germantown call, etc. After the guests had left I conferred a little longer with the provost concerning Germantown and York and submitted the letter which the York church council had sent to Pastor Gerock and which he had sent on to me. During the night I felt very ill.

JUNE 14. Visited sick Peter Draess; spoke and prayed with him. His wife, who was lying in childbed, asked me to remind her sick husband to have his last will drawn up because she had a brood of children, etc. From there I went to good friend Mr. Handschuh's, conferred with him with regard to my necessary journey to the country congregations, and took leave of him.

About two o'clock in the afternoon I drove to Germantown with Mr. Christler and stayed overnight with Mr. Jacobi, who received me hospitably. I learned that in the previous week Pastor Rapp had lost his case against Martin Kreuter and had had to pay the costs. The reason why I had left the city on this day was that I did not care to be present at the laying of the cornerstone of a factional Reformed church on the following day, as it is a dangerous thing to mix in party affairs. Meanwhile, at home, my wife received £1 for George Adam Mayer's grave fee and 10*s. pro labore.*

JUNE 15. I was summoned from Germantown to old Michael Eckert. He was dying and was trying to say something about where he had hidden some money, but could not express it, and since he had lost his hearing it was also impossible to make him understand anything. He had willed something to the Germantown church and it was this that he wanted to tell Mr. Jacobi.

JULY 7. Visit from Captain de Haas who had received news that the Indians had taken some more small forts from us and murdered all the garrisons, etc.; that in the region of Shippensburg there were several thousands of women and children scattered in the woods and fields who would simply starve because they had fled so far from their homes to escape horrible massacre at the hands of the Indians.

JULY 8.   Summoned to pray with a sick woman beyond Pool Bridge, outside the city, which I did, and because she was so poor she asked me whether I would not give her a contribution with which to buy some medicine. From there I went back to the city and stopped for an hour and engaged in edifying conversation with Mr. Jacob Graef's family. Thence went to visit the Reverend Commissary Peters, of the English church and president of the Academy, who showed me a letter from the *chancellor* in England, which gave the information that under the present confused circumstances abroad they could not and dared not approach His Majesty on behalf of the German charity schools in this country because he is occupied with so many burdens; consequently the charity schools must be discontinued immediately. Hence I was at once to give notice of this fact to the *deputy trustees* and the schoolmaster in Providence, Hanover, and Pikestown. Thus this arrangement, which has for several years contributed especially to the good of the poorest German Protestants and their children, has come to an end.

All kinds of political party writings concerning the revolutions in Europe are being reprinted and promulgated here. So, on the one hand, things look distressing in Europe and, on the other, they look perilous here on account of the savage nations. However, that there are still a few people even here to whom the merciful God reveals his determinate counsel may be presumed from the following example. There was brought to my house for criticism an English *manuscript* entitled *Remarkable Relation of a Visionary Sight, as it was seen Pennsylvania Febr. the 14th 1763*. No one could really have dreamed then that in so short a time a bloodbath would be inflicted upon the inhabitants of North America. The beginning of it coincides exactly with the manuscript, and if the outcome should also correspond with it, sword and hunger will make many widows and orphans and fill the streams of the hinterlands with blood. God is supremely just and holy. Since the war and the recent peace, a mortification has set in on the body of North America and speedy *amputation* will be necessary if the rest is not to die altogether.

JULY 18. Early in the morning had a visit from Mr. Ebelin, who said he heard from English people that I was going back to Europe; he begged me to take him along with me, etc. There is a spirit of confusion among the German people. The old Reformed party is being served in the old church by a Reformed preacher from Germantown who is under the authority of the Reverend Synod of Holland. The separated Reformed party is holding services in a large, newly begun church, which so far has only one story of masonry, and the party is being served by a Swiss pastor, Mr. Rothenbuehler. Since our church is too small and there is not enough room or seating capacity for several hundred Lutherans, these people are going to the new Reformed church. Consequently our church was very sparsely attended yesterday afternoon at Mr. Handschuh's service and the new Reformed church was crowded. Besides, Pastor Hartwick now appears to be working against us inasmuch as he is preaching on Sundays in the suburb called Kensington and intends to cut off our members from St. Michael's Church. Moreover, some of our Lutherans are riding and driving to Germantown on Sundays to hear Mr. Kurtz, who began his ministry there a week ago yesterday.

Visit from Mrs. Klemmer, the midwife, who gave 7*s*. 6*d*. for her daughter's confirmation. Juerg Michael Riem gave 7*s*. 6*d*. for his step-daughter's confirmation. About 6 P.M. went to the Rev. Mr. Duché's, where I took part in an edifying conversation until nine o'clock. Those present: Messrs. Roberdo, Dr. Clarkson, Charles de Wrangel, D.D., Mr. Jacob Duché, *minister,* Mrs. Hopkison, and another aged Englishwoman, Mrs. Duffil. The subject was the working of God's Spirit upon the soul, illustrated by examples from experience and judged in Christian simplicity according to the Word of God as the *principium cognoscendi.* After nine o'clock I stopped in at Leopold's, intending to admonish him, but he was not at home. Blasius Beck died today. My wife visited the Martin Riess family. His Reverence Dr. de

Wrangel communicated to me a letter from Pastor Weygand, of New York.

JULY 20. In the forenoon George Loh, from the country, brought his sick child and had it baptized with the name Jacob. In the afternoon had a pleasant visit from Dr. de Wrangel which greatly cheered me, but I also heard that in the previous week an assembly, gathered for prayer in an English Reformed church in Virginia, was attacked by the Indians and thirty persons in the church were murdered and scalped. Thus the judgment begins at the house of God.

AUGUST 5. Visited poor Michael Weissinger, who was sick, and gave him a small gift of alms from my alms box. Afterwards set out with my wife and my daughter Margaret to cross the Delaware River in a boat. We were unable to push off until twelve noon, but crossed safely and at half-past two went on by wagon in great heat. We had thirty-five miles to go and finally arrived safe and sound at Mr. Jacob Fries's after midnight, near one o'clock.

AUGUST 6. Troubled by dysenteric movements owing to the heat of the previous day and the cold night air. Gradually our poor, scattered brethren began to come in, people who live five, ten, and fifteen miles away. They had not heard a sermon since the previous June, 1762, and exhibited a fervent desire to hear the Word of God and receive holy communion. At twelve noon we went to the church, a building that trembled because of its weak foundations and whose roof served to keep out the sunshine better than the rain.

Only a few of the members live near the church and school-house; the majority are scattered at great distances. The soil is very poor and sandy, and the Germans are accustomed to spend the summer months in the regions where they can make barrel staves and tar in order to make a bare living.

The church was full and I gave them an exposition of the hymn, *"Treuer Gott, ich muss dir klagen,"* etc. After this had been well taken to heart, we proceeded to confession and absolution. Anna Margaret Roller, a single person, desired to renew her baptismal covenant and be confirmed. I examined her privately and found that she had a sufficient knowledge of the chief doctrines necessary for salvation and received good testimonies concerning her life in the presence of the congregation, had her answer questions concerning the articles of faith, and confirmed her. She was born in this country and had been in service among English people who had paid no attention to her spiritual welfare, until she reached the age of understanding, learned to read, and through reading the holy Scriptures acquired a desire to become a member of Jesus and the Christian church. Likewise Mr. J. Kientsch applied for confirmation of his wife, who had grown up among English Quakers. He had given her good instruction in the chief doctrines of God's Word. I examined her, prayed with her, and confirmed her. Toward evening we visited an upright, well-disposed member of the congregation and his Christian family.

AUGUST 7.   A large crowd gradually assembled from far and wide. I recorded those who desired to commune. After the crowd had gathered in and around the church, I became very much concerned as to how I was going to baptize the children who had been registered for baptism, for there were twenty-two children to baptize and the church was so crowded that there was hardly any room left for me. The twenty-two children were crying so loudly that the noise was wretched. After I had baptized all of them and dismissed them in peace, the mothers hurried out with them into the open air; others crowded in and we went on with the service. With God's help and the co-operating grace of his Spirit I preached on Luke 19:41ff. I found the listeners inside and outside the church to be very attentive, which is usually the case with those who very seldom have an opportunity to hear a sermon. After the sermon the people had to be moved again so that those who had today declared their intention to commune could be inside the church. For these people I held confessional service and delivered an exhortation. About one o'clock in the afternoon we celebrated holy communion with some ninety members.

After this was completed in proper order, the women were dismissed and the men stayed. I read out the reckoning of the offerings made at the Sunday gatherings at which a sermon was customarily read by the schoolmaster. This totalled £5 and some shillings, so that the church treasury now had a balance of £34 and some shillings, which could be used in the near future for the enlarging and repairing of the church. They very urgently and fervently besought us to visit them from Philadelphia or to send others from our Ministerium to see that they were provided with the means of grace. They begged me in particular to confer with the Swedish provost in Philadelphia, and with the Swedish missionary pastor at Raccoon, so that the latter, too, might come to their assistance, since we Germans were able to get away so seldom.

Toward evening, accompanied by my family and the school-master, I visited the first and oldest settler who twenty-four years before had helped to build the church, namely, Jacob M. Miller. He made mention of several things I had said in my sermon and spoke of old times, especially of Pastor Schultze, whom he had brought from Ansbach to this country in 1732.

When we got home in the evening I conducted devotions with the numerous members of the family and some others. I asked each one what impression he had received today, and from the answers I observed that simple people always retain things better when one gives edifying examples to illustrate the explanation of the Word. For example: Satan plays with some souls as children play with birds. They take a long piece of string, tie the end to the bird's leg, and hold the other end in their hand. The bird may flutter as best it can, but when it goes too far it is pulled back. Application: Satan will allow a lot of external things, like going to church, as long as there is no true turning from darkness to light, from the power of Satan to complete freedom in and through the Son of God, etc.

Another example which I cited was likewise easily compre-hensible: I was summoned to go to a neighborhood inhabited by English people who had purchased, as servants, many of our poor

Germans who had been shipped to this country. Since these Germans had not for several years heard any preaching at all in their own language and had expressed a desire for it, their masters were Christian enough to invite me to preach, first an English sermon in their church and afterwards in German for their servants. I did so to their pleasure. Afterwards when the German service commenced and the Germans sang beautifully and harmoniously, the English people sat back in their pews and the expressions on their faces showed that they were entranced. When the service was over and I had stepped outside the church, the Germans gathered around me and wept aloud, partly for joy at having again heard the Word of God and partly for sorrow that they had so little opportunity to hear it, whereas in Germany they had had plenty and did not make good use of it. Some of the masters asked me what was the meaning of their servants' crying. Were they complaining over lack of food and drink or clothing? When I told them the real reason, some of them wept also and expressed the wish that the servants might soon learn the English language and be able to worship at the English services. An old gentleman who was born in Wales came up and said, "The German people can sing like the holy angels, but some of them live like the devil." He said he had been in a place where he had seen the Germans coming out of church with tears in their eyes, but they went right over to the next tavern and dried their tears with material spirits. The application was easy to make: how heinous the sin and great the offense to hold the truth in unrighteousness in the very light of the Gospel!

During the night we had one shower of rain after another.

AUGUST 8. Made preparations for the return journey, though it was raining hard, since I had to be in Philadelphia on the morrow, God willing, for the day of thanksgiving for the peace concluded in Europe. We set out from Mr. Fries's at nine o'clock in a country wagon and kept on going through rain and shine until about six o'clock in the evening, when we reached the Delaware River after putting thirty-five miles behind us. We had asked a couple of friends in Philadelphia to take us by land from the Delaware to Philadelphia. However, since it had rained so terrifically in Philadelphia, they had been in doubt as to whether we would come, so we found only one *chaise*, Mr. Christler's, when we crossed the river. This was sufficient to carry my wife and daughter and luggage, and I was obliged to walk the five miles home that evening. Arrived home near nine o'clock overheated and fatigued.

August 10. A visitor came on account of matrimonial troubles, and another on account of a man sick with dropsy; he desired me to use my good offices for him with the overseer of the poor. Visit from two overseers of the poor to whom I gave a few lines addressed to the doctors regarding the dropsical man. Visit from a sick woman who desired advice with regard to her illness. Visit from Frederick Sachs. Summoned to the dropsical Michael Weissinger when an English doctor was tapping him. Near 6 P.M. my wife and I went to the home of the English-woman, Mrs. Hopkison, on Walnut Street, where we attended a devotional hour conducted by awakened English people. Dr. de Wrangel, Mr. Duché, Dr. Clarkson, and others were present. Came home about ten o'clock. Dr. de Wrangel expressed his regret that it had been impossible for any preacher to be at the Kingsessing church on the afternoon of the recent day of thanksgiving, for about fifteen hundred people had been present in vain.

August 26. Alexander Murray, the new missionary of the English in Reading, came to visit me right after my arrival and engaged me in a long conversation concerning the English Church. He deeply regretted that a *coalition* between the German Lutheran congregations and the English Church had not yet been effected. He expressed the opinion that this was just the most suitable period in which to establish a bishop in America. And if this were to come to pass, native German sons of good intelligence and piety could be educated in the English academies, ordained, and usefully employed for the best welfare of the church of Christ in both the German and English languages, since, as it is, strife and factiousness prevail in the German

Evangelical and Reformed congregations and the people are gradually joining with the Quakers or might even fall back into heathenism if preventive measures are not taken.

I told him that I would think just as he did if I were in his place. I said that one could travel from one pole to the other in a few minutes on a map, but in practice things went much more slowly and laboriously. It is something fondly to be hoped for that all the walls of partition made by human hands may be done away and Christ be all in all.

SEPTEMBER 21. In the forenoon I went to the Rev. Commissary Peters and spoke with him in regard to the late Mr. Heintzelman's child. I also learned from him that Mr. George Whitefield had arrived yesterday and requested the permission of the *vestry* of the English Church to preach in their church.

SEPTEMBER 24. Three men from the Goshenhoppen congregation came to secure testimonials for naturalization. About eleven o'clock I went to Mr. Daniel Roberdo's, where Mr. George Whitefield, who arrived from Virginia last Tuesday, September 20, was lodging. I just happened to find Mr. Whitefield alone and was able to speak with him for a while. Among other things he spoke with great veneration of Court Preacher Ziegenhagen, called him a father in Christ, etc. He also said that he had recently received a letter from Dr. G. A. Francke, of Halle, which had strengthened and cheered him uncommonly, etc. He said that it was a great blessing that the most gracious God had till now preserved these two old fathers for the good of Christ's kingdom, etc. He asked me to let them know that he had arrived here and that he felt very weak in body, that he was at home hardly anywhere any more, that he desired release if it pleased his Master, etc.

I responded by saying that some years before he had said in a sermon here that he did not desire to be taken home in a whirlwind like Elijah, etc. I said to him, further, that awakened and pardoned souls could still bar the way to his departure by believing prayer. He said, however, that he believed that his own prayers would have precedence because his earthly tabernacle had become too weak and unfit to serve his Master. I related to him an example from the time of the Reformation, namely, how Superintendent Myconius was once very sick and the blessed Luther gained eight more years of life for him by his believing prayers, etc. And if Mr. Whitefield could no longer trumpet forth the Gospel because of the weakness of his lungs, he might retire to some corner and write for edification; thus awakened and pardoned souls would thereby receive equally as much profit.

I heard that he is to preach in the English High Church tomorrow morning for the first time, as the church council has requested him to do so.

At home I found Mr. Jacobi, of Germantown, who brought news concerning the church's lawsuit; he reported that the matter is to be settled by the *Supream Court* next Thursday. O help me, gracious God! How such affairs which have to do only with the outer fences around the untilled vineyard oppress me!

Toward evening Mr. Jacobi returned and brought the report that no session of the *Supream Court* would be held at this time because the chief judge, Squire Allen, had gone to England and the next in line was sick. Consequently all the preparations made for this session have been in vain.

OCTOBER 9. In the evening, from six to nine o'clock, I attended a gathering of awakened souls from our congregation in the home of Mr. Leonard Kessler. I noted some unusual traces of grace at this meeting. This forenoon, from ten to twelve o'clock, Mr. Whitefield preached in St. Peter's Church on Matthew 3:11, "I indeed baptize you with water, . . . he shall baptize you with the Holy Ghost and with fire," a text which had been suggested to him. There were tears and much emotion. He was again very sick and weak during the week.

Last Thursday we received a report that the Indians had won a victory over our English soldiers near Niagara. The Indians horribly murdered almost seventy of them and pillaged the *provisions* and *ammunition* that were destined for Fort Detroit. Thus does the Lord God visit our territories with goodness and severity.

OCTOBER 22. Our poor *diaconus* and catechist Mr. Friderici unexpectedly came from the scattered sheep beyond the Blue Mountains and reported that on account of the Indians he had fled to this side of the mountains with his wife and six children, leaving behind his cattle and the crops he had harvested for the winter. He gave me an account of his laborious pastoral work among many small congregations. Since he had worked so hard to serve our poor, scattered brethren with the means of grace, I felt I ought to give him something in his hour of need, so I asked him in Pastor Kurtz's absence to preach for me, God willing, tomorrow forenoon at Barren Hill and in the afternoon at Germantown. He was willing to do this and gave me support in my weakness.

Today there was a rumor going around the city that our Six Nations Indians, who have so far been loyal, have declared war against the English subjects, that now all the savage nations in America have united to destroy all white subjects under the scepter of Great Britain in North America, and that they will begin near Philadelphia within three full moons. Today we also received by messenger the news that the Indians had massacred a number of our settlers at the newly founded place near Wyoming Valley. It is said that the Indians are depending on a French fleet for support.

OCTOBER 30. About eight o'clock in the morning Mr. Gaub fetched me with his *chaise* and took me to Germantown, accompanied by Mr. Greiner, a deacon there. We arrived in Germantown at half-past nine. At ten-thirty the service was begun. Just as we were praying the Lord's Prayer in closing and everything was in deepest stillness and reverence, we suddenly heard a noise as though several coaches were going by. Then followed a shaking and trembling of the earth that shook the whole church, and my pulpit swayed back and forth.

I stopped in the middle of the third petition and realized for the first time that it was an earthquake. The faces of the whole crowd of people suddenly went pale and several women cried out in broken voices, "O God, it is an earthquake!" Whereupon everyone took alarm and was about to take flight, which in the great crowd would surely have caused great loss of life and many injuries. I immediately shouted to them to sit still and remain quiet, that it was the hand of God, that it was better to fall under his hand here than outside, and that I still had to pray. Everything grew quiet again and they broke out in tears, so that I was able, praise God, to begin to pray the Lord's Prayer again. Half crying and half speaking, we sang *"Christus, der ist mein Leben,"* etc. Before the benediction I reminded the congregation of what I had so urgently preached to them the week before from the text, Proverbs 1:24, "Because I have called, and ye refused, I have stretched out my hand, and no man regarded." Since the Lord had just now stretched out his hand, each one was to go home and into his chamber, bow beneath the mighty hand in penitent prayer, and bring with them the true Surety.

In the evening I had visits from several awakened souls. Today our new governor, John Penn, Esq., landed with Captain Budden and set foot on land at the very hour of the earthquake.

NOVEMBER 22. I heard that an expensive flour and oil mill was burned in Bethlehem, and it is thought that it may well have been done by neighboring inhabitants who were much embittered against the Moravians because they suspected that the Bethlehemites and their Indian friends had some part in several murders and burnings of their homes and farms. However, it is very difficult to prove, and still more difficult to remove the people's suspicions. O God, what confusion everywhere! More and more murders and burnings are occurring on the frontiers, and almost daily there are robberies in and around the city. The poor settlers are fleeing naked and destitute farther and farther into the country, and winter is upon us. The country people are becoming embittered because the authorities are taking no adequate measures for defense. So now we are beginning to hear that the people from the country are about to come to the city in droves and destroy everything in *revenge*. The city itself is swarming with unruly mobs which are ready to join with any hostile group and wreak havoc. In short, the cup of sin is full!

The Year 1764

JANUARY 15. At 5 P.M. I went out to the poorhouse with Mrs. Graef inasmuch as I had been requested to visit a soldier who was suffering from consumption. I spoke with him and another German concerning repentance and conversion. Since there were a number of other English paupers, cripples, and blind persons living in the same room, I prayed in English.

JANUARY 31. In the forenoon I went out in the rain to the *hospital* to visit a German woman, Maria Elizabeth Ripp, who was suffering from *mania*. I could accomplish little, however, as she had no understanding. She is constantly praying and screaming about spiritual things which she learned in her youth. The caretaker and his wife asked me to preach an English exhortation there occasionally for the patients.

FEBRUARY 1. This afternoon all citizens were summoned to the state house by the governor and *counsel* through the *conestable*. There the governor made a public proclamation:

1) That it had been learned that a large mob of frontier settlers, who had killed several Indians in Lancaster, were coming to Philadelphia to kill the Indian families who had been brought down from Bethlehem and taken under the protection of the government.

2) That since such procedure could be considered as being none other than a breach of the peace, revolution, or rebellion against our gracious king and the law of the land, the *Act of Riot* was invoked and one hundred and some regular soldiers were set apart to guard and protect the Bethlehem Indian families in the barracks.

3) That the governor and *counsel* called upon citizens who were willing to lend armed assistance and resist the rebellion to band themselves together and hand in their names.

4) That because there was a pouring rain at the time and the Germans did not enlist and sign their names with the rest, the governor and others were much offended, conjecturing that perhaps the Germans might be making common cause with the malcontents or so-called rebels, etc.

As far as I can learn, the opinion and sentiment of various ones of our German citizens is as follows:

1) They were of the opinion that it could be proved that the Indians who had lived among the so-called Moravian Brethren had secretly killed several settlers.

2) That the Quakers and Bethlehemites had only used some of the aforesaid Indians as spies and that they had in view only their own selfish interests, without considering at all that they had murdered their fellow Christians.

3) Indeed, that they had loaded down the said Indians with presents and taken them, their secret enemies, to their bosom only for the sake of this selfish interest, which explained why the Quakers, etc. in Philadelphia did not exhibit the least evidence of human sympathy, etc. when Germans and other settlers on the frontiers were massacred and destroyed in the most inhuman manner by the Indians. On the contrary, these Bethlehem Indians, despite their congenital craftiness, etc., were brought to Philadelphia and maintained and supported at the expense of the inhabitants. Besides, the young male Indians had already escaped and were probably doing harm while the old men and women and children were living off the fat of the land at the expense of the province.

4) And now because there was a rumor that the remote settlers, some of whom had lost their wives and others their children and relatives through these atrocious Indian massacres, were intending to come to Philadelphia in a corps and revenge themselves upon these Indians, and therefore our German citizens should enlist to fight, resist, or even kill their own flesh and blood, their fellow citizens and fellow Christians, and seek to protect the lives of the Bethlehem Indians! Why, they say, that would be quite contrary to nature and contrary to the law of

Christ, for he did not say, "Thou shalt hate thy friend and love thine enemy." That is the general *tone* among some. They would unhesitatingly and gladly pour out their possessions and their blood for our most gracious king and his officers, but they would not wage war against their own suffering fellow citizens for the sake of the Quakers and Moravians and their creatures or instruments, the double-dealing Indians.

It is difficult in such a crisis to say anything or give any judgment in such a strange *republick* which has caught a fever, or, rather, is suffering from *colica pituitosa.*

FEBRUARY 5. Toward evening the rumor sprang up that a corps of backwoods settlers—Englishmen, Irishmen, and Germans—were on the march toward Philadelphia to kill the Bethlehem Indians at the barracks outside the city. Some reported that they numbered seven hundred, others said fifteen hundred, etc. The Friends, or so-called Quakers, and the Moravians ran furiously back and forth to the barracks, and there was a great to-do over constructing several small fortresses or ramparts near the barracks. Cannons were also set up. Some remarked concerning all this that it seemed strange that such preparations should be made against one's own fellow citizens and Christians, whereas no one ever took so much trouble to protect from the Indians His Majesty's subjects and citizens on the frontier.

Toward evening His Reverence Dr. Wrangel came to preach in our church as he had promised to do. Pastors John Haeggblad and Paul Brycelius were with us at my house. We conferred hastily concerning the rumor which was circulating and what it might be necessary to say about it in our church. The principle is clearly and distinctly expressed in Romans 13:1, 2; Titus 3:1; I Peter 2:13, 14; Proverbs 24:21.

After two o'clock at night the watchmen began to cry, "Fire!" I asked our watchman, who is a member of our congregation, where the fire was. He said there was no fire, but that the watchmen had orders to cry out, "Fire," because the above-mentioned backwoodsmen were approaching. Thereupon all the alarm bells began to ring at once and a drum was sounded to summon the

inhabitants of the city to the town hall plaza. The ringing
sounded dreadful in the night.

I asked a German neighbor to go to the town hall and bring
me news of what was happening there. He reported that the
market place was crowded with all sorts of people and that arms
were being distributed to those who would take them. He had
not, however, seen many Germans. The sounding of the tocsin
continued on through the night until near dawn, and the
inhabitants were ordered to place lights inside the doors and
windows, which was done. Meanwhile, all sorts of rumors were
flying in every direction: The rebels had divided into three groups
and were going to attack the open city in three places simultane-
ously; then they were near; then they were still far away; now
they were coming from the east, then from the west, and so on.

FEBRUARY 6. The alarm bells finally ceased at daylight.
About nine o'clock Dr. Wrangel came and told us that he had
been invited to attend upon the governor and *counseil* and that
the *venerabile concilium* was annoyed because few or none of our
German church people had reported on Saturday or last night to
take up arms against the rebels, which might give rise to evil
reflections, etc. Dr. Wrangel therefore felt himself compelled by
motives of the common good, and especially the good of our
German nation, to urge our Germans who had stood idly in the
market place to take up arms. Because I was still weak from my
illness and was unable to go out, Dr. Wrangel ordered Pastor
Brycelius, who was still with me, to drive to Germantown with
all haste and in our names (a) warn the elders of our congregation there not to join the approaching rebels, but rather to stand
on the side of the government, and (b) since it had been bruited
about that there were many Germans among the so-called rebels,
Mr. Brycelius was to try and see whether he could not give them
an earnest and kindly admonition, etc.

Dr. Wrangel left us and roused up a number of our Germans.
Mr. Brycelius rode to Germantown because the word was going
around that the mob was coming toward Germantown from
Whitemarsh. Several hours later Mr. Metzger and other crafts-

men gathered together, formed themselves into a small mounted company furnished with proper arms, sounded the trumpets, and made a several hours' tour in and around the city. They were almost shot by inadvertence, for cannons loaded with small balls had been placed here and there and the ignorant *constable* was just on the point of blazing away at them because he thought they were rebels. It seems almost inconceivable, but a number of older and younger Quakers also formed themselves into companies and took up arms, etc.

At any rate, it was a strange sight to the children on the streets. A whole *troup* of small boys followed a prominent Quaker down the street shouting in amazement, "Look, look! a Quaker carrying a musket on his shoulder!" Indeed, the older folks also looked upon it as a miraculous portent to see so many old and young Quakers arming themselves with flintlocks and daggers, or so-called murderous weapons! What heightened their amazement was this: that these pious sheep, who had had such a tender conscience during the long Spanish, French, and Indian War, and would rather have died than lift a hand for defense against the most dangerous enemies, were now all of a sudden willing to put on horns of iron like Zedekiah, the son of Chenaanah (I Kings 22), and shoot and smite a small group of their poor, oppressed, driven, and suffering fellow inhabitants and citizens from the frontier!

Pastor Brycelius returned from Germantown at evening and came to see me after having delivered his message to the governor. He reported what had happened, namely, that when he arrived in Germantown he had delivered the warning to the elders of our congregation, but they had not seen, nor did they know anything of, the so-called rebels. He therefore rode all the way through Germantown, over Chestnut Hill, and up to the point where the dwellings stop, and there he suddenly and unexpectedly ran into the vanguard of these people. He realized his mistake and was about to turn and flee, but he was stopped and ordered to remain with them.

They asked him where he had come from.

Reply: From Philadelphia.

Question: Where was he going?

Answer: To Philadelphia.

They told him that he must now stay with them.

Mr. Brycelius answered: "If I must, I will do it." When they dismounted at an inn in Germantown Mr. Brycelius struck up a conversation with several of them, Irishmen and Englishmen who appeared to be respectable, and they asked him why he had come out from Philadelphia. He replied that his home was not in Pennsylvania, but that he was a preacher in New Germantown in Jersey. He said that he had formerly spent several years in Dublin, the capital of Ireland, and thus cherished a love for the Irish nation. Being on a visit to Philadelphia he had heard that there were some Irishmen coming down from the frontier, and love of the common good and peace had impelled him to see them and speak to them. He innocently asked them what was the purpose of their coming. They replied that it was not their intention to do any injury to the least child of their fellow inhabitants nor to anyone else. It was rather their purpose:

a) To demand the custody of the Bethlehem Indians, not to kill them, but only to conduct them out of the province; they were ready to put up a bond of ten thousand pounds that this was their intention.

b) The people in and around Philadelphia lived a pleasant, protected life and had no feelings for the great need and tribulation which the poor settlers on the frontier had to endure. They lacked protection and even the barest necessities. So, since they had a number of weighty *gravamina* to present to the government, which must of necessity be redressed, they had set out on this journey to settle their grievance in Philadelphia.

Mr. Brycelius replied that it was his opinion that as far as their first point, regarding the Indians, was concerned, they would not achieve their purpose because of the following reasons:

1) The government had taken these Indians under its protection, and after it had learned that a company was coming down with the intention of murdering them, just as they had murdered

the Indians in Lancaster, it had on the past Saturday publicly proclaimed that this was a case of illegal assembly and forthwith the *Act of Riot* was read, declaring that if they did not desist they would be declared outlaws.

2) Furthermore, the government had hired, from His Majesty's general, a large company of royal soldiers who were now under arms and guarding the remaining Indian families in the barracks. Yesterday (Sunday) the soldiers had completed a number of defenses and placed cannons in order to destroy any attack upon the barracks, etc. Besides these measures, as soon as word of their coming had arrived last night, the tocsin had been sounded and there had been a great mobilization of arms, etc. And now, since, by their own admission, they had already endured such great affliction and danger on the frontier, and their poor women and children who escaped the Indian massacres were still back at home, Mr. Brycelius said that he pitied their wretched and miserable condition from the bottom of his heart, but that he urgently begged them not to plunge further into utter destruction and not to take one step farther toward this *precipice,* but rather to commit their case into the hands of God and the government.

Regarding the second point, he said that he did not think it at all advisable that they should go to Philadelphia armed, inasmuch as this would cause a great and horrible blood-bath. They ought rather to send their most intelligent men into the city as unarmed deputies to the governor, and in this way, it was to be hoped, their grievances would be remedied and under God's blessing peacefully settled.

All this appeared to give them pause and to make an *impression* on them. They replied that so far only two hundred and fifty of them had arrived and that they expected to have the rest of their comrades with them by twelve o'clock at night so that they would then number about fifteen hundred, although three thousand inhabitants had enlisted. At that time they would consider the matter further.

When Pastor Brycelius, with good intention, remarked to them, among other things, that even the Quakers had taken up arms, they laughed heartily and were amazed at such a *phenomenon*. Mr. Brycelius offered to give them something to drink for refreshment, but they refused absolutely to accept it, saying that they were used to nothing but the most extreme want. They had a rule among them that if anybody discharged a flintlock without a command, he was immediately to be shot by the person next to him. While Mr. Brycelius was there, a flintlock went off unexpectedly and the others immediately shouted, "Shoot him dead!" Several others, however, immediately objected that it had been done unintentionally. They were so trustful of Mr. Brycelius that they even gave him the password for the night. He therefore also asked them who their captain or leader was. But here they were shrewd and replied in the phraseology of the Indians that they were all brothers and that they also had among them some old persons whose advice they followed. After Mr. Brycelius had done what he could, besides the efforts made by two English preachers of the High Church and a Presbyterian professor from the Academy, who had likewise been requested by the governor to see what they could do among these people, he departed and returned to my house. He judged that there were very few Germans among them, that most of them were English and Scotch-Irish *dissenters*. For the rest, he said, they appeared to be resolute and soldier-like, but withal decent and substantial, most of them furnished with horses, muskets, a pair of pistols, and Indian hatchets.

Here in Philadelphia the militia drilled in the largest meeting house of the Quakers on the market place.

FEBRUARY 22. Early in the morning I went to see the two doctors who have charge of the hospital and spoke to them with regard to the lunatic in Providence. From there I went to a *trustee*, Mr. Greenleaf, and he referred me to another *trustee*, Israel Pemberton, who replied that I might come to a meeting of the *trustees* at the hospital this afternoon and there I would receive a full answer. About eleven o'clock I went to the *hospital* with an English friend and secured the admission of the lunatic. I also visited several Germans who were in the hospital. The leading *trustee*, Israel Pemberton, remarked that I might come out occasionally to give an admonition to the patients.

MARCH 4. After the service, about five o'clock, I went out to the *hospital*, as I had agreed with Dr. Wrangel that one of us would give an admonition in English to the patients. When I arrived I found Dr. Wrangel already there. This made me very happy because I felt weak and *catarrhal*. His Reverence Dr. Wrangel delivered an excellent address on Isaiah 53:4, "Surely he hath borne our griefs," etc. The sight of so many different patients, some of them in bed and others up, some in chains and others walking in circles, the exceedingly appropriate subject matter, the fluent and truly devout manner of address, and the vivid portrayal of the faithful Saviour and Friend of man—all this was certainly moving, gripping, and enchanting. Those who were chained exhibited all sorts of convulsions and made strange gestures, but not one of them made a sound.

MARCH 10. Afterwards I was requested by several English gentlemen to go to the prison and examine a German doctor or chirurgeon who had come from London a few months ago. He is locked in irons because a band of thieves recently broke into the shop of an English merchant at night and stole a large quantity of silverware and gold. Part of the stolen goods had been found in the possession of the doctor, and the ringleader, an Irishman, gave king's evidence and testified against him. The English gentlemen expressed the opinion that if the doctor were honestly to expose his accomplices and reveal to me the whereabouts of the remaining three parts of the stolen goods, he might be accepted as a king's witness and escape with his life.

I spoke to him alone in a private room. He said that his name was Frederick William Autenried, that he was born in Esslingen in the Duchy of Wuerttemberg, that his parents were still living, that he had a wife and children, and that he had been a chirurgeon in Germany, Austria, Hungary, etc. But he would not admit to me that he had taken part in the burglary. He disclaimed any knowledge of complicity or even less of the remaining unfound goods and insisted that the Irishman had given him the silver-

ware that was found in his possession for safekeeping. He said
he knew nothing more about the matter and refused to denounce
innocent people in order to gain freedom for himself. I imparted
this information to the Englishmen and went home.

MARCH 29.   I had a visit from a fellow member of the Evangelical faith who lives on the frontier, nine miles beyond Easton.
Among other things, he wanted to present a memorial to the
governor and *assemblee* but found that the *assemblee* had already adjourned and that the governor had gone on a journey
to the lower counties, Newcastle, etc. The outlook is very confused and dangerous. For the provincial government, on order of
His Royal Majesty's general, had promised one thousand men
as its contingent for a spring expedition against the hostile
Indians, and had even gone so far as to pass an act for the print-
ing of £55,000 worth of paper money to support the military
forces. Now it comes to light that the governor and the *assemblee* cannot agree and have fallen into a quarrel, each putting
the blame on the other. They have broken off their sessions. The
consequence is that they cannot furnish the promised one thousand men; and the provincial troops, numbering seven hundred,
who were supposed to be guarding the frontier up to this time,
are also leaving their posts because they are getting no pay.

Thus the frontier is completely unguarded and the poor country people are wholly exposed to the bloodthirsty Indians. The
assemblee pushes all the blame on the *proprietaries* and the governor and has resolved to place the *province* under the protection
and government of His Royal Majesty. Since well-founded
charges against the proprietors in England and their delegated
governor are required in order to bring this about, the local
assemblee has drawn up the *gravamina* and prepared a *supplique*
addressed to His Majesty which they intend to have subscribed
by local English and German citizens, etc.

The man from the frontier urgently besought me to send a
circular letter to our preachers, requesting them to warn the
members not to sign the *assemblee's* charges and *supplique* because it was the opinion of the hard-pressed frontier settlers that

back of it was a Quaker invention. That is, they were pretending that there would be a royal government, which was something that could not be put into effect very quickly, and since in the meantime all provision for protection of the frontier would cease, the poor frontier settlers would be left in the lurch and the door would be flung wide open for the Indians to massacre a large number of them before His Majesty so much as heard about it.

I told him that we preachers could not permit ourselves to interfere in such critical, political affairs. Our office rather requires us to pray to God the Supreme Ruler for protection and mercy and to admonish our fellow German citizens to fear God, honor our king, and love our neighbor, etc. He accepted this in good part, but felt that the poor frontier settlers would suffer indescribable horrors for it, because now was the time when they must till their fields and gardens if they and their children were not to starve. But since they were not safe from assassins and bushrangers for a single day or hour and had to remain together in groups with their families, their fields were lying idle; and as soon as the attacks by the barbarians were resumed the frontier settlers from four counties would flock to Philadelphia by the thousands and speak to the government for themselves, etc.

APRIL 10. I was flooded with visits from country people who desired testimonials for naturalization. About eleven o'clock I was called outside the city to visit some sick people.

In the evening I was obliged to go to the city jail to speak to the German chirurgeon, Frederick William Autenried, of Esslingen in the Duchy of Wuerttemberg, who is imprisoned as a delinquent for burglary and is to appear before the criminal court tomorrow. I took Mr. Henry Keppele with me and spoke with him for fully a half-hour. He was more concerned, however, about the preservation of his physical life, about which we can do little or nothing except to leave it in the hands of the court. I therefore told him at my departure that if there was anything I could do for the good of his soul, I would do it gladly.

APRIL 13. Had several visits from Germans who thought that we ought to present a *supplique* to the governor begging a *pardon* for the Autenried who was condemned to death for theft. Others are opposed and say that this might possibly do harm to the man's soul and cast more dishonor upon our German nation, as he is said to have been pardoned once before in England and relegated to America as a condemned criminal.

APRIL 16. In the afternoon I was obliged to go to the jail to speak to William Autenried, the prisoner who had been condemned to death. He was brought up from the dungeon to a private room. But he acted very wild and unruly and would speak of nothing else but that he had been innocently condemned to death and that I and others should petition the governor for a pardon. He was willing to undergo every imaginable punishment, but not the infamous death of the gallows; he would rather commit suicide than die on the gallows.

I replied that I had a fair appreciation of his situation and that I was sympathetic because, as I had learned, he had been born of respectable, Christian parents, had been baptized, and had had the benefit of instruction in the Christian religion in his youth. But since he had not followed up those good impressions, but rather given place to the evil spirit, he had by frequent repetition of transgressions brought himself to dereliction and become a temple of Satan and sin and, finally, as he became completely hardened, he became the dwelling-place of unclean spirits. The light and grace of a higher revelation concerning redemption had disappeared. The rest of his corrupted nature was trying to help the *preserva-te-ipsum* by lying, denying, and boasting in order to save its life. And now he was making it a *point d'honneur* to rebel against the manner of execution, namely, the gallows, when, after all, he had not resisted coarse outbreaks which deserved the gallows, etc.

The delinquent listened for a while, but then began at once to protest his innocence all over again. I replied that I had heard from his own countrymen that his parents in Esslingen were respectable people, but that he had never obeyed their admonitions, rather causing them heartache even in his youth and grieving them by his rude outbursts, etc. He seemed to be touched by this and wanted to know the names of the countrymen who had said these things, saying that it might possibly have been one of his two brothers.

I told him further that I had read today in the printed magazines from England that in the previous year William Autenried had been condemned to death for theft, but had been pardoned and transported to America, and that during his imprisonment he had smashed a chair and set fire to the door with it, etc. Did this perhaps also refer to his brother, or to himself? Then he began to wish that he had never been born and cried out passionately, "God has forsaken me! The English condemned me to death unjustly, and now the Germans are slandering and persecuting me besides!"

My reply was that just the opposite would be the truth. He was the one who had forsaken God and followed his own lusts. The English have such excellent laws that none can be so easily condemned by them if they are innocent. And as far as the Germans were concerned, I myself am witness that a number of prominent Germans went to no end of trouble to save his life if only they could have found anything of consequence in the circumstances that might be in his *faveur,* but his circumstances are altogether too black, and his countrymen would have to make themselves accomplices in injustice and thereby bring disgrace upon the whole German population, as though they had no sense of the distinction between *bonum et malum, justum et injustum.*

Delinquent: Oh, hanging is a terrible, infamous death! I cannot bear such a thing.

Reply: Christ the Saviour of the world died on a cross between two malefactors. "Thou hast made me to serve with thy sins, thou hast wearied me with thine iniquities," etc. The thief on the cross said, "We receive the due reward of our deeds," etc. How many thousands of Christians suffered terrible forms of martyr's death for the sake of Christ and the truth, and how many die in their beds and endure much more? All these things are to be endured, if only the soul is at peace with God through Christ.

The delinquent began again to burst out in exclamations and howled with impatience. I told him that such conduct would not improve his situation one whit but only kept him from the utterly necessary work of repentance. I told him that he was not of the *genus femininum* but *masculinum* and since he had learned the art of chirurgery and also practiced medicine, he surely ought to know that death by strangulation was not much different from that by apoplexy. He should not dwell on the manner of death but rather seek grace and life for his undying soul. Squire Kuhn, of Lancaster, was with us and he, too, admonished him sympathetically. But he always kept coming back to the first point, that we should beg the governor to spare his life. In conclusion I prayed to God for him.

APRIL 24.   Had a great many visitors. At 11 A.M. I went to the jail and spoke with the condemned William Autenried. I found a good many difficulties still in the way and indications that the usurper was seeking to preserve his palace.

MAY 12.   About nine o'clock in the morning I went to the jail. I was very much afraid, fearing that if Autenried should not be certain of grace in his heart he might become desperate in public and cause an abominable spectacle. I found him somewhat anxious, but withal resigned and composed. He begged me to give him holy communion once more, which, for certain reasons, I did. He then put on his death clothes, and while he was doing this, I spoke with him, pursuing the purpose we had in view. We then went into the other room, where we found Dr. Wrangel, Mr. Duché, and Dr. Clarkson. We sang *"Jesu, meines Lebens Leben"* and spoke on the verse, "Take this child away, and nurse it for me." The three of us accompanied the three delinquents on horseback. Autenried conducted himself well. Brinklow was pardoned, much to his astonishment. Williams and Autenried were hanged. Both bodies were buried in the potter's field, Dr. Wrangel and I being present at the burial.

JUNE 14. Today we received the sad news from our frontier and from Virginia, etc., that the hostile Indians have horribly massacred many settlers and carried others away as prisoners into the wilderness. The storm is drawing ever closer.

JUNE 17. Today the city authorities ordered the *constables* and undersheriffs to patrol the watersides because complaints had come in that grown and half-grown boys were gathering in large crowds, stripping naked on the banks, and bathing in the river, thus giving great offense on Sundays during divine service. It is really dreadful in this large, open city, teeming and swarming with young folk of all nationalities who are permitted all freedom and frivolity, for there is no strict policing or discipline. If the spring is not soon healed with salt, the corrupt flesh will soon gain the upper hand and will shortly become a carcass! The otherwise noble and good laws are too lenient, and by comparison it is like trying to govern and check horses, mules, oxen, wolves, bears, swine, dogs, and cats with silken threads. It is most dangerous of all for the children and young people, and in this respect it is like Sodom and Gomorrah, for the best and most devout parents have their troubles trying to guard their children against the poisonous, pestilential plague.

I was obliged to make public mention of this in church today, as the deacons complained that they had told several boys to be quiet and not disturb the others during catechization, and the impudent rascals had clenched their fists at them and poured out English curses such as *"Go to h..l!" "You son of a b..ch!" "God d..mn you!"* etc. And what is more, they said that their parents would protect them against deacons, etc. I gave the parents to understand that if they were going to strengthen their children in their wickedness, we would be compelled to resort to the law of the land and have them forcibly ejected from public worship or, following our Saviour's example, we would make a scourge of cords and drive out such godless boys from the bethel, the temple, and the house of prayer in order that there might be quiet for the rest.

SEPTEMBER 30. Early in the morning six fathers announced

their children for baptism; others requested that their sick be included in the general prayer. In the forenoon conducted divine service, baptized the children, and preached on Matthew 6:24. Toward evening several hundred German settlers from the country came to the city on account of the election of the *assembly* tomorrow. In the evening I was besieged with visitors.

OCTOBER 1. In the forenoon I was called out of the city to administer communion to Phillip Mey's sick wife and baptize her sick child. At one o'clock in the afternoon I had to go to the schoolhouse, where all the citizens who are members of our Lutheran congregation assembled to discuss the election and then proceeded to the *court*house in an orderly group. It was so packed with country people, however, that our people were not able to get in until four o'clock. During this time, at home, I had numerous visits from country people.

OCTOBER 2. I was summoned to the courthouse to cast my vote, as the rest of the preachers had already been there. I did so and returned home. In the afternoon I had to go three miles outside the city to visit John Klein's sick wife; found her well-composed and desirous of and prepared for a blessed departure. In the evening I was again summoned to the courthouse to cast my vote for the election of two burgesses or city members of the *assembly*. There was such a crowd, however, that I was not able to cast my vote until after ten o'clock.

OCTOBER 3. About nine o'clock I went to see Mr. Whitefield and conveyed to him the greetings and best wishes sent to him by His Reverence Court Preacher Ziegenhagen through Mr. Pasche in the letters of January, *a.c.* He was delighted and expressed the wish that he might still have the opportunity of seeing the institutions in Glaucha [a suburb of Halle] and their heads before he died. At ten o'clock I went to St. Paul's Church and heard Mr. Whitefield preach on Zechariah 12:10, "And I will pour upon the house of David, and upon the inhabitants of Jerusalem, . . . as one that is in bitterness for his firstborn." A large crowd of people was present, and he preached in a manner that was so orthodox and practical that I have heard very little like it outside of Kensington, Halle, and Wernigerode. It certainly cheers one to hear such a man.

There was great rejoicing and great bitterness in the political circles of the city, since it was reported that the German church people had gained a victory in the election by putting our *trustee,* Mr. Henry Keppele, into the *assembly*—a thing which greatly pleased the friends of the *proprietors* but greatly exasperated the *Quakers* and German *Moravians.* Never before in the history of Pennsylvania, they say, have so many people assembled for an election. The English and German Quakers, the Moravians, Mennonites, and Schwenkfelders formed one party, and the English of the High Church and the Presbyterian Church, the German Lutherans, and the German Reformed joined the other party and gained the upper hand—a thing heretofore unheard of.

The Year 1765

JANUARY 22.   I was called to go to the *hospital* outside the city to visit a dying man. The man was born in Eutin and served at sea as a sailor, having come here from Kitts. He was sick in the *hospital* for several months without my knowledge. As far as he was still able to speak, he told me how he had been born of Evangelical parents, baptized in infancy, and instructed and confirmed as a youth. And now, after being away from home for seven years, sailing to and fro on the ocean, he regretted his past life and sighed that the merciful God might accept his poor soul, forgive his sins for Jesus Christ's sake, and not cast him out. Truly, it is a hard thing to die in a strange land among strange people whose language one does not understand.

JANUARY 23.   Many visitors running in and out. I went out to the *hospital* again to visit the man from Eutin once more, but learned from the English nurse that after my departure yesterday he had covered up his face and, when she uncovered him toward evening and asked him how he was, he replied that she should not disturb him in his meditation and prayer, and shortly afterwards he fell softly and quietly asleep. He had already been buried today.

The nurse asked me also to speak to a German Reformed preacher who was confined there. He was the Rev. Dominicus Bartholomaeus, who was sent to this country twelve or fourteen years ago by the Reverend Synod of Holland but has been suffering from *mania* for several years past. He was well-behaved, but I was able to carry on little sensible conversation with him because what he said was confused and clouded with heterogeneous matters. I tried to see whether he remembered any Latin, but found nothing but confusion.

As I was going back home toward evening and passed the

public cemetery outside the city, the so-called potter's field, two German women told me that a coffin had just been brought to the cemetery and the people had gone away leaving the coffin without a cover and without having dug a grave, and it was therefore to be feared that dogs would devour the body during the night. The affair looked suspicious to me, for it might have been that such a person could have been killed and brought there secretly. So, though it was evening, I was obliged to go to the caretaker of the cemetery and inform him of the matter. He already knew about it, however, and said that it was the body of a poor English woman who had died of smallpox and had been ordered there by the overseers of the poor, though they had forgotten to make arrangements for the digging of a grave. I was very much relieved because such things can involve one in a great deal of *trouble* and I would have been obliged to give testimony in court if a legal investigation had been necessary.

FEBRUARY 4.   In the evening went to a merchant's house and heard Dr. Wrangel expound part of John 4 and 5. There were two ministers of the English Presbyterian Church and two Lutherans present. The English Presbyterian Church is growing so rapidly among the English in America that in a few years it will spread and surpass the Episcopal and all the rest. Its *progress* is due to the fact that they have established seminaries in various places, educate their own ministers, keep strict discipline, and tolerate no ministers except those who have good moral character and the ability to speak, and who are content with small salaries and able to endure hard work. Those denominations here which do not have these characteristics, but just the opposite, are consequently decreasing and making room for the Presbyterians. However, the Presbyterians push the doctrine of absolute predestination and the hypotheses connected with it too far, and their pastoral staff is well tipped with steel.

FEBRUARY 15.   In the morning I went out on pastoral duties and when I got back home I found at my house two gentlemen from the *Assembly*, Messrs. John Hughes and Henry Pawling. They desired to speak with me. The visit alarmed me somewhat as they are both leading men in the party that is opposed to the *proprietors* and I have no desire to have anything to do with their bitter strife. It is so easy to let fall a word that may do harm and be misused. Mr. Hughes begged the privilege of presenting a number of questions which he desired me to answer.

Mr. Hughes: You are familiar with the controversy between the two parties, one of which is for a direct government by the king and the other for the old regime of the proprietors?

Reply: During my stay here I have had little or nothing to do with political affairs, and it is not my sphere even now, as my office is concerned with other things.

Mr. Hughes then began to explain the present *charter* rights and liberties and how these had been abused by the *proprietors* and their governors, etc.

Reply: I am obliged to you for wanting to give me your explanation of the affair, but I will tell you frankly what my attitude is in these political matters. When I first came to this country I was asked by various lawyers, etc. whether I would not render assistance and prepare the members of the German congregation for the coming election day in behalf of one or another interested party. I replied that my call was limited to the welfare of souls and I could not engage in any political activity whatsoever. Ever since that time I have observed in this province that our German inhabitants have been previously prepared and instructed every year in the public newspaper by the German newspaper publisher, the late Mr. Christopher Sauer, as to how they should vote and whom they should elect, and the chief proposition of the exhortations and instruction was always this: Whatever you do, you German inhabitants, take care to elect assemblymen who will not relinquish one tittle, yea, one hairbreadth, of the ancient privileges, rights, and liberties granted by King Charles II to the proprietor, William Penn, and through him to the people. Accordingly, the Germans would rather have given up their lives before they would have elected anybody but Quakers to the Assembly. For the Germans had been so inculcated with the idea that if they failed to keep the Quakers in the government and elected in their place Englishmen from the Episcopal or Presbyterian churches, they would be deprived of their ancient rights and liberties and then they would be saddled with laws forcing them to engage in military drill to assist in defense against enemies, and also to pay a tithe to the ministers of the Episcopal church.

Mr. Hughes: But why, then, were the German Lutherans so active at the last election to eliminate those members of the *Assembly* who have been petitioning for a royal government and to elect other members who are fighting for the old regime of the *proprieteurs?* By doing that they openly declared that they are enemies of our king!

Reply: According to the original rights, granted by Charles II, every inhabitant has the power and liberty to cast his vote for any man whom he deems most suitable for the *Assembly;* His Majesty suffers no injury from that. As a Hanoverian I am a subject of His Britannic Majesty, and more than that, I am a naturalized citizen and freeholder, and according to the fundamental laws of this province, as long as they remain *in esse,* I have the right and liberty to cast my vote annually for the gentlemen of the *Assembly* and the *sheriff* as I see fit. And when all our members were called by our church council to attend a meeting in the large schoolhouse on election day, and they unanimously decided that it would be a good thing if several German citizens were elected to the *Assembly,* I approved it because we German citizens are not bastards but His Majesty's loyal subjects and naturalized children. We have to bear taxes and *onera* just as much as the *English* inhabitants, and therefore we have the right and liberty to have one or more German citizens in the Assembly and to learn through them what is going on.

Mr. Hughes: That was not unfair.

Reply: But it is unfair and scandalous that the two parties, one contending for the *conservation* of the old form of government and the other striving for a new form, should depart from the main point of the affair and descend to personalities and carry their bitter enmity to such lengths in anonymous writings and

115

engravings, the like of which have never been heard of in so-called Christian countries, for religion and politics are thereby mortally poisoned and wounded. From the bottom of my heart I desire peace, and I beg you, honored sirs, not to involve me in the affair in any manner whatsoever through your visit and conversation because I have never been of any other mind, nor have I ever found any other disposition in our congregation, except to remain loyal to God and our king.

Mr. Hughes and Pawling: We assure you that our visit was made from sincere motives and will not be abused. *A Dieu.*

FEBRUARY 25. Had visitors from the country and the city coming in and out practically the whole day with this or that inquiry or arrangement to make. For example, a group of Dutch and German Lutherans from a certain region reported that their English neighbors were about to build an Episcopal church. Since a number of Lutherans were living in the neighborhood, the English people had offered to permit them to participate and give them the privilege of holding German services in the church if they would raise and contribute part of the cost. They desired advice concerning this.

These questions are easy to answer but more difficult to resolve, as the *dubia vexata* are not so easily settled and the universities are too far away that one might secure a *responsum.* When one listens to a *collegium polemico-disputatorium* at the universities and the dissenting parties are before one only on paper, one wins every time and carries off the victory. But when one must confront the authors personally, it is not so easy, for they, too, have their arguments and they hold them fast. The late Professor Paul Anthon was doubtless a redoubtable *polemicus* because he always searched out and began with the root and source of the *status controversiae* and dealt rather too much in abstractions. But when one takes it in the concrete, it would probably be difficult to debate with the pope in Rome.

MARCH 8. Early in the morning I was obliged to give to the city authorities an account of the *status controversiae* with regard to a German orphan girl whose father died in the war. The girl had been bound out to English people for a term of six years and seven months and was supposed to learn to read and write. Now the term of servitude has elapsed and she can neither read a letter nor pray a single word and has been so completely debauched that she prefers to remain with her mistress because she is satisfied with her brutish life, etc.

Because I know a little English, I am plagued by poor German folk to do all kinds of writing in addition to my other burdens. What is needed is that the congregation should retain a special agent or notary, for there are many cases concerning the poor and orphans that are *remote* from the care of souls and require someone who understands the laws of the land and both the German and the English language. It would be easy enough to find such a person if the position did not concern the affairs of the poor and orphaned which offer nothing but reproach for compensation.

MAY 10. At nine o'clock in the morning Brother John Andrew Krug and I went to *St. Pauls* Church and listened to *Common Prayers,* which lasted until after eleven o'clock. Afterwards Mr. Whitefield preached on Daniel 5:25-30, "And this is the writing that was written," etc. He directed his practical meditation to the balances, that is, the Bible, and weighed in the balances all the numerous religious parties in Philadelphia, the denominations, High Churchmen, Presbyterians, Baptists, Quakers, Lutherans, Calvinists, etc., the deists, naturalists, etc.

The church was crowded to capacity. He would admit no weight to be sufficient except that which Christ bestows in true repentance of heart, in justification of a poor sinner in the sight of God, and in sanctification by grace. It was all very practical and impressive, with the exception of one statement which grieved me sorely, namely, that the claim that regeneration takes place in baptism is an error, etc. Here he himself was weighed in the balances and found wanting. The statements concerning baptism in holy Scripture speak far too strongly of regeneration for anyone to be able to say that it is an error, much less a *grand error.* The term "regeneration" must not be confused with conversion. After the sermon I went with Brother Krug to Mr. Whitefield's lodgings and introduced Mr. Krug to him.

JUNE 5. Toward evening I had a visit from, and a conversation with, an English justice of the peace. He told me that my petition had been granted by the Philadelphia *court,* which is now in session, and that an obnoxious tavern in New Hanover has been closed. It was a tavern located immediately opposite the church in New Hanover, and Satan conducted his school there. On Sundays and festival days before the service began, a mob of people always gathered there. They were people who had come from near and far to go to church, but they were lured inside and then came to church half-drunk. When church was out, they went in again, and many a time they became completely intoxicated. Since revelry, dancing, etc. on Sundays are punishable, they reveled all the more frivolously on the days after holidays—such as Christmas, Easter, Whitsunday—tippling, fiddling, dancing, and engaging in all the other abominations that go with them, and the poor young people were especially drawn into them.

My co-worker and I have often warned and begged them with tears, but it was in vain. I therefore spoke to the chief judge in the city and begged him to have some consideration and put a stop to such a soul-corrupting nuisance. This evening I learned that the matter has been before the *court* and the innkeeper has been deprived of his tapster's rights.

JUNE 20. I was sick and depressed because the night before in a dream I had a strong premonition of impending tribulation. It happens quite against my will that I occasionally experience a strong impression in my sleep and see a *scene* in which future events and circumstances are represented to me in certain images, whenever anything in the nature of trials, sufferings, and tribulations is at hand. How it happens I do not know, because I do not yet know all the powers of the soul, but I have learned from experience that it always turns out as foreshadowed. The only thing I can do in such a case is to beseech God to avert the blow, or pray that the blow may be softened.

AUGUST 2.   In the forenoon I visited the king's agent and desired also to speak to members of the government, but found none of them at home, as they are all staying at their estates outside the city during this hot season of the year.

AUGUST 4.   Because it has not rained in and around the city for a long time and everything is dry and burnt, a number of people have been finding fault because we have had no special prayers for rain in our church, except the Litany. I therefore purposely took a text from Amos 4:6-12 this morning, and set forth the causes whereby the Lord is moved to discipline his covenant people and the divine purpose of this discipline, namely, the true repentance of the people. If this repentance does not ensue, it is useless to pray for rain and fruitful seasons.

AUGUST 5.   The gracious Lord bestowed upon us a fine, soaking rain, which continued until near evening.

SEPTEMBER 23.   Had fresh work to do inasmuch as naturalization papers are to be granted at the *Supream Court* tomorrow and may still be obtained for two dollars, whereas after the Stamp Act goes into effect it will probably cost £9 or £10, and this has been announced in the newspapers throughout the country. The church people who desire to be naturalized are required to submit an English certificate from their minister and two deacons. We have about a hundred from our Philadelphia congregation who desire to be naturalized, and an equal number from the Lutheran congregations in the country who applied to me for their certificates.

OCTOBER 1.   I had to hide myself, partly because of my illness and partly because of the excessive hubbub and running in and out.

OCTOBER 2.   Now that the country people have caught their breath somewhat and cast their votes, the city people are beginning to vote today. At nine o'clock in the morning the bells on our schoolhouse were rung and within a few hours about six hundred German citizens assembled in and before the schoolhouse and marched in procession to the *courthouse* to cast their votes. They conducted themselves very soberly and honorably and acted in a body to the delight and also the dismay of the English nationality, depending upon which of the two parties the people belonged to and what their sympathies and opinions were.

OCTOBER 4. There were two large funerals to conduct in our congregation. I was again loaded with fresh burdens by city and country people who desired to be naturalized today, and I suffered a *relaps* of the chest inflammation. I also heard that the Quakers and the parties which adhere to them won the election *per fas et nefas* and that they are jubilant over it.

OCTOBER 5. Had some relief because the fever is becoming intermittent. Visitors from the city and country running in and out. The leading English merchants of the city sent two deputies to report that a ship from London, under the protection of a warship, would land near the city with the high tide in the afternoon, and that it would unload the stamped papers by authority of an act of the royal parliament. Accordingly, inasmuch as all the bells on the High Church as well as those on the State House were to be tolled in mourning, all the ships lying at anchor in the roadstead were to give signals of distress and mourning, drums covered with crape were to be sounded throughout the city, and a general gathering of citizens was to assemble at the State House for further discussion, they asked whether we too would not muffle the bells on our schoolhouse and toll them in mourning.

I replied that I was unable to grant permission of my own accord but must first ask the church council. I therefore had members of the church council and congregation who live nearby called together and asked for their opinion. They wanted to know what I thought of the affair. I replied: Be subject to the authorities that have power over you. The proposed movements in regard to the landing of stamp materials will be noticed and reported in detail in the newspapers. Since, apart from this, we Germans are already being painted black enough by the envious opposing party in England, we would be sensible to guard ourselves against this act; this is good advice to the wise. We would do better to remain quiet and let the English act as they see fit.

As much as at all possible, let us warn our members not to appear at the State House and to have nothing whatsoever to do with any uprising or tumult. And this was what was done by our people.

The ships arrived in the afternoon, and the English tolled their bells and beat the drums until evening. Several thousand citizens gathered at the State House, where a number of leading English merchants and lawyers harangued the people and the people echoed them with their yeas and nays. They sent several deputies to the receiver of excise, or stamp-master, who had been appointed by England, a wealthy tradesman named John Hughes, and demanded to know whether he was going to accept the office or resign. The stamp-master, however, was very ill at the time and was unable to make up his mind immediately concerning such an important matter affecting his personal interests, and he asked for time to reflect on it until next Monday.

When the deputies came back with this answer, the moderators and orators had all they could do to pacify the people and beg them to go back to their homes and await the reply on the following Monday, for a single spark would have been able to kindle and set the whole dry, inflammable mass in flames and the houses of the stamp-master and others would have been demolished and not one stone left on another. The good Lord prevented, however, and the mob dispersed. The warship took the stamp materials on board from the merchant ship for safe-keeping. Grumblings were heard here and there about the fact that we Germans had not rung our schoolhouse bells, but I was glad that it had not been done, for the English, etc. are prone to incite and egg the Germans on and then put the blame on us.

DECEMBER 16. There is a proverb here, and I know from my own experience that it is true, which declares that the Germans who come from Europe are blind the first seven years they are in this land. It is exceedingly difficult for the theologues who come from Europe to get a practical understanding of the distinction between the *ecclesia plantata* [church already planted] and the *ecclesia plantanda* [church being planted].

121

Some of the people here ought to be educated by us and given a catechetical and practical training. The English Presbyterians have done this, and still do it, and they have made unbelievable progress throughout North America. One old preacher, named William Tennent, who lived in a log hut in the country, started with his own sons, and a large institution, the *seminarium* in Jersey, has grown out of it [later, Princeton University]. Between one and two hundred men trained in this way are laboring in various parts of North America. They get along on meager salaries and know how to adapt themselves to circumstances here.

Muhlenberg was kept busy in the years 1766 to 1769 with pastoral duties in Philadelphia and with finding pastors for the increasing number of congregations elsewhere. Frequently he had to try to mend the relations between pastors and congregations following quarrels. Construction of a large church, Zion, was begun in 1766 by the congregation in Philadelphia with the smaller St. Michael's continuing in use.

The Year 1769

APRIL 27. Set out from Philadelphia at nine o'clock in the morning with the Rev. H. Helmuth and Mr. Frederick Kuhl. I had Mr. Heil's mare, and Mr. Helmuth also had a satisfactory, easy-going creature to ride. But the road was muddy and slippery as a result of the previous heavy rains, which caused me no little concern and fear, for our colleague was not yet accustomed to riding, and the journey we had before us was long and quite perilous for a complete novice. It was raining now and then, but by twelve o'clock noon we had succeeded, with God's help, in crossing the Schuylkill River and putting twelve miles behind us. After we had refreshed ourselves somewhat, our dear escort, Mr. Kuhl, took leave and rode back to Philadelphia, leaving the two of us to continue our journey.

It was now four o'clock in the afternoon, and we had traveled thirteen miles farther—twenty-five miles in all—under God's protection and preservation. We rested a little and deliberated on our strength and how far it might take us before nightfall. The inn in which we had planned to put up for the night was eight miles farther. To reach it we had to cross a broad river, which is usually swollen in rainy seasons and dangerous to ford, and I had misgivings about this. But my dear companion was still stouthearted and courageous, and he offered the well-considered advice that it would be better to try to cross the river today because it might rain during the night, which would make the river harder to ford tomorrow. We made the venture and, praise God, we got through safely before nightfall and reached our destination.

APRIL 28. Up early and, after praying and committing ourselves to the gracious protection of God, we would have been glad to proceed, but it rained harder and harder in an uninter-

rupted downpour. I encouraged myself with the vain hope that
a wagon, returning to Lancaster without a load, might pass by.
Such wagons are generally covered with coarse canvas, which
gives a measure of protection against the rain. Some wagons
actually passed, but they had heavy loads and did not have room
for two additional passengers. The drivers said that an empty
wagon, carrying our chests of clothing and books, had passed
them about an hour and a half before, and they advised us to ride
after it in the hope that the wagon would perhaps stop at the
next *station* for fodder, etc. We set out in God's name, and
within three hours, under an unrelenting, cold rain and in the
face of a wind storm, we covered seven miles and met the empty
wagon at the *station,* where we had time to eat a little lunch and
dry ourselves somewhat before the fire.

We still had twenty-five miles before us to Lancaster. I
requested the driver to take Mr. Helmuth into the wagon. He
was willing to do so, made a seat out of his feed bag, and tied
Mr. Helmuth's riding horse to the rear of the wagon. My dear
brother was quite pleased, although, on account of the deep ruts
and holes in the road, such a ride is very rough; a passenger is
severely jolted and thrown from side to side, and this, being
somewhat similar to an ocean voyage in a storm, causes seasickness. I rode on ahead for eight miles, and when I reached another
station seventeen miles from Lancaster, I had the special pleasure
of encountering two honest elders of the Lancaster congregation
who had come out to meet us and take us all the way in to our
destination in a covered carriage. An hour later Mr. Helmuth
pulled alongside in his wagon. Since the heavy rain was continuing and evening was approaching, we had to spend the
second night on the journey. We were well cared for by our two
benevolent old friends, the Hubeles.

APRIL 29. It was no longer raining today, and all of us set
out together in the carriage. But we had all we could do to get
started because of the deep mire and muddy roads. Finally we
crossed the swollen Conestoga River on a ferry and arrived in
Lancaster safely at one o'clock in the afternoon.

APRIL 30. Several men from the four small vacant congregations in Maytown, Donnegal, Middletown, and Hummelstown came to see me today. They had previously expressed their desire for a preacher. A fairly strong congregation in Warwick, twelve miles from Lancaster, was also represented by these men; this congregation was never one of the United Congregations but had allowed itself to be served for several years by two notorious and ill-famed preachers who adhered to the so-called pure doctrine of the unaltered Augsburg Confession, and these preachers took great pains to browbeat the poor sheep into believing that a union with the preachers sent from Halle would be dangerous, that they were fortunate to be able to attain to heaven in the unaltered way, etc.

MAY 3. Clear weather returned, but I did not propose to undertake the journey because the rivers were high and the roads muddy. In spite of this an honest old man, a deacon in the little congregation in and around Maytown, came and inquired if I would go with him according to my promise. I decided to go along by horse. At four o'clock in the afternoon I set out from Lancaster with the old man, rode twelve miles, crossed two rivers unharmed, and reached his home in the evening. Only two families of the Evangelical Lutheran religion live in this region, and they dwell among rigid Irish Presbyterians and German Mennonites, etc.

MAY 4. Set out early in the company of the aforementioned two families and rode four miles to Maytown on rough roads. A goodly number of our brethren in the faith were assembled there in front of a wooden church which was still uncompleted. It was a pleasure to conduct the service, and I preached on the Gospel for the Ascension of our Lord, baptized a child, and explained the doctrine of infant baptism. The simple people were very attentive, which is usually so in the case of those who seldom have opportunity to hear God's Word and become hungry for it. As far as their material circumstances are concerned, they are newcomers in this region and most of them are poor; hence they are able to contribute only a little to the support of a preacher.

The service was ended at twelve o'clock noon. An elder, named William Bischof, was there to escort me to his small congregation in Donnegal. We did not have time to eat lunch, but set out at once, and within two hours we reached the place. A considerable number of German Protestants was assembled there, and I tried to edify them on the basis of a text from Psalm 110:3. At the conclusion of the meditation I had the young people and the children come forward. They were very timid about standing up, and I had to employ all the tricks I knew to gain some measure of their confidence. All the adults remained and, although they let me catechize the youth alone, they silently gave me to understand, by their eyes, ears, hands, feet, look, and demeanor, that they enjoyed and approved of the proceedings.

I lodged for the night in the home of the leader or elder of the little congregation. A specially prepared building on his farm served as a meeting place for the congregation.

MAY 5.   Set out early and, accompanied by my dear host and his awakened brother-in-law, rode nine miles, on roads that were rough and full of holes, to Middletown. This is an established town or village located where the Swatara River and the Susquehanna River form an elbow or triangle. The inhabitants of this town are also young newcomers and for the most part poor. Some well-disposed German Lutherans have collected alms and mites of charity in Philadelphia, Lancaster, and elsewhere, and they have undertaken the construction of a church of rough stones, forty-six feet long and forty feet wide. The roof has been laid and the building is protected from the weather, but they have not been able to complete the church because their means are inadequate and they have no pastor to gather and encourage the congregation.

Before we came to the town we had to cross the swollen Swatara River on the ferry. We arrived at nine o'clock and learned that the announcement concerning a service had not reached them on account of the rains and bad roads and that the people did not know of my coming. The deacons, elders, and *trustees* immediately assembled and sent out their children and servants to announce the service wherever they could. By eleven o'clock a fair number had already gathered in a large house, and I preached to them on the basis of Psalm 73:25, 26.

At two o'clock in the afternoon, after we had had a bite to eat, the most prominent landowner of the village of Hummelstown having come to fetch me, we set out on our journey. Once again we had our horses ferried across the river, and on the other side we were met by six elders and deacons who accompanied us. At 3:30 P.M. we reached the village. There I found a nice, large wooden church, the construction of which had been completed. It was located on two *lots* which Mr. Hummel had provided as a free gift, and he had also contributed some farm rent, amounting to 1*s.* sterling from each house lot. Only a few pounds of debt remain on the church and schoolhouse. The people desire to stay together with the other three congregations and are willing to provide the necessary support for a faithful laborer from our United Ministerium, if someone can be found. At four o'clock we went to the church and I preached in a practical way on Hosea 2:14. After the sermon I called up the children who were present and catechized them.

Where can we get help? And where can we find men who are adapted to the circumstances? As yet we have no *seminarium* here, and the dearly beloved laborers who are called and sent from Europe with so much care and trouble are for the most part, especially in their first years here, not in a position to put up with our work and manner of life. It is impossible to have a clear conception of this in Europe.

In the aforementioned four little congregations, a preacher would have to preach and catechize the first Sunday morning in one congregation and that afternoon in another; then on the following Sunday he would have to conduct services morning and afternoon in the two remaining congregations. During the week he would have to seek out the sheep, develop a Westphalian stomach to digest hard fare, and be equipped with a great soul and with love toward Christ and his lost sheep, for this is an *ecclesia colligenda* here. It is exceedingly sad and heart-rending to be in such places, see the conditions with one's own eyes, and not know what to advise or how to help.

The small villages were not founded until after the [French and] Indian War, and then they were established to enable the poor people to live closer to one another so that they might have a better opportunity to defend themselves against the treacherous murderers, etc. In former times these remote regions were inhabited almost exclusively by Scotch-Irish settlers, but wherever the Germans become deeply rooted, work hard, and manage to make both ends meet, the Irish gradually withdraw, sell their farms to the Germans, and move farther to the west. Within the last ten years the Germans have increased considerably in these regions.

MAY 6. Set out early from Hummelstown, escorted by an elder of the congregation, a man who had learned chirurgery in Germany, had gone to war as regimental chirurgeon, had come here to this land sixteen years ago, also practiced his profession as chirurgeon in some military campaigns and expeditions here, later bought a farm from an Irishman and got his livelihood ever since from farming. He escorted me fifteen miles to a point where a well-disposed elder of the aforementioned strife-ridden congregation (Warwick) was waiting for me. This elder had ridden out to meet me and accompanied me seven miles farther to an iron foundry, where I was to put up for the night.

At this iron foundry [Elizabeth Furnace] lives a German gentleman [Henry William Stiegel] who came to this part of the world as a young man without means. At first he served some prominent English merchants in the capacity of clerk, but as a result of his crafty mind and great ability, and also as a result of his first marriage, he succeeded in establishing an iron foundry. With all his extensive and large business affairs, this man has been a very zealous Lutheran and promoter of the Evangelical religion. He has a large and splendid house, like a nobleman's palace. He employs German laborers almost exclusively in his iron foundry. And in order that he might further the spiritual welfare of these poor people and edify his own family, he set apart a large hall on the second floor of his house for public worship, furnished it with an organ and seats, and has for several years been retaining one or another member of our Ministerium to conduct German Evangelical services in the said domestic church or chapel about every fourth Sunday in order that his family, workmen, and also German neighbors might have an opportunity to be edified. A few miles from this iron foundry he established a village, and there, too, he dedicated an imposing house, containing a hall furnished with a pulpit, organ, and seats, for German Evangelical services. In the home of this patriot I was hospitably received and entertained, even as I had been on previous occasions.

MAY 7. It was a pleasure to attend early morning devotions which the aforementioned gentleman conducted with his family. About ten o'clock I betook myself with the family a mile and a half to the church which I have already referred to as being located twelve miles from Lancaster. Since it had been announced that a service would be held in this church today, a large number of people had assembled. I preached on the text, Isaiah 5:1-4, "My well-beloved hath a vineyard in a very fruitful hill," etc.

In the company of friends from Lancaster, I rode three miles with the well-disposed elder who had ridden out to meet me yesterday, and we ate a noon meal at his house. From there we proceeded toward Lancaster. After riding seven miles we came to a little town called Lititz, which the so-called Moravian Brethren founded several years ago and are still developing gradually. It is located in a pleasant, rich, and productive region and has several large, imposing public buildings constructed of massive stones, also an inn in which travelers are entertained in friendly fashion and clean surroundings at a modest price. From Lititz we rode eight more miles and arrived safely in Lancaster in the evening. Toward noon I rode with others to the home of an elder five miles away. There I ate and then, at two o'clock in the afternoon, continued the journey. We crossed the Susquehanna River, rode twelve miles farther, arrived in York at eight o'clock in the evening, and lodged at the home of an elder.

MAY 19. Early in the morning it began to rain heavily, and it continued to rain all day, so it was very inconvenient to go out. Service was appointed for ten o'clock. This was the first time I preached in this church, which is durably constructed of massive stones and adorned with all kinds of paintings, including one of the blessed Dr. Luther, which is life-size and fairly recognizable because his name is written underneath in large letters. Even if the picture does not resemble the sainted Luther, this should not be surprising, for a like dissimilarity may have appeared some years ago between Luther and those who bear his name and claim his faith.

MAY 20. Set out again from York with my dear companions. At 2:30 P.M. we arrived in Lancaster, safely, praise God, albeit tired.

MAY 22. At 2:30 P.M. I set out on my return journey and was accompanied by the Rev. Mr. Helmuth and several elders to the other side of the Conestoga River. One of the elders, Mr. Brenner, who had to go to Philadelphia on business, afforded me company, and we covered twenty-five miles by nine o'clock in the evening.

MAY 23. Since we still had forty-one miles before us, we set out early. At seven o'clock in the evening, under the gracious protection and mercy of God, we arrived in Philadelphia, safely and tired of traveling.

The Year 1770

MAY 7. Early in the morning I heard that Mr. George Whitefield had arrived in Philadelphia yesterday from South Carolina. Went to his quarters and bade him welcome. He was hale and hearty and promised to preach in Zion Church some time after my return from the journey into the country. At eleven o'clock I set out alone on my journey, put twenty-six miles behind me, and in the evening reached New Providence, tired and stiff but, under God's gracious protection, safe and sound.

MAY 8. Rode on, covered thirty miles, and reached Reading.

MAY 11. Rode fourteen miles farther to the district of Heidelberg, where I spent the night with my relatives. There I encountered an Indian chief of the Six Nations whom I used to know; in his own way, he was very friendly and cordial toward me. I have had various conversations with his deceased father, a *regulus*. The princely clothing of this chief, of his wife, and of their son, who was with them, consisted of woolen blankets which they wrapped around themselves. Their sole ornaments were rings in their noses, etc., for they receive no contributions, *revenues,* or the like from their subjects, but must support themselves as well as they can by hunting, or when they are among Europeans, by making baskets and brooms.

MAY 16. Accompanied by my host, I rode ten miles to church in Heidelberg, in Berks County, where I had made an appointment, God willing, to preach. A large number of German Protestants were assembled there. My chest complaint and hoarseness were worsening, and this made it difficult for me to speak. Nevertheless, I preached with pleasure because my auditors were attentive and eager for the Word.

Since it had been arranged that I was to conduct divine service tomorrow morning, God willing, in the Northkill congregation, a true Israelite took me four miles farther to his home, where I was to spend the night. Here I found a patriarchal family, for the father fears God and believes with all his house.

Just when we were about to edify ourselves further, a schoolmaster, who far surpassed us in learning and experience, arrived. He had gathered quite a store of the polemical theological writings of the last century which abound in Latin phrases and words, and he requested me to explain such as he had noted down in a catalog which he had with him. I replied that we possess the saving Word of God in the Holy Bible, pure and clear in our mother tongue, and that we can attain to life and light in the order of repentance and faith without Latin scraps, if we are earnest about being saved, and that we have also been blessed in this century with many edifying works in our mother tongue which show us the way to life, etc. He replied that he also has a good store of these more recent books. We tried, in every possible way and with goodness, love, and earnestness, to refer him to his own heart and to the primary roots of true conversion and change of outlook, but he had already experienced all that we could tell him, and more besides.

He said that he lacked only this one essential thing, that he might understand the Latin words *Festum Nativitatis, Circumcisionis, Epiphaniae, Resurrectionis, Trinitatis, Dominicae Ascensionis, Pentecostis,* for he had long harbored a secret desire to be a minister and for this purpose had purchased, at great cost, the famous Erdman Uhsen's very instructive *Redner mit oratorischen Kunstgriffen,* etc. We again urged him to begin by learning to experience what Christ prescribed in Matthew 5 concerning poverty of spirit, mourning, purity of heart, hunger and thirst, etc. But neither friendliness nor earnestness was of any avail. He stuck to me like a bur on a coat, called me aside, and would not rest until I had revealed to him the Latin mysteries. Then, in the evening, he bade us farewell with a relieved conscience and left us, tired out, to ourselves.

MAY 18.　My chest was tightly congested and I was perplexed as to how I could preach without a voice. Rode three miles to the house of mourning, where a large number of people was assembled, and I escorted the funeral to the cemetery in Heidelberg. I preached on Psalm 73:25, 26, "Whom have I in heaven but thee?" I had to force myself almost beyond my ability to utter a sound and to clear my throat with a dry cough. After the sermon a raw, cold wind began to blow, and this suddenly stopped up my previously dilated pores, giving me a fresh fever and nausea.

Betook myself to the home of my brother-in-law, Samuel Weiser, where I met the aforementioned Indian chief. I asked him, since some of the Indians are excellent *botanici,* if he did not know of a remedy for my chest. He replied that if he were in his own country he would quickly find an herb which would be good for me, but here in these settled regions he could not find anything. I entered into a conversation with him through an interpreter and began by asking him about his family, some of whom were with him, living in the woods. He recalled that he had been in my home in Providence several times with my late father-in-law and that, some seventeen years ago (which he counted on his fingers), a number of his people's most distinguished chieftains had traveled through Providence on the way to Philadelphia, had received bodily refreshment from me, and had on this account conferred a name on me.

Question: What is this name in your language? Answer: *Gachswungarorachs,* which signifies a saw used for cutting wood or boards. I wondered what the profound meaning might be. Did it have reference to my office or to my person? It was said that it referred to both, for in olden times they had had a distinguished *sachem* or chief with this name. As regards the office, a seer or priest must be a saw in the hand of a mighty one who is able to cut hard, knotty, intractable hearts and transform them into something useful. This sounds good if a strong and wise hand uses the saw and the jagged edge is and remains sharp, tough, and firm.

He was asked why he had run out during the heavy windstorm and had shouted with such a mighty voice. Answer: The windstorm was brought about by the large, thick head of a forest god, equipped with long, heavy hair like iron chains, who flew across the tops of the trees and in his swift movement caused the din and shaking. If the head had flown too low and the strong locks of hair had turned around and become entangled in the tops of the trees, the trees would have been torn out by the roots. For this reason he had called to the head in order that it might fly high enough over the treetops and not uproot the trees, and this is what happened, etc. This is very artful and ought to furnish the critics of mythology with additional material for a dissertation for a master's or doctor's degree inasmuch as all the fields of investigation are largely exhausted.

Before we were able to refute this, the Indian inquired if I was not cross and displeased with him. Counter-question: Why? Answer: Because in the days when he lived among our people he occasionally drank a glassful too much and was too gay. Answer: As a rational man and the son of a famous *regulus,* he ought not to drink more than is required to meet his needs and slake his thirst. The irrational beasts, as he knows, do not permit themselves to consume more than necessity and thirst demand; how much less ought rational creatures transgress the laws of the great God? He said: When he is in his own country, he lives soberly and temperately, but when he is among the people who came from beyond the great water, he is led astray. Answer: From this he can deduce that there is confusion and corruption in human nature. He conceded this and apologized for being so poorly clothed; he said that he was ashamed to sit beside me, etc. Answer: We hold that clothes do not make a man virtuous, even less that they make man acceptable in the sight of God; only an upright heart does this. He leaped up, pressed my hand, and said: That is good teaching; his heart is upright. Answer: Without redemption the uprightness is inadequate. Here we broke off because there is a want of expressions for making spiritual things plain.

Toward evening I rode seven miles farther in the cold to my quarters, and this aggravated my catarrh.

MAY 20. Set out early with two friends and rode eight miles to Atalaha, where a very large number of people had assembled at the church. Had to baptize two children, and this was harder and more painful for me than preaching all day at any other time. I requested the congregation to be patient and indulgent, whereupon I forced myself to speak for a quarter of an hour on the words in John 14:18, "I will not leave you comfortless: I will come to you." Rode off two miles to one side to a deacon's home. In the evening I arrived at my brother-in-law's, F. Weiser, in Heidelberg, and finished by baptizing two Negro children belonging to his slaves. Felt a violent throbbing of blood and a stinging pain in my chest. United the Negro Richard Sloan and the Negress Martha in marriage.

MAY 21. Set out on my return journey. Rode fourteen miles to Reading, and from there my honest colleague, Pastor Krug, accompanied me by horse to New Hanover, twenty-two miles beyond. We arrived there in the evening.

MAY 22. After Pastor Voigt had refreshed us with prayer and breakfast we took leave. Brother Krug set out on his return journey, Brother Voigt betook himself to his congregation in Pikestown, across the Schuylkill, and I went toward Providence. I stopped in at Widow Marsteller's and edified myself with her. The rest of the day I spent in continuing my journey, and in the evening I reached the Rev. Michael Schlatter's home, where I was hospitably received and entertained.

MAY 24. Rode four miles off to one side, to Barren Hill. There I found a numerous gathering, baptized three children, preached on the Ascension of Christ, etc., and rode all the way to Philadelphia in the afternoon.

JULY 3. Bade farewell. My generous host, Gottfried Klein, took me to Easton, where the aforementioned major, Squire Arndt, was awaiting me. I visited the Reformed pastor and was then taken by the major to his home three miles from Easton. Here I enjoyed Christian conversation, which was edifying for the soul, and also every imaginable provision for my bodily well-being.

JULY 4. Squire Arndt drove me in his *chaise* fourteen miles to a little town named Allentown, where the rural preacher Mr. Friderici is living at present. This preacher is in wretched circumstances because he is growing old and weak, has a large family of children, and has a small income. Friends who know his circumstances told me that he has piled up more debts than he is able to pay, and they are very fearful that he may be imprisoned for this reason. Here in Allentown I learned that our co-worker, Mr. Jacobus van Buskerk, having been apprised of my arrival, drove to meet me, and that he and Mr. John Daniel Gross, this year's president of the Reverend Reformed Ministerium, were awaiting me in Bethlehem, the Moravian *settlement*. Since we had already passed through Bethlehem, we missed each other; accordingly we tarried in Allentown until they returned from Bethlehem.

I had already heard a great deal about Pastor Gross's learning, gifts, diligence, and efforts among his own people to put the Reformed congregations in good order, and also, as far as our preachers are concerned, that he lived in love and harmony with our laborers in his neighborhood. Now I had the pleasure of making his personal acquaintance face to face. His animated, edifying, and wise conversation pleased me very much and confirmed the good reports I had before heard concerning him.

JULY 5. Squire Arndt and Pastor Gross bade an affectionate farewell and set out for their respective homes. Squire Lewis Klotz, Mr. Buskerk, and I conferred as to whether or not I should remain in this district another Sunday. I should have preferred to press on to Philadelphia because my faithful colleague Mr. C. E. Schultze was left alone under the burden there. I had expected to be away only two Sundays; three Sundays had already passed, and now I was to remain away a fourth, etc. But they insisted so strongly upon my staying that I could not refuse. They sent an express to Philadelphia, more than fifty miles away, in order to make the necessary report, and this put me at ease.

They also prepared a plan according to which the congregations in this district could be visited, although the most pressing harvest season had already begun. Next Sunday I was to preach in Macungie in the morning, in Salisbury in the afternoon; Monday morning in Weissenburg Township, and that afternoon in another church in Weissenburg Township; Tuesday morning in the Albany church and that afternoon in the Rosendale church. This schedule was put in writing and was announced in the various districts either by special messengers or by others as opportunity offered itself.

JULY 11. In the afternoon our worthy friend, Squire Klotz, who traveled with us since Monday and endured all the heat and hardship, bade us a tearful farewell, promised to send me his horse tomorrow to help me on my way to Philadelphia, and rode seven miles farther to his home. Mr. Jung decided to escort me to Philadelphia, and toward evening he rode with me seven miles to Mr. Buskerk's, who had arranged to take me to Germantown in his *chaise* with Squire Klotz's horse.

JULY 12. Set out on our journey. We had hard work on account of the rock-strewn roads, stifling heat, and the showers. On the way we stopped in at the home of a regular pastor of the Reformed congregations in Old Goshenhoppen, Mr. John T. Faber, who received us in very kindly fashion.

JULY 13. We visited our dear colleague, Pastor John Frederick Schmidt, in his home and were received with kindness. Mr. Buskerk set out today from Germantown on his return journey. Mr. Jung continued to provide me with company on my way to Philadelphia. There I found my family well, thank God.

The Muhlenberg sons had come home from Germany. Frederick and Henry were ordained as pastors by the Ministerium in 1770. Peter, in response to a call from a congregation in Woodstock, Virginia, went to England for Episcopal ordination, as required by Virginia law. Two of the Muhlenberg daughters married young clergymen who had come from Germany, John Christopher Kunze and Christopher Emanuel Schulze.

The Year 1774

My beloved patrons and friends in London, etc. urged me to undertake a journey to Georgia and attempt with God's help to effect a reconciliation between quarreling parties there. It was my wish to do so if the Lord would show me a way in which I could get there. In June, 1774, God so ordained that my youngest son Henry was elected and called from Jersey to be the third pastor of the Philadelphia congregation. Thus one impediment was removed.

There still remained the obstacle of my sick wife, whose attacks were becoming more frequent from day to day. I thought of sending her to her aged mother, who is still living in the country, for nursing and care and then setting out on the journey to Ebenezer alone, but I could not obtain her consent. After she had been told by several of her English women friends who had suffered from similar illnesses that a sea voyage had given them relief, she formed the resolution to travel with me by sea to Charleston, and from there to Georgia, and to live or die with me. This pleased me, in a way, but I was also somewhat apprehensive because she had never in her life been out on the open sea, and a sea voyage is an uncomfortable, hard, and wretched experience for healthy and strong persons, to say nothing of old, weak, sick, and helpless people, especially women.

As my wife had decided to travel with me, I was also obliged to take along my grown, unmarried daughter to attend and care for her helpless mother, and in love and childlike obedience toward her parents she gladly gave her consent.

After thinking about and feeling some concern about traveling through other provinces where one is unknown and strange and where the English governments do not understand German credentials, especially in these critical times when even respect-

138

able people are occasionally looked upon as spies and vice versa, and also reflecting that it was quite possible that I might have need of the protection of the provincial government on account of the angry factions in Ebenezer, I asked my old friend and patron, the Rev. Dr. Peters, to procure for me from our governor a *passport* and *recommendation* for the journey. This he did gladly after I had explained to him the circumstances of the commission I had received.

AUGUST 27. In the forenoon a faithful friend, Mrs. Graef, took my sick and swollen wife in a *chaise* to the vessel and I bade farewell to several more persons. Various friends sent us victuals for our comfort on shipboard. Before the vessel sailed, many friends, both men and women, came to the roadstead and took leave. A number of friends and relatives fastened three boats or skiffs to the ship and accompanied us five or seven miles down the Delaware.

AUGUST 28. In the morning we came to anchor with the ebbing tide at New Castle, about forty miles from Philadelphia. Since yesterday my poor wife has been suffering severe pains in her swollen feet and it appears that it may become an inflammation. Most of our passengers went ashore. My wife's painful illness gave me great anxiety because remedies and conveniences for such patients are unobtainable on board the ship. But the Lord provided for even this trifling detail. A man who is a member of our Philadelphia congregation, Mr. John Heidt, whose line of business is on the water, came over to see us in his shallop, and when he learned our predicament, he sent his people back to land to procure a quantity of elder bushes to be used for the inflammation. The application gradually relieved the inflammation and pain.

AUGUST 29. We arrived opposite Cape May. I had an opportunity of writing a few lines and sending them to my children in Philadelphia, for a vessel from Jamaica was sailing past us. During the night we finally reached open sea, but had contrary wind which continued till the evening of September 5, which caused varying degrees of fiendish seasickness in my daughter, myself, and other passengers. My wife, however, was spared, but she had just that many more attacks of *passio hysterica*.

Because of my sickness I was unable to observe the latitude, the winds, and variations, which, I trust, will do no harm to the commonweal, since, even without this contribution of mine, contrary and foul winds can be found in superabundance in Pierre Bayle's dictionary, in Voltaire's writings, and also in German and English books, and are no less abundantly observed and communicated, at a price and according to taste, to the Christian world in all sorts of learned magazines, journals, newspapers, and reviews.

SEPTEMBER 7. This evening we reached within ten miles of Charleston. There being no *pilot* at hand, and being in a region of sand banks in the darkness of night, we sailed to and fro the whole night, used the lead repeatedly, and by the goodness and mercy of God were preserved from misfortune.

SEPTEMBER 8. We forged ahead, secured a *pilot*, passed the sand banks safely, and at about 10 A.M. arrived at Charleston, South Carolina, in the same month in which I landed here thirty-two years ago in Captain McClellan's *brigantine* from London. As soon as my unexpected arrival became known, a number of members of the honorable church council of the local German Evangelical congregation came, helped us off the ship, welcomed us with uncommon friendliness, and refreshed us with bodily comforts. We immediately felt the difference in the climate; here it was oppressively hot and the inhabitants' faces were sallow, pale, or yellow, as if they had come out of the graves or the hospital. At first it strikes one as strange to see so many Negro slaves, for here, it is said, there are twenty blacks for every white man.

SEPTEMBER 12. My friends said that in Carolina and Georgia September was the most dangerous month of the year for epidemic sicknesses and deaths. They said that one English doctor had declared that at the present time he alone had about six hundred patients suffering from acute fever, diarrhea, dysentery, etc. In the afternoon I did not feel very well, but went out with my wife to visit Mr. Michael Kalteisen, a well-read and experienced elder of our congregation. He knew a great deal about the circumstances of the local congregation and was inclined to tell me all about them. He is a useful man in civil society and is therefore burdened with many offices. Among the elders here, as well as among the members of the congregation, one finds many who are steadfast, intelligent, and well-disposed Lutherans, men who are eager to promote and propagate the Evangelical Lutheran confession and willing to give time, labor, and money; but they lack a preacher who is powerful in proclaiming the truth of the Gospel and is exemplary in his conduct. The great majority, however, is satisfied with the mere outward *opus operatum* and the shell; the preacher may live as he pleases so long as he has a good voice and knows how to console people. The form is still there, but the power of godliness is unknown. The best teacher and pastor will have to have patience and begin here with the first elements of the true Evangelical religion and its practice.

OCTOBER 7. During my stay here the young discharged preacher, Mr. Frederick Daser, visited me several times and also attended my services on Sundays, doubtless in the hope that I would be able to bring about a reconciliation between him and the church council and congregation and get him settled for life. I therefore informed myself somewhat more fully concerning the affairs of the church and the pastors it had had, consulting not only the church records but also the elders, deacons, and intelligent members of the congregation, and found out the following facts:

1. The first preaching of the Gospel in the German language here in Charleston was doubtless done by Pastor John Martin Bolzius.

2. In October and November, 1742, Henry Muhlenberg stayed here for several weeks and conducted German services on Sundays in a private house with the few German inhabitants who lived here at that time.

3. Pastor Christian Rabenhorst and *Magister* J. S. Gerock arrived in Charleston about twenty-one years ago and conducted services during their sojourn here.

4. Candidate John George Friedrichs came, gathered the Germans together and ministered to them for several years in the French church, whose deacons were good enough to permit our Germans the use of the church between their services and their cemetery for burials. The Rev. Mr. Friedrichs worked hard and, with the help of the elders and deacons, was able to secure a place in the city for a German Lutheran church, schoolhouse, and cemetery. He was known and loved among the English inhabitants for his honest character and he collected among them for a church building. The Rev. Mr. Friedrichs laid the cornerstone of this first Lutheran church on December 17, 1759. Before the building was completed, however, he left Charleston to gather congregations in the country. Afterwards they accepted as pastor a Mr. Wartmann, an educated minister, who is said to have been an uncommonly lively speaker but a fiery and grossly extravagant *cholericus* who had worn himself out with several congregations in Pennsylvania and Virginia. He remained here about two years and then went farther into the country. The elders and deacons in Charleston called Mr. Nicholas Martin, an autodidact who entered upon the office in November, 1763, and served for several years. On June 24, 1764, the church was dedicated by Messrs. Friedrichs and Martin and named St. John's.

5. After Mr. Martin, the autodidact, left the congregation and moved on, the elders and deacons turned to His Reverence Dr. G. A. Wachsel, of London, petitioned for an educated, regular teacher and pastor, and soon afterwards secured the Rev. John Severin Hahnbaum, who entered upon the pastorate on June 14, 1767. Unfortunately, however, he lived only a few years and died on February 10, 1770, after an illness of about six months.

6. While Pastor Hahnbaum was still living (that is, in 1769), a young *artium magister,* Mr. Daser, arrived in Charleston from the Duchy of Wuerttemberg without credentials, clothing, or money, because, as he said, his trunk containing the said

valuables had been stolen from him in Holland. Mr. Kalteisen, a kind-hearted local elder, took pity on him, paid for his passage, and provided him with clerical clothes. And since Pastor Hahnbaum was already ailing at that time, he engaged the said *magister* as a vicar with the approval of the honorable church council, examined him, and had him installed and presented to the congregation by two elders.

The said vicar received not only good instruction from the *pastor ordinarius,* but also his daughter in marriage, as well as his theological books and sermon notes, so that he was well provided with adminicles and might have become a real *theologus* if he had been in earnest about his own soul and the souls of others. After the Rev. Mr. Hahnbaum's passing, the honorable church council allowed the young *Magister* Daser to administer the office conditionally for one year in the hope that he would be diligent and carry on his ministry with earnestness and zeal. When the year of probation was up, having no other alternative they renewed the agreement for three years.

Both of them were still young and, besides, somewhat inexperienced in economy. They failed to balance their income with their expenditures, and, it is said, frequented societies where the so-called *adiaphora* are indulged in or at least present the appearance of evil. For example, when a person indulges in all too sudorific dancing at frolicsome weddings, studies the fine points of morality in the current comedies, runs the streets at night, bombards doors and shutters with sticks and stones, gets into debt, and even loses his reputation as a citizen and practices his weighty office as a mere side line, etc., how can this awaken any love on the part of intelligent people? When the three years of the contract drew to a close, the church council gave notice that his services would terminate.

In the meantime, *Magister* Daser had procured from the local lieutenant governor and the English minister of the High Church a *recommendation* addressed to the *Lord* Bishop in London, requesting *Episcopal ordination and a competent living* in country congregations.

Mr. Daser postponed his journey to see the bishop in order first to find out whether I would support his party, provide him with an adequate salary from the congregation, and install him as preacher for life. The church council party, however, absolutely refused to consent to this. They would have nothing further to do with him as a minister, much less assume the debts he had incurred. Under these circumstances I could not conscientiously side with Mr. Daser and his party, which, of course, caused them to show secret ill will toward me and to say that I was being partial and leaning too much toward the church council's side.

OCTOBER 13.   Our host received a visit today from a German family of our religion who live in Old Indian Swamp, fifty miles away in the country. The man's name is Philip Eisenmann and he has a plantation of his own, but no Negroes. He and his wife cultivate the place themselves in the sweat of their brows and prove thereby that a man can live and find food and clothing without the use of black slaves, if he be godly and contented and does not desire to take more out of the world than he brought into it.

They lamented the great lack of schools and religious services in their neighborhood. They have been using their barn for public worship and have taken on as preacher a young man who recently arrived from Germany and spent some time teaching school in Charleston. The man said that the pastor works the whole week on a sermon, gathering it together from books and writing it all out, and then on Sunday dryly reads it from the paper without the slightest expression in his voice. He even has to read the Lord's Prayer, not knowing it from memory, and gives as his excuse the fact that the Lord did not give him the gift of a good memory. The good Lord is always the one to be blamed when these sluggards remain uncircumcised in heart and ears. The only credentials he brought with him from Germany were a pair of black breeches. The other fragments, such as bands, etc., he obtained from his countryman, Pastor Daser.

OCTOBER 19.   The local so-called German Friendly Society

held its quarterly meeting today. According to Mr. Kalteisen, it was founded eight years ago, January 15, 1766, and its membership has grown to upwards of eighty members living in the city and the country, of whom more than fifty are still living. The society possesses excellent printed rules and regulations and its object is to establish a fund from the interest of which it hopes to support members who have been impoverished by misfortune, or their surviving widows and orphans, and as far as possible to bring them up as Christians and useful citizens. This commendable society is, so to speak, the flower of the German nation in these parts.

The heads of this praiseworthy society bestowed upon me a special honor by kindly inviting me to attend their meeting today and to dine with them at noon. I could not very well decline because it would afford me an opportunity to become more closely acquainted with the most civilized and prominent members of our German nationality in this place than is possible in church gatherings, where, as a rule, only one speaks while the rest listen. The *vice-president* and treasurer came for me at 1 P.M. after I had first been shaved and my peruke had been dressed.

OCTOBER 22. Today our good hostess treated us to a great rarity which had been sent to our host by a good friend from Philadelphia on Captain Wright's ship, namely, sauerkraut, which to me and my family was like the gift of a costly medicine. Since such things are rare and not easily preserved in this warm climate, the whole family derived great sensual gratification from it, and I cannot deny that I shared in it. For I have not arrived at that *état d'abandon* which, in my younger years, the fanatical French and German moralists taught and insisted upon so stoutly, to wit, that if a man would be a perfect Christian, he must bring self-denial to the point where he becomes indifferent alike to heat and cold and sour and sweet taste.

OCTOBER 26. At last the vessel is about to sail for Savannah. A prominent English lady offered to convey us to the ship in her coach, but we politely declined, preferring to go on foot because we could expect to have enough swaying motion on the sea-coach. As I learned, the ship, called a *schooner,* was to make its last voyage and then be discharged because, like myself, it had become old and decayed. It was heavily laden with animate and inanimate creatures.

I immediately betook myself and family into the so-called cabin, as did the English lady also. There we found four bed-steads ingeniously contrived like cow cribs. The lady and her little son took one, an old English sea captain who was a passenger took the second, the third was taken by my daughter, and the fourth remained for my wife and myself. There was an almost insupportable stench in the cabin, as though rats had been decaying in it.

We could not sleep because, besides the overpowering stench, we had a swarm of poisonous, stinging gnats, called *musquitoes,* about our heads, and on the floor were innumerable *cackrotsches,* a species of insect about the size and shape of a beetle, black in color, which searches for victuals, gnaws at clothing, and even bites human beings in their sleep. I wished that they were all in the curio cabinets of Europe. Beneath, above, and on all sides of the cabin, between the old wainscoting, the rats and mice scampered and fought and squealed; and the vessel tossed to and fro and up and down like a drunken Frenchman dancing a rustic minuet.

OCTOBER 27.   At half-past eight the sun shone through the mist and the Lord showed us a door through which we could escape. We sailed along comfortably until two o'clock in the afternoon, when we anchored safely at Savannah and landed.

OCTOBER 30.   I preached morning and afternoon in the local German Lutheran church. A considerable group assembled, and the auditors were very attentive. About ten years ago they bought a lot for £150 sterling, and a wooden building which had formerly been a courthouse for £18 sterling, which they moved to the lot and adapted for worship, providing it with a steeple and bell. They are furnished with the means of grace every six weeks by the Rev. Mr. Rabenhorst. They use the Halle hymnbook and sing well, but the pastor himself must lead the singing because they do not have a cantor.

OCTOBER 31. In the afternoon, about four o'clock, I had the pleasure of meeting personally for the first time in my life the two pastors of Ebenezer, the Rev. Christian Rabenhorst and the Rev. Christopher Frederick Triebner. After cordially greeting one another and inquiring about the state of one another's health, we touched on the subject of the various natural temperaments of different men, whose temperaments had been sanctified, it is true, by the grace of God in conversion, but not exterminated. I illustrated this with an example from times past, namely, the three differing temperaments of the three late godly teachers in Halle, Francke, Anthon, and Breithaupt.

After this I let them read the warrant I had received and read to them an extract from the two letters of instruction from His Reverence Senior Urlsperger. I then asked them whether they acknowledged them to be authentic, whether they recognized me as being empowered, and whether they would permit me to act in accordance with my authority as far as God would enable me. Pastor Rabenhorst replied, "Yes, most willingly." Pastor Triebner seemed to have some hesitation. However, when I assured them that they would find me very faulty but nevertheless without guile, his assent also was forthcoming. Accordingly I requested them to add their written approval to the warrant, and this was done.

The pastors stayed with me until evening. Mr. Triebner remained an hour longer than Mr. Rabenhorst and told me a long string of one-sided things about the whole sad affair. I had to listen, but could say nothing in response because *altera pars* was not present and each party believes itself to be absolutely right. One point in the narrative secretly alarmed me, however. It is a point concerning which I am not yet certain, but if true it means that Jerusalem Church, the principal church in Ebenezer, was, in a *grant* from His Excellency the Governor and the *Council,* assigned under seal, with all its ground, parsonage, and cemetery, to the *jurisdiction* of the Church of England. If this should be the case and cannot be altered, and if representatives of the High Church should obtain a footing, then Ebenezer and its appurtenances will fall into an entirely alien channel, all the many benefactions and labors will be abortive, and my presence here will be useless and in vain.

NOVEMBER 2. My host was kind enough to lend my daughter a horse to ride along with them to Ebenezer.

NOVEMBER 7. Now the passion weeks were to begin. Squire Stephen Millen gave me his *chaise*; his servant drove and he rode along on horseback. We had covered twenty miles by about four o'clock, arriving safely at Pastor Rabenhorst's residence but damp from the rain. Found my wife and daughter fairly well.

I had imagined from various descriptions of this preacher's plantation that I would find a large, costly residence or palace, but found instead a little house made of wood, set on four blocks several feet above the sandy ground, with a cramped sitting room and bedroom on the first floor, under which the geese, etc., have their abode. They very happily vacated their bedroom and went to sleep in the upper floor under the roof.

NOVEMBER 11. About ten o'clock in the morning we three preachers met at the appointed place. I began with prayer and then said, among other things, that today I was going to make a test to see whether grace was really at the bottom of their lives and in which of them it was preponderant. I asked them to advise me as to how they might most quickly and best be reconciled with each other. We would now reduce their mutual complaints to the minimum and talk them over by word of mouth. Pastor Rabenhorst was to begin first. He did so and set forth several complaints. Mr. Triebner brushed them all aside and began to harangue, saying that he had done everything in God, in the sight of God, according to the instructions of the Reverend Fathers, and according to his best knowledge and conscience, and appealed to witnesses from his own party, etc. I became alarmed and said that this was not the way to achieve reconciliation and the best solution. His reply was that he wanted to defend his innocence in writing. I said that to do that would take a year and a day, use up paper, time, and strength, and still would do no good.

We stayed there from ten o'clock in the morning until four o'clock in the afternoon. I used the most moving appeals. I begged and besought them to forgive each other. I said that it was undeniable that Mr. Triebner had gone too far and accused Mr. Rabenhorst of things which he could not prove, etc., and that Mr. Rabenhorst might also have wronged Mr. Triebner in some instances, but that at least they could and should forgive each other their personal failings. Mr. Triebner replied that he had already said publicly at the last congregational meeting that he might possibly have been wrong in the mode or manner of his procedure, but not in the matter itself, for he had acted in accord with the Fathers' instructions and according to his best knowledge; but the opposing party had not been satisfied with this statement and locked him out of the church, etc.

It was impossible for me to believe that the Reverend Fathers could have instructed him to treat Mr. Rabenhorst as he had. But he intimated that Mr. Rabenhorst had been characterized to him long ago in Augsburg and London, or Kensington, as being the kind of man that he had actually found him to be here. I was still less able to believe this; for when the Reverend Fathers are assured by credible witnesses, and not by slanderers, of gross errors or faults and weaknesses on the part of one of their missionaries, whom they themselves have chosen, called, and sent, they seek in fatherly love and earnestness to set him straight, and they make use of the various degrees of admonition. They certainly would not give any neophyte and inexperienced minister instructions and orders to mistreat an older minister without his having been heard, or to cast suspicion on him behind his back.

I was unable to accomplish any more, however, except that he did say that he was willing to forgive Mr. Rabenhorst for the injury he had done to him. Pastor Rabenhorst saw my perplexity, disappointment, and sorrow and began to weep bitterly. He stood up, extended his hand to Mr. Triebner, and offered him forgiveness and peace. As an evidence of the reconciliation he went with us to his house and had a little to eat. In the evening he took me to his house five miles away. At evening devotions the dear man prayed very fervently and touchingly for all, but especially for his colleague, Mr. Triebner, which gave me a deep, inward joy.

NOVEMBER 20. Last night the ice froze to the depth of a finger-breadth, and now a few flakes of snow and cold rain are falling, which is something very unusual here, and the people feel it more sorely than the bitterest cold is felt in the North.

NOVEMBER 30. In the evening one message after another arrived from Pastor Rabenhorst's plantation. It was almost, in miniature, like the messengers who came to Job. (1) A fire in the fields had destroyed the necessary winter fodder of the cattle. (2) One of his most useful Negroes had been crushed and injured while felling a tree. (3) A negress was suddenly stricken with *colick*. (4) A calf died by accident. And so forth.

It is a burdensome, expensive, and hardly profitable business managing a place with Negro slaves, especially when one tries to maintain them in a Christian or at least humane manner, as Mr. Rabenhorst does. The way most of the English planters keep their slaves, they may well derive greater profits, for they make them work six days and give each of them a half-measure of maize without lard or salt and little or no clothing. They keep taskmasters over them who employ all sorts of instruments of torture, and on the seventh day they let them off to plant and sow for themselves and raise a bit for their own livelihood, if they are not too old and worn out.

The Year 1775

FEBRUARY 1. An old stooped, worn-out Negro has a half-grown daughter whom Mr. Rabenhorst wanted to give to me. I asked the father whether he was willing to let her go with me, promising that I would treat her as my own child, but he showed by his fearful countenance and gestures that he would rather lose his own life than be separated from his daughter. I was only too glad to desist, for I had not been in earnest.

As far as moral evil is concerned, they have this in common with white-skinned people, namely a fleshly mind and an enmity toward that which is spiritual and heavenly, and especially they cherish a secret rancor for having been snatched from their homeland and sold into everlasting slavery in a strange land. I was eager to secure their favor and asked Pastor Rabenhorst by what means this could be done. His answer was tobacco leaves, of which the men, women, and children are extremely fond and which make them as friendly and fawning as does a piece of meat a dog.

FEBRUARY 17. Took affectionate leave of my dear host, Squire Millen, and his family, who entertained and cared for us so lovingly, for which may the Lord recompense them. A number of Christian friends, men and women, of Ebenezer and Savannah accompanied us to the ship with tears and good wishes. The captain having some further business to transact, the ship remained at anchor till toward evening, so we were able to put our civil prison in some order and each one was able to occupy his berth. In the evening we sailed a few miles with the current on the Savannah River. The entire ship's company consisted only of four passengers (my wife and daughter and I and an English tailor), five sailors, a steersman who was making this voyage for the first time and was still strange, and a German captain who is cautious and careful in the duties of his calling on the water.

FEBRUARY 18. We were becalmed most of the time and progressed only a few miles with the current.

FEBRUARY 19. We had opportunity to collect our minds and edify ourselves with God's Word. We reached the region, called Tybee [Island], near the open sea, where we could see the oyster banks on one side and the lighthouse on the other.

FEBRUARY 20. We obtained the first serviceable wind, which carried us out to sea and also immediately gave me a violent seasickness which necessitated my going to bed. The sickness was all the more grievous because the ship was so small and I suffered all the more from its violent movements and lurches. Within three days we reached the Florida Gulf Stream, which flows toward the northeast, and here we had a favorable wind. My sickness and my daughter's continued, but my otherwise sickly wife was spared seasickness, which was somewhat of a relief to me since in such circumstances nobody can help his neighbor.

MARCH 2. Toward evening we were still about sixty English miles from Cape Henlopen, and we thought we could steal quietly into the bay and cast anchor. But suddenly a violent northwest wind arose and drove us toward the northeast. The wind grew stormier, and the dark night made the situation even more fearful. The sails had to be quickly hauled down to save the masts, the rudder was secured, and the ship was left to the mercy of the roaring waves. The little ship quivered with strange epileptic paroxysms and made such wild and erratic leaps upwards, downwards, sidewards, backwards, and forwards that it was impossible to walk, stand, sit, or lie, and one knew not how to live or die. We had secured the window shutters, but we nevertheless shipped waves several times from above and were partly soaked. Each of us passengers grasped something secure in the cabin and held on to it, as in ancient times people grasped the horns of the altar and let themselves be killed.

In such a situation, mere sensual faith, as well as philosophy which is built only on sand, is washed away; then the only thing that counts is, "Blessed are they that have not seen, and yet have believed." The conscience confronts the poor sinner with the sins of his youth, of his office, of his station, the sins of omission and the sins of commission, and places him, naked and condemned, at the gates of eternity!

Toward morning the storm subsided and we commenced sailing again, but we could go in no direction except eastward, farther and farther away from Pennsylvania. When the latitude was observed it was found that we were about one hundred and sixty miles from the cape; thus we had been driven one hundred miles since the night before. Soon afterwards the good Lord granted us a favorable wind so that we were able to steer our course for the cape, and we reached it within thirty hours.

During the night of March 4 and 5 we had already reached Reedy Island, about sixty miles from Philadelphia. But here again we had to undergo another little trial. The sailor who cast the lead during the night had unwittingly tangled his line, which made it somewhat shorter, so when he cried out, "Five fathoms," it was only about four or three. The pilot, depending upon this, got too far over to the left side where the ship ran aground and stuck fast.

MARCH 5. Early in the morning. The captain and the sailors were embarrassed because the ship was stuck fast, but they hoped that it could be worked loose at high tide some six hours later. But when high tide came, the ship still remained fast and immovable. By the providence of God four strong pilots came to our rescue in their shallops from Reedy Island, having seen our plight from afar off. They tried all possible means, but in vain. Finally they lifted five thousand pounds' weight of barrels of rice from the ship to the pilot boat and then set to once more with all their might and main, while I prayed in secret in my cabin; and finally, about three o'clock in the afternoon, through prayer and work, the ship was brought out of the hole and into the river. We sailed onward with a favorable wind until, under God's gracious protection, we anchored safely at Philadelphia on

Monday noon, March 6, and stepped off the boat to meet our children. We were welcomed on the streets by many old friends who accompanied us to the parsonage.

MAY 28.   A large number of Lutherans from the country and the town assembled in order to see and hear the old bugbear [Muhlenberg] once more. On account of my departure for South Carolina and Georgia, my prejudiced enemies and unfair detractors spread gross slanders against me among the ignorant people throughout the whole colony and the neighboring provinces. These calumnies were first hatched here because I was not willing to leap to the service of several bigwigs and envious persons and remove honest Pastor John Andrew Krug, etc.

It was said at first that I was conducting a correspondence with the royal chaplains in London and that I proposed, through their mediation, to levy the tithe here, etc. This arrow was forged in order to injure our poor Ministerium. Finally, when in the following year the Acts of Parliament came and laid the ax to the roots of the tree, and when I had journeyed out of the province with a part of my family, all the foul vapors from the father of lies were let loose and spread *methodo mathematica* in every direction. Among other things it was said, "The king has become a papist, and old man Muhlenberg has gone abroad to celebrate Mass for him." Others said, "No, he made a hasty exit in order to escape being hanged by the people," etc. Still others said, "The avenging God would not permit him to live, for he suffered shipwreck and was drowned between South Carolina and Georgia," etc. Real friends were depressed and half-believed that it might be so. Envious persons accepted the report as true and their rejoicing was the crackling of thorns under a pot [Eccl. 7:6].

When at last I returned, the crudest rumors subsided. But it was still believed in the country that I had been tarred and feathered, driven about in a cart, and drummed out of Philadelphia. And several friends far out in the country inquired anxiously whether this was true. The story had some appearance of truth, for this did happen recently to a prominent *doctor medicinae* because he had spoken against the measures of defense.

JUNE 11. This morning I was fetched at my lodgings by several prominent men who were delegated by the honorable church council. They escorted me in procession to the church after the old German manner which used to be practiced ages ago in the ancient and distinguished Hansa towns and imperial cities. The church was crowded, but a couple of companies of the recently organized civil militia were able to squeeze in too; they left their weapons outside of the church, where they posted a guard. Inside the church the elders were kept busy preserving order. The schoolmaster and organist and cantor—all in one person—had prepared some vocal and instrumental music. I preached on today's lesson, John 3:1ff. The auditors were as attentive as the intense heat and the crowded quarters allowed. After the service I was escorted home again in the same extraordinary fashion. It is hard to adapt oneself to the curious variations between good and bad fortune. It is like the description in the hymn, *"Ach wie nichtig, ach wie fluechtig,"* etc. First Haman wants to put Mordecai and his brethren out of the way, then he takes him on horseback through the streets of the city and has men proclaim before him, "Thus shall it be done to the man whom the king delighteth to honor."

JUNE 12. Every place through which I passed or in which I stopped for a while on my short trip to Reading, I found the male inhabitants under arms. The exceptions were women and the various kinds of sectarians who believe that the millennium is now at hand and that they will reign completely. The objection may be raised that there is hardly prospect that this will come from England in the present golden age.

The inquisitive question, What is the purpose of the military exercises? is answered thus: It is not our purpose to harm anyone or seize rights which are not ours, but to defend the liberty and rights vouchsafed by God and stipulated by earlier governments and to obey the admonition of the world's Saviour that every right-minded housefather should protect his house and property against thieves who may be presumed to come not only to steal but also to slay and destroy. It is difficult and even dangerous for

155

preachers in this crisis to attempt to lead men back to the original cause of the present divine discipline and judgment, that is, the abuse of noble freedom, a false security, and the sins and evils which arise therefrom. If one tries to explain and clarify this, foolish people at once declare one to be a traitor of their rights and liberties and lay the blame on *causae secundariae,* etc.

The local natural philosophers cannot comprehend how a mother can devour her own children except in cases of extreme hunger and despair, when implanted love is overcome, of which there are a few examples, as in the siege of Jerusalem, etc. Some of the local natural philosophers go even further and declare that it is known from experience that in the animal kingdom a sow often devours most of her offspring after birth, but they are not in agreement as to whether this is done out of love or hate. The wisest, however, conclude that, inasmuch as animals have something analogous to reason, it is to be accounted as being in accord with a fundamental rule of society if a mother keeps only a few and feeds these few so much the more in order that those remaining may have so much more to eat and may live in abundance, etc.

Simple people who have never experienced the bitter fruits of an interval of domestic war take it lightly and expect that an all but universal martial spirit will spread among the inhabitants of North America and will seize upon all adult males and youths and even children in their cradles so that practically everyone, old and young, will begin to drum and fife and shoot, albeit without lead and powder. This will probably not settle the matter, and it would be better if the immoderate rage and fury of the mother subsided, if means of reconciliation were found, and if fathers did not entice their children to anger, to rebellion, or to "barking in reply." For when one shouts into the woods, the echo comes back.

Some say that it is consequently a very grave possibility that England might urge her neighboring and otherwise envious powers not to send any armaments and weapons to her children for their defense, inasmuch as she herself often sends over fire and sword instead of scourges, taskmasters instead of fathers, and, in addition, hires and eggs on the neighboring, barbarous, and inhuman heathen, the black servants, etc. in order to visit temporal and eternal destruction upon the bodies and souls of their children and devastate the property they have with bitter sweat secured. In the towns one sees boys, who are still quite small, marching in companies with little drums and wooden flints to defend their inherited liberty. And pious mothers trust, with respect to their dearly beloved babes in their cradles or at their breasts, that the Lord God of Sabaoth, guardian of infants, who is today despised throughout the world, will graciously protect them and fight for them.

DECEMBER 26. On the strength of available news and in the light of all appearances, it seems that the flames of war will spread farther over the united North American provinces during the coming year, unless the Lord God, the supreme Ruler, determines otherwise.

Inasmuch as our Lutheran congregational establishments, although small, are involved in all that happens, it is necessary to ask if reason and revelation counsel that we conjugate in the active, passive, or neuter. Cities like New York, Charleston, Philadelphia, etc., which are closest to the ocean and which possess inflammable materials of superior moral and physical character, are, according to human reckoning, most exposed to trial and danger. And if the temples should burn along with other things, Vespasian will say, "We have no need of priests!" What, then, shall we do with the wives and children of poor preachers? When storms and tempests gather, a clucking hen, albeit only an irrational little creature, instinctively seeks some spot in which she might find shelter for her young ones. I often reflected that, if I still had my farm in Providence, one or another of my fleeing colleagues might, in addition to myself, find refuge there, at least in the first *paroxismum,* and might recover his breath until a better solution is offered, etc.

Troubled by such thoughts, which came not from unbelief but from concern, I happened by chance upon a notice in the English newspaper, offering a place in Providence for sale. The property consists of seven to eight acres adjacent to the street, most of it laid out in orchards and vegetable gardens. There is a large two-story dwelling, built of massive stones more than twenty years ago, with four rooms on the lower and four on the upper floor. Nearby is a one-story stone house and workshop, together with two draw-wells and a large stone barn and stables. The buildings were erected twenty and more years ago, when I was still living in Providence, by one of our parishioners, and must have cost him from £500 to £600. During the construction he was overtaken by a continuing delirium and ran into debt, as a result of which his *creditores* had the *sheriff* put up the place, etc. for auction. After the purchaser had resold the place to an Irishman, who rented it for several years to tradesmen and artisans, the buildings, etc. were allowed to get out of repair and go to ruin.

I hardly knew what to do, for I do not trust my own ideas and picturesque fancies. In consideration of its nearness to one of our original congregations, which has no parsonage although it has a debt-free church and schoolhouse, in view of the decline of our oldest congregation in New Hanover, and because a place (neither too near the city nor too near the Indian frontier) is needed in the present *crisis* as a refuge for fleeing pastors, their families, widows, etc., I resolved to buy the place. Meanwhile I placed the matter in secret before the overruling Saviour, who does not exclude trivialities from his providence and direction, with the humble petition that he might further the matter if he holds it to be good and useful, but that he might obstruct it if he does not, for I am ignorant and cannot foresee future events.

By observing the circumstances I was able, though not without difficulties, to purchase the place in my name, and as my estate and landed property, for £340. The following was my plan: (1) I wished to apply to this purpose a certain sum from the Count Solms-Roedelsheim legacy—neither too much nor too little—in order that this part of the legacy might be secure and bear interest. With this in mind, I took £280 from the £1,160 belonging to the legacy and in keeping of the local *corporation* and placed this amount on the aforesaid property. (2) My kinsman by marriage, Mr. David Schaefer, advanced £100 for his son-in-law, Frederick Muhlenberg, with the idea that the said Frederick Muhlenberg might in an emergency flee thither with his wife and children and might enjoy shelter, proportionate to the interest on this sum, until other arrangements might be made. (3) Now wanting to raise the full purchase price were £40 currency. According to the estimate of intelligent builders, the execution of the contract of sale and the repair of the buildings and property would require at least £180 currency, if the interest was also to be deducted. My helpless wife agreed to apply to the place a sum of about £120, which she had saved as a widow's mite from the inheritance from her father. She did this because, if she outlives me, she will probably wish to choose Providence, God willing, as her permanent place of residence when she is a widow. Thus the whole sum amounts to £500 currency, which, at 6 per cent, the highest rate of interest, will cost £30 a year, and at 5 per cent, a moderate rate of interest, will cost £25.

The Year 1776

MARCH 17. Was obliged to undertake a journey to Providence. My reasons for undertaking this journey during such severe winter weather, when the roads were still bad, were as follows:

1. The disturbances of war were on the increase.

2. Between March 6 and 9 two warships had proceeded so far up the Delaware River that they were only twenty English miles from the city. The Philadelphia galleys, or rowing boats, each of which carries a cannon, were ordered to go out to meet them. They engaged the enemy in action, which lasted two days and nights in succession, and the firing of the cannons could be heard and counted quite easily, which caused considerable tumult and alarm in the city. Those who were able to flee, fled from the city—especially well-to-do families, women, and children—and the streets were so crowded with wagons, chaises, and carts that they had difficulty passing one another. This was particularly so because they did not flee like John Bunyan's imaginative Christian but took with them the best objects of their tender consciences and the most important evidences of their religion. Although the warships did not accomplish their intended purpose this time, a severer visitation was expected soon.

3. The wife of my son Frederick, on the advice of prudent friends, fled from New York with her two small children in February of this year. She found refuge in the home of her dear parents in Philadelphia, where she was soon confined with her third child.

4. My third son Henry and my son-in-law John C. Kunze in Philadelphia also had pregnant wives, and I had a sick and timorous wife. Since it seemed as if God in his gracious providence had directed us to a little place in Providence as a refuge from the first onslaught, we preachers planned to stay with our

congregations in their extremity but to transport our wives and children, as weaker vessels, to Providence until the storm passes. Since the dwelling which had been purchased in Providence was uninhabited and uncared for, in need of repair, and requiring reconstruction, I was obliged to undertake the establishment of a new household there.

This is the eighteenth time, within the thirty-four years of my pilgrimage here in America, that I have had to change my residence. I have been like an Arab who pitches his tent first here, then there. If I had remained a confirmed bachelor, I might have been able to move my household in a small bag with little effort or expense. Yet there is an advantage, for with all the moving about our household goods have become lighter and lighter.

MAY 17. The day of prayer and fasting decreed by the Continental Congress was observed today. The Quakers protested beforehand openly and in writing that they were unable for reasons of conscience to obey such human ordinances, and some of them opened their stalls and shops on this day in order to express their defiance of so-called human ordinances. Before one knew it, however, a crowd of half-grown boys and students began to riot, walked up and down with clubs, etc., and ordered the conscientious Friends to take down their signs and close their shops for the day. The obedient ones listened to the voices of the boys; some who were stubborn were compelled by stones to listen.

JULY 4. Today the Continental Congress openly declared the united provinces of North America to be free and *independent* states. This has caused some thoughtful and far-seeing *melancholici* to be down in the mouth; on the other hand, it has caused some sanguine and short-sighted persons to exult and shout with joy. It will appear in the end who has played the right tune. This remains as a comfort to believers: There is One who sits at the rudder, who has the plan of the whole before him, to whom all power in heaven and on earth is given, and who has never yet made a mistake in his government. He it is who neither sleeps nor slumbers and who has asked his people to pray, "Hallowed be thy name, thy kingdom come, thy will be done."

JULY 8.   Today the united North American provinces were proclaimed independent from the *state* house. Psalm 127:1. An election is being held in Philadelphia, and in the whole province. The inhabitants are to elect their delegates *per plurima vota* to a *convention,* which *convention* is to have its first *session* in Philadelphia on July 15 (unless the city is taken by surprise before that).

JULY 11.   Inasmuch as Pastor Kunze's strength is largely restored and my presence on the property is very necessary, I hired a wagon and moved to Providence with my sick wife and very young daughter Salome—to remain there until a better solution presents itself.

I met a company of men from Reading, a hundred strong, on the march to the *province* of Jersey. Most of them were settlers and young men born in this country and recently enlisted with others to form an army of observation in Jersey, since Rehoboam's thick finger [I Kings 12] has entrenched itself on Staten Island (the island between New York, Jersey, and Pennsylvania) and requires watching as well as counterpressure. The company camped overnight here in Providence, some in the woods but most of them in two inns.

Had a letter from *Magister* Christian Streit with the announcement that he intends to accept service as an army chaplain in Virginia and the request that his congregations be cared for by a minister from our Ministerium.

JULY 23.   Since Sunday I have had a kind of colic, which may be due to drinking water and milk. In the city I was accustomed to *covent,* or small beer, which quenches my thirst best in the hot summer days; but this is not to be had so conveniently in the country until one procures the ingredients and utensils. Again, in the evening, there arrived here a company of riflemen, or sharpshooters, from Reading on their march to Jersey. Most of them are native youngsters from in and around Reading who learned bushfighting like that of the Indians. They

are also clad in Indian fashion and are armed with rifles and
tomahawks. Their outer shirts are shaggy, almost like the
pictures of satyrs, fauns, or sylvan spirits of ancient times.

AUGUST 2. Toward evening Colonel Grub arrived with his
battalion of five hundred militia men, who camped tonight in
the open field in order to march on to Jersey early in the morning.
As it is now time that the farmers should be preparing their fields
for the sowing of winter crops and the men must go to war, there
is much lamentation, and the women and gray old fathers are
obliged to complete the gathering of the late harvest and put
their hands to the plow.

AUGUST 9. Received letters and newspapers from Frederick
Muhlenberg, who had come back to Philadelphia from New
York the day before, after narrowly escaping from New York
and leaving some of his household furnishings behind. Today
he sent up a wagonload of his household furniture and books
and sent word that he would come up with his wife, three
children, and maid next week, God willing. It is hard for young
beginners when they suddenly lose their scanty support and are
forced to flee with wife and little children, lose part of their
necessary household furnishings, and finally have the rest of them
smashed to pieces on the journey.

AUGUST 22. This morning, about eight o'clock, two companies of Colonel Pott's battalion from up in the country stopped
at the Providence church. I was asked to give them a word of
admonition in English and German in Augustus Church, for they
were on the march to the camp in Jersey and were members of
the Episcopal and Protestant churches.

Since I could not with good conscience refuse, I acceded to
their request, for one should in charity be impartial and emulate
the heavenly Father, who makes his sun to rise on the evil and on
the good and sends rain on the just and on the unjust. I have
not been charged with the task of investigating and compre-
hending the matter in controversy, nor is it possible for me to
determine which party has the highest and best right, whether
the one has a better right to make serfs of the inhabitants of

America by force and to reap what they have neither plowed nor sowed, or whether the Americans have as good or even better right to defend the rights and privileges granted and stipulated to them by the highest God and by former crowned heads. Contending parties cannot be their own judges, and private persons possess no infallible scales to weigh without error the preponderant arguments of both sides.

This is evident in this controversy in the many writings *pro* and *contra,* indeed, even in the speeches made on both sides of the conflict in parliament. Therefore, since the ministers neither can nor should be judges or arbitrators in such a conflict, they do best if they commit the whole thing to the only and highest Judge of heaven and earth and follow the rule of the Spirit of God given through the Apostle Paul, Romans 13, "Let every soul be subject unto the higher powers," etc. If God's governance ordains or suffers that a king or a parliament or a congress should have power over me, then I must be subject to and serve two discordant masters at the same time.]

The English address I based on I Samuel 17 and the German on Psalm 27. The mothers and relatives wept over the departure of their loved ones.

SEPTEMBER 16. I had a visit from the president of the English Academy in Philadelphia [later, University of Pennsylvania], William Smith, who conferred with me about the following serious matter. Since the esteemed Congress of the United North American Provinces has declared independence and thereby dissolved the previous government, and since a convention of this province has been in session for some time to draw up a fundamental plan for a new government, it has become evident from the printed draft which has been submitted to the public for criticism that the Christian religion is paid scant or no respect, but is rather considered an indifferent, arbitrary matter.

Any member of the future new government will be sufficiently qualified if he merely acknowledges by word of mouth a Supreme Being as the creator and upholder of all things. Moreover, every religious party and persuasion shall, without distinction, have equal freedom to believe and teach what it pleases according to its own so-called conscience or judgment.

The members of this provincial convention, sitting as delegates from each district, are doubtless for the most part honorable, loyal citizens and mechanics. They have a good understanding of farming and trade and, as far as religion is concerned, are of various denominations, nationalities, languages, and persuasions. But those who are doing the speaking and bear the most weight appear not to be favorably inclined toward the Christian religion.

SEPTEMBER 17. At noon I was summoned to a house where there were two prominent members of the Academy and one from the Episcopal Church. I pointed out that it would be most surprising if several hundred thousand souls in Pennsylvania would allow themselves to be governed under a new form by men who did not profess the Christian religion. No matter how much inhabitants might be divided into religious parties, they nevertheless profess the Christian religion. Are these many thousands of souls to be governed by men who neither believe nor confess the Saviour of the world and his Word?

One of the two, a vice-provost and doctor of theology, replied that the form of government had nothing to do with the matter of religion and expressed the opinion that it was sufficient if members of the new government merely confess faith in a Supreme Being as creator and upholder of all things. The old form had given occasion to abuse, since high officials were required to swear upon the Trinity and the Bible and receive the Lord's Supper when for the most part they did not believe in those things.

Another replied that the abuse of a thing was no argument against the right use of it. I said that clergymen were supposed to be the pillars of the Christian religion, with a command of learning and language, and that if they were to remain silent now and not defend this good cause, they would surely be held accountable.

One man remarked further that there was no provision whatever in the new plan concerning the *charters,* privileges, and legacies which the congregations, corporations, or societies possessed under the former constitution and now might lose. It was deemed advisable to petition the convention to amend the forty-seventh section of the fundamental plan. . . . Accordingly, one of us was appointed to speak with the honorable president of the convention, Mr. Benjamin Franklin, and ask him whether we might not wait on him. He was condescending enough to come to us, and he took our written draft and promised to lay the matter before the convention when it reached Section 47.

OCTOBER 29. The interim government of the Americans has so many machines and wheels that it moves slowly, and at one time it is driven ahead of itself, at another behind itself. It was decided long ago that an army of observation of ten thousand men should be enlisted in the United States. Then when the British army landed on Staten Island, the provinces of Jersey and Pennsylvania lay open and unprotected; but since the army of observation had not been raised, the associated militia was obliged and forced to take the place of the army of observation, and this came just at the time when the farmers had not yet harvested their crops and still had their fields to prepare for sowing. In the city the mechanics were snatched from necessary trades and their families deprived of subsistence. In the country the most indispensable heads of families and workers had to leave their work, though they were anxious to sow seed for the coming year. The inhabitants who make a matter of conscience of the defense of their liberties and property stayed at home, laughed at the associators, and meanwhile raised the price of all necessities and amassed money for their tender consciences. Thus shillings are made into pennies, new patches are put on old, rotten garments, diapers cut from napkins, and the horse put behind the plow.

NOVEMBER 8. Bought a quarter of pork for the household for 13*s*. 6*d*. One hears complaints upon complaints among the inhabitants of the city and the country over the dearness of things.

The finest salt, which before the war could be had for 2*s.* a bushel, has already risen to 25*s.* and is hard to obtain. A pair of shoes which usually cost 7*s.* 6*d.* now costs 15*s.* A pound of butter, which used to cost at most 1*s.,* is now from 2*s.* to 2*s.* 6*d.* Wool is three times as expensive as formerly. Linen that was usually bought for 3*s. per yard* now costs from 9*s.* to 12*s.* A pound of meat that once cost from 4*d.* to 5*d.* now comes to 8*d.* or 10*d.* A cord of firewood which formerly could be had for £1 now costs £2, and bread flour is also beginning to rise because the last harvest did not turn out well and the wealthy Quakers are buying up large quantities, for with their tender consciences they prefer to gather up and hoard crops rather than Continental paper money. Thus the Lord is gradually pulling the breadbasket higher and higher away from us in order that we may not become too independent.

Several Hessians were brought to Philadelphia as prisoners. One of them happened to meet an inhabitant who was his aunt. The aunt asked him what had made him come here to do violence to his own flesh and blood. He replied that he had been torn out of bed, away from his wife and children, and forced into the service. This was incredible to the bystanders who had been born in this country; they said that that was the way the farmers in this country treated their horses, oxen, and cows which they sold to the horse copers and butchers.

Others were asked why they had fought so violently against the Americans in the battle on Long Island and treated the prisoners and the wounded so pitilessly. Answer: The English officers had told them that the Americans were savage cannibals, especially those who were shaggily clad, whom they must exterminate first of all if they were not to be tortured and eaten alive by them. This was therefore a minor stratagem of war; for the American chasseurs or sharpshooters, who shoot with rifles and are called *riflemen,* have a peculiar form of dress, much like that of the savage Indians, and most of them are enlisted native-born men of English and German extraction. Hence the Hessians, etc. were, and are still being, incited to set upon men of their own race and blood, for the crafty British would rather fill the graves with hired, foreign fascines than with their own native and lordly flesh.

DECEMBER 18. The provincial militia, which, to be sure, has been "associated," has been most urgently called up time after time to take its place along with the others in the breach, but it is like electricity in dark, wet weather. The glass globes must be turned and rubbed for a long time before they give off fire. In short, it is said, to the joy of many and the terror of many more, that the British armies will eat their Christmas dinner in Philadelphia and that for their encouragement they have been promised three days of liberty to plunder, etc. Men, women, and children are still fleeing the city for the country daily and are having to do so under unusually hard conditions.

The Year 1777

FEBRUARY 15. In the evening several companies of soldiers returned here to Providence from Ticonderoga after serving their stipulated time. It was difficult for them to find quarters. Frederick Muhlenberg took in seven of them, gave them a warm room for the night in the adjoining house, and supplied them with supper and sauerkraut, which pleased them very much and for which they were thankful because they had not had anything warm for a long time. Afterwards four German coachmen arrived and requested something warm to eat; they, too, were given supper by Frederick. Although the soldiers' stipulated time has expired, most of them have enlisted again to the end of the war.

MARCH 11. Had all sorts of English and German visitors who sought help for the sick, for there are no practitioners in the art of conjecture in this whole region inasmuch as they have gone to the military hospitals. I cannot help them because the Halle medicine is exhausted. What there is left of it is so expensive that poor people cannot afford it. The proverb says: Do not meddle in other people's business, etc. However, the command to love one's neighbor goes beyond the *sensus litterae,* so that one may put out a fire in an emergency, even on the Sabbath, or may haul an injured dumb animal out of a well, even if it is not done according to the *methodus mathematica.* The *Aesculapii* [physicians] dare not take offense, for they are not here. As long as the Halle medicines lasted, I used them according to the accompanying printed directions. But since I must do without these medicines I give people, who ask for it, counsel from the blessed Dr. John Samuel Carl's *Apotheke* and Dr. Tissot's *Haus-Arzenei-Buch,* and I show them the remedies which the great Benefactor causes to grow on their land or before their doors without payments or interest. Perhaps the physicians will soon return and I will be relieved of this burden.

APRIL 3. Today the day of fasting, prayer, and repentance recommended by the *Congress* and appointed by the provincial council and president was observed throughout the land. Romans 13, "Let every soul be subject to the authority that has power over him." This is an infallible rule for Christians who will not suffer other readings, variants, or the like and who do not need textual critics, for it carries its own meaning. This time it was quiet in the city—and also in the country, it is said. Only a few members of sullen sects declared that their consciences were oppressed if they were expected to observe a day which was appointed only by men. They opened their merchandise and huckster shops for business, but they were not strong enough to suffer for the sake of their consciences, for some half-grown zealots came along and, at the bidding of their own opposite conscience, hurled stones into the shops, as a result of which the shops were soon closed.

MAY 3. Prepared several baptismal certificates because the Militia Act requires all inhabitants from their eighteenth to their fifty-third year to engage in military exercise and to be ready, in emergency, to help defend the land. Accordingly parents must prove when their sons were born.

MAY 12. Today Frederick Muhlenberg was occupied with the troublesome task of packing, for he intends, God willing, to move tomorrow with his family to the little parsonage in New Hanover. Trouble and unrest in this world, and especially now in time of war. Last night, at twilight, the neighbors heard and saw a large number of ravens and crows crying and fighting, something very uncommon in this region. I observed that one should not ascribe significance to the cries of birds, but that one may reasonably conclude that wheresoever the carcass is, there will the eagles be gathered together.

It is reported that His Excellency General Washington has sent an order to Philadelphia, requiring that all doctors and surgeons report to camp without delay. One may conclude that the destroying angel has bloody work in mind at God's command, if the Lord God commands or permits it. Lord, Lord, enter not into judgment with thy servant, for in thy sight shall no man living be justified.

MAY 16. At eight o'clock in the morning the deacon set out with me after I had asked several neighbors to make my necessary trip to Philadelphia known as much as possible and to have me excused because I announced last Sunday that, God willing, I would preach in Augustus Church on Whitsunday, German in the morning and English in the afternoon, and now I cannot fulfill my promise. Our journey was quite uneventful until we were within five miles of the city. Then the *chaise* broke down. This put us in straits because I am not in a condition to walk one mile, to say nothing of five miles, while carrying my bundle. Before we knew it, a prominent Catholic man of the city with whom I was acquainted came up behind us in a *chaise*. Without being asked he came to our aid. Fortunately he had a long rope with him, and with this he helped us tie the broken *chaise* together in such fashion that we were able to proceed slowly to Philadelphia. Thus divine providence extends even to little trivialities; a Samaritan had to assist an orthodox priest and Levite in order to point out that we should do likewise.

MAY 30. Early this morning my wife began again to take a new medicine for her illness—a mixture of molten sulphur and steel. One takes a piece of raw sulphur and a piece of glowing steel; the two are held over a pan of water and the mixture is allowed to drip in; afterwards it is made into a fine powder. Now and then an amount that can be placed on the point of a knife is taken with honey or *molasses*. Dose: Three knife-points mixed with honey and taken straight, once a week when the moon is waning. This has helped some patients whose epileptic *motus* came from worms. A person in trouble looks for release and is glad to try anything. Because the cause of sickness is so difficult to determine, many remedies are used in vain and they disturb Nature rather than help.

MAY 31. When I was obliged, in 1761, to move from

Providence to Philadelphia and to sell my farm, of this property I kept a lot of three acres near Augustus Church and forty acres of woodland. But when, in 1771, I was pressed by need on account of my large family and heavy expenditures, and inasmuch as my woodland was lying idle, as it were, I was compelled to sell the forty acres without the lot near the church. Only now have I realized that I made a mistake, for wood is becoming very scarce hereabouts and is becoming more so elsewhere; yet some is needed every year to maintain the fences around the orchard, the vegetable garden, and the buildings. Accordingly, I asked the owner today to sell me ten acres at the increased price. He promised to do so on condition that I and my heirs keep it and do not sell it to friends.

JUNE 20. In the afternoon I had myself cupped by a man who lives five miles away and paid 7s. 6d. I must continue to do this because, on a journey to Jersey in March, 1760, I caught cold in my back when I became wet. When this condition persisted stubbornly, the physicians recommended that plasters of Spanish fly be applied in the month of July. A plaster had hardly been applied when news came unexpectedly of my father-in-law's death and I was obliged to attend the funeral. In this hot season I spent three days traveling up and back without having opportunity to take care of the plaster and a *mortification* resulted. Although this was later healed, ever since that time I have had to be bled several times a year. Perhaps the British will finally do this for nothing if Providence decrees, or permits, that this should be the course of events.

JULY 1. New troubles and alarms. Our *assembly,* the new state government, has passed and published an act which requires all white inhabitants of Pennsylvania, eighteen years of age or over, to swear an oath of allegiance and acknowledge the new government as the lawful authority within a short time. Anyone who fails to do so within the appointed time is to forfeit all rights and privileges in the *Republic* and be subject to imprisonment and, if these measures do not help, be exiled from the country. There is no way out now except to follow the counsel of Romans

13:1-4: Be subject to that power which rules and offers protection, or, as it is put, which has the strongest arm and longest sword. There is no power but of God.

JULY 24. We learned of a distressing case. Our present state government had passed a law requiring all white inhabitants from eighteen to fifty-three years of age to be ready to serve in the militia and to engage in military exercise for the defense of their rights. Those who did not obey, either willfully or for reasons of conscience, were to pay a fine of £3 10s. at the close of the year. All at once more tender consciences were discovered in the state than had ever before been noticed. Inasmuch as many, especially among the sects, appealed to their tender consciences and refused to obey and mocked and ridiculed others who obeyed the government, a *collector* appointed by the government was obliged to take several armed men of the militia and begin to collect the fines. It is reported that a regularly appointed, decent, and honest *collector* went with two armed men to the home of a wealthy inhabitant of tender conscience and demanded the £3 10s. fine. The man seized a plowshare which he had at hand for this purpose and split open the *collector's* head with it, so that he died at once. One may well ask what kind of conscience this is if it induces a man to refuse to defend his goods and property, his body and life, and yet induces him to murder his fellow citizen rather than pay £3 10s. out of his abundance. A strange picture of a tender conscience!

AUGUST 5. Yesterday and today a large number of empty freight wagons passed; they were ordered by the government to go to Philadelphia to take the poor women and children into the country. They will only be in the way and will offer an impediment when the battle begins. We had the good fortune to get a needed servant in the wagons. In one of the wagons we got our hired maid, Susanna Klein, whom we promised to pay £12 a year, i.e., 5s. a week or £1 a month. Servants are so rare that they will not work for less than a wage of £18 to £20 a year. This is so because, since the war, none are being transported from Germany, England, etc., and the cost of clothing is high.

AUGUST 11. The heat is almost unbearable. Here and there people suddenly collapse and die when they are not careful in drinking cold water. Another company of state militia passed. Several officers stopped in and refreshed themselves with milk and water, which is the only drink that really slakes thirst. Some privates visited our orchard and knocked down the apples, which had survived the spring frost, for their refreshment. There is still an old custom here, not unlike the Mosaic law, to the effect that travelers may enter an orchard and pick up or knock down as much fruit as they wish to eat, but they are not allowed to carry the fruit away. I did not begrudge my countrymen—Hanoverians, Waldeckians, Anspachers, Hessians, etc.—the last drop of milk and water, the last apple and cabbage for their refreshment, as long as they came peacefully, did not sell them, and did not offend against the second table of the law.

AUGUST 13. Heard another company of militia march by. What one used to hear in the country at this season of year was the music of the swish of flails in three-quarter time, but now one hears drums, fifes, and war cries instead.

AUGUST 18. I wrote a letter to Philadelphia in order to get some needed salt, and also one to Reading. So many thousands of inhabitants cannot live without salt. The seaports are closed by British war vessels so that one cannot go in or out. The people living along the sea coast in Jersey and Pennsylvania are making salt out of sea water, but one must ask with Andrew, John 6:9, What is this among so many? Yet even these small salt-making houses have been raided several times by the enemy. In Philadelphia, as a consequence, a bushel of salt has risen to twenty-six dollars (that is, £9 15s.) when in former times it could be bought for 1s. 6d.

Today I also learned that a band of thieves and murderers is roaming about in our neighborhood, that they have broken into several houses at night, bound up the people, and then stolen whatever they found to be valuable. I am especially subject to danger because my relatives in Philadelphia have placed several hundred pounds' worth of household goods here for safekeeping and I have nothing but sick and frail females about me. The Lord God is sufficiently powerful to protect his weak and helpless creatures when they pray for his protection. It has also pleased him to supply every living creature with defensive weapons; accordingly it is proper, especially for rational creatures, to employ the means which reason and revelation have ordained and allowed. Matthew 24:43. In cities there are watchmen at hand, and perhaps also garrisons. But in the country people are scattered; they often live a quarter, a half, a whole, or several miles apart; and thieves can break into a house, rob, and murder before the nearest or farthest neighbor learns of it. The neighbors who live near by have agreed that anyone who notices a forced entry should shoot out of the window and thus call others to his assistance. The Lord is still the keeper of Israel, who neither slumbers nor sleeps, and except the Lord keep the city and the house, the watchman waketh but in vain. Meanwhile we must do our part, as far as it goes, and commend ourselves to his almighty and gracious protection.

AUGUST 19. Last month, in July, it was a year since Congress declared the *independence* of the thirteen united states. The Philadelphians observed the day with special solemnity according to the advanced taste and sensuous magnificence. The air was filled and shaken by artificial fireworks and thunderclaps. Empty skins were bloated with food and drinks of health. Houses with their artificial *illumination* outshone the moon and the stars. And the newspapers indicated that everything proceeded in the most orderly fashion.

The celebration was immediately followed by one distressing report after another. For example, (a) the chief navy captain of the States, Commodore Manly, was captured, together with his frigate of thirty-some cannons, and taken to Halifax. (b) The two principal fortresses, Ticonderoga and Mount Independent, which are the main gateway by land to the states of New England, Jersey, New York, Pennsylvania, etc., were abandoned with all their ammunition and provisions before the British fired a shot at the fortifications, and thus the British richly harvested what they had not sowed. Luther had already said, in his time, that no fortress is invincible if asses can reach it with golden bullets.

SEPTEMBER 6. Today I am sixty-six years old and am entering upon my sixty-seventh year.

This summer I beheld a scene or *portrait* at my small dwelling place. A scrawny, unattractive hen, or pullet, laid eleven eggs in a hidden place amid a great cackling. For several weeks the hen sat on the eggs, suffering hunger and thirst and hardly taking a few minutes during the day to search for food in order to preserve life. Finally the little creature came out and brought eleven chicks to my door and asked for feed for her helpless offspring. She broke the bread for her young ones, warmed them at her breast, protected them against storms, warned them when she spied a bird of prey from afar, drew them after her when she wished to stray, fought men and strong beasts who approached too near to her young ones, cut a figure with her wings as if she were wearing a hoop skirt, and brought her young ones to my door or under my window five or six times a day and asked me to feed them. When the young ones had grown enough to help themselves, there was not one among them which showed enough gratitude to bring the mother a kernel of corn or share a chance crumb. Moreover, the mother ceased calling them, became quiet, modest, shy, and timid, and withdrew into solitude. Let the application be made to poor, aged parents and preachers, children and congregations.

SEPTEMBER 11. This morning we heard heavy and long continuing cannonading some thirty miles away on Brandywine Creek, where the two armies were engaged in a hard struggle; both sides suffered great losses and the British held the field.

SEPTEMBER 12. This afternoon six wagons with guards passed by; they are to take the most prominent Quakers of Philadelphia, who have been arrested, to Augusta County, in Virginia. Now prepare thyself, Pennsylvania, to meet the Lord thy God!

SEPTEMBER 14. A noisy Sabbath; there is no end to the

riding by of *chaises,* coaches, and freight wagons with refugees. An intelligent *gentleman* told me where the British army is encamped and conjectured that a division will cross the Schuylkill near us and proceed by the highway toward Philadelphia. Accordingly our neighborhood in Providence may be marched through or may even become the battlefield.

SEPTEMBER 15. Early in the morning a large number of freight wagons crossed the Schuylkill and passed by our place. They had loaded ammunition from a magazine in order to take it to safety in the direction of Bethlehem because the British division had approached the magazine last night. Further news came to the effect that the main camp was set up near Chester last night; also that the second division of the British intends to come across the Schuylkill at Swedes' Ford, eleven miles from our house, and that the third division will pass our home. Consequently the American army must also divide: one part near Philadelphia to meet the British from Chester, another at Swedes' Ford, and a third to meet the British coming from Providence. Chester is fifteen miles south of Philadelphia, Swedes' Ford sixteen miles west, and Providence twenty-three or -four miles northwest of where the American division has stored its supplies today near Philadelphia. Accordingly I (together with the people who have fled from Philadelphia to my house) am just midway between two divisions which are preparing to do battle against each other. I shall have nothing left except what God in his providence, grace, and mercy for Christ's sake has appointed in the other world. Now we shall have to practice what the sainted Luther sang,

> Let goods and kindred go,
> This mortal life also;
> The body they may kill,
> God's truth abideth still,
> His kingdom is forever.

SEPTEMBER 16. God in his goodness and mercy protected and preserved us during the night. We have reason to hope that the division of the British army will not come across the Schuylkill today either.

The imprisoned Quakers who were taken past here on September 12 reached Pottsgrove, ten miles from here, in the evening and were guarded by only a few men. It is reported that they were to move farther on September 13, but they refused. The guards therefore sent for help to the nearest commander of the militia, who despatched six men. Still they refused to go on, for they hoped, as it is said, that a number of British light cavalrymen might come and release them. But meanwhile a report was sent to Reading and a number of light cavalrymen of the American militia were sent from there the following day and took the defenseless sheep from Pottsgrove to Reading.

The Quakers protest that they are suffering for Christ's sake, etc. But this meets with little or no approval on the part of otherwise-minded people, for it is objected that (a) if they were really concerned about Christ, the Saviour of the world, and his kingdom of grace, they would not mutilate and reject his order of salvation and means of grace—for example, the whole Gospel, baptism, and holy communion. (b) If they were only concerned about their own Quaker society, it is objected, they would not have engaged in political affairs but would have submitted to the authority which now has power and offers protection. Inasmuch, however, as they have hitherto been protected by the present American government and have not been disturbed but rather preserved in their freedom of conscience, and yet have criticized and fought against the defensive measures of the Americans, both publicly and privately, in writing and orally, have refused to contribute their share even in money, have spoken for and rendered every possible assistance to the enemy, etc., they cannot be tolerated as members of a *republic* but must be excluded and be deprived of protection until God in his providence appoints or permits another government to wield the sword in place of the present one. If they followed the teachings of Christ and his apostles, had not set themselves up as partial judges between two parties, but had remained quiet and had borne their share of the burden until God, the chief Ruler and Judge, had himself resolved the conflict, they would have been tolerated. Accordingly they did not suffer for Christ's sake but on account of their transgression as traitors, etc.

SEPTEMBER 17. Since yesterday, and through the night, it has stormed and rained, and it still continues to rain. The poor men of both armies are in a bad way, for they must be out in the cold wind and rain, without tent or roof, and thinly clothed. This can cause grave illnesses, especially in this time of the equinox. I am sitting here, old and worn out, with a sick wife who is afflicted with hysterical paroxysms, surrounded by two daughters, two daughters-in-law, two little children, and my son's parents-in-law, etc., and I expect that any day or hour a British division will cross over the Schuylkill to our home and treat us, without distinction, as divine providence decrees or permits. One cannot well flee, for no place is safe. Where the two armies do not go, one finds thieves, robbers, and murderers who are taking advantage of the present times and conditions. For there are generally two parties, as is customary in such wars—parents against children, children against parents, brother against brother, neighbor against neighbor, etc.

SEPTEMBER 18. Yesterday and all night we had cold, stormy wind without rain. This has lowered the high rivers and gives both armies opportunity to march in either direction.

I have often been advised to flee farther away because the British treatment of preachers is barbarous and merciless, etc. But whither? What God has decreed for me in the course of events I cannot escape, no matter where I go. Psalm 139:7, 8, "Whither shall I go from thy Spirit? or whither shall I flee from thy presence?" etc. I had locked up my most important documents, such as *deeds,* obligations to the Solms-Roedelsheim legacy, etc., in a small chest and had the schoolmaster take them into the loft of the church. But since, as is well known, the British burn churches too, I had them taken down again. One thing may as well be where the other is. Everything is in God's hand to give or to take through intermediaries or through the elements which are in his service.

SEPTEMBER 19. Received news in the afternoon that the

British troops had marched across toward Providence on the other side of and farther down the Schuylkill. Their camp could be seen, I was told, through a fieldglass. The American troops then marched through the Schuylkill, four miles from us, and came out on the road to Philadelphia at Augustus Church. They had to wade through the river up to their chests. His Excellency General Washington was himself with the troops who marched past here to the Perkiomen. The passage of the troops lasted through the night, and we had all kinds of visitors, officers, etc. To get wet up to one's chest and then to march in the cold, foggy night while enduring hunger and thirst, etc. is hard for the poor men. It takes courage, health, etc. But instead of prayers, what one hears from many of them is the horrible national vice: cursing. At midnight a regiment camped on the street in front of my house. Some vegetables and chickens were taken, and a man with a flint came to my chamber, demanded bread, etc.

SEPTEMBER 20. The marauders who are following the American army are still stopping in to complain of hunger and thirst, etc. Isaiah 58 may also be applied here in the sense, "Is it not to deal thy bread to the hungry?" The two armies are near each other, the American on this side of the Schuylkill and the British on the other. Our weak vessels baked bread twice today and shared what little there was with the sick and wretched without charge. In the evening a nursemaid came with three English children of a prominent family which is fleeing from Philadelphia. Since night had fallen, they could not go on and pleaded to be put up; we took them in and gave them such accommodation as we had. "Given to hospitality," Romans 12:13, especially toward little children who are as angels. There were also two *Negroes,* servants of the English family. They secretly wished that the British army might win, for then all Negro slaves will gain their freedom. It is said that this sentiment is almost universal among the *Negroes* in America.

SEPTEMBER 21. In the afternoon we received the news that the British army is in motion on the other side of the Schuylkill. Certainly it is to be conjectured that the army will march across the Schuylkill, will come out on the highway at our house or a half-mile above, at Augustus Church, and will attack the American army. We were earnestly advised to flee because a battle may be fought here in this region and our house, etc. plundered and burned. It is expected that the American army will return tonight. Our relatives who have fled hither—Mr. Hall and his wife, my son Henry and his wife and child—decided to flee farther up to New Hanover. They wished to take us two oldsters along, but I saw no possibility of going. It would have pleased me if my sickly wife had gone along and left me here alone, but she was not to be persuaded by any means and insisted on living, suffering, and dying with me in Providence. While we were thus taking counsel a heavy rainstorm arose and prevented the departure. It was decided to leave at midnight when the moon went up. At twelve o'clock at night the vanguard of the American army passed by with its field pieces. Some of the troops pounded on our door as if they wished to break it. Our house guests jumped up and asked what they wanted. Answer: Fire. A German captain happened to be among them and drove them away.

SEPTEMBER 22. Beginning last midnight the whole American army returned and encamped about a mile above our house because it was reported that the British were crossing the Schuylkill and coming out at our house and that the battle would take place in this neighborhood. Early in the morning Henry Muhlenberg's parents-in-law, together with wife, child, and maid, drove off for New Hanover with their wagon and horses. But they were not able to get through the army and had to make a detour. My son Henry set out for Philadelphia, and I stayed behind with my wife to await what divine providence had decreed for us. The British did not cross the Schuylkill, and at two o'clock in the afternoon the American army broke camp and proceeded toward New Hanover, as far as my son Frederick's dwelling place. Accordingly the British have an open way to Philadelphia and can reach the city in a very short time. The wind is uncommonly cold and biting today. This, together with the equinoctial season and the other circumstances, has upset me.

All day hungry and thirsty soldiers, etc., have been stopping in and calling on us.

SEPTEMBER 23.   Last night a corps of American light infantrymen, a *scouting party,* was chased across the Schuylkill toward us by the British. They camped near our house. During the night an old English neighbor came to my house and asked me to get up and speak in his behalf with General William Maxwell. He, his sister's son, and another man had wished to go to their relatives who live near the British *camp,* etc., but they were picked up by the American patrol, taken for spies, and held in custody on this account. However, since, because of my catarrhal fever, I had taken something to induce a sweat, I could not venture to go out into the cold night. This morning, in response to a repeated request, I went to the general and told him that I have known this old neighbor more than thirty years, that he is a member of the Anglican church and an honest neighbor, and that, as far as I know, he is not a man of evil character. More than this I could not say. If it helped I have not yet learned. It is a delicate matter in this kind of war in which father is arrayed against son, son against father, brother against brother, neighbor against neighbor, etc. No one can trust another.

The militia troops who are encamped here must have wicked men among them. Some of them have broken into the house of the man who now owns my former farm, have broken chests and boxes to pieces, and have wrought havoc on the place. Others have smashed fences and rails and burned them, etc.

O poor Philadelphia! It is reported that the British army set out last night by moonlight and marched to Philadelphia. Meanwhile the main army of the Americans is up in New Hanover, thirty-six miles from Philadelphia, because it was supposed that the British troops would go farther up the Schuylkill toward Reading.

SEPTEMBER 25.   At two o'clock in the afternoon it began to rain hard and become very cold. The rain lasted almost all night. The poor soldiers have to endure a great deal because they have no tents with them. Our barn was crowded with those who sought some shelter. The little hay which we stored for the winter is carried away and spoiled. It is reported that the British soldiers have moved somewhat farther down toward the city.

SEPTEMBER 27. I was to bury a deacon's child at Augustus Church. When I arrived there I discovered to my sorrow that a regiment of the Pennsylvania militia had taken possession of Augustus Church, schoolhouse, etc. The church was crowded with officers and privates with their guns. The organ loft was filled, and one man was playing the organ while others sang to his accompaniment. Down below lay straw and manure, and several had placed the objects of their gluttony, etc., on the altar. In short, I saw, in miniature, the abomination of desolation in the temple. I entered but did not deem it advisable to speak to the mob because they at once began to jeer and several officers called up to the organ-player, "Play a Hessian march," etc. I sought out Colonel James Dunlap and inquired if this was the protection of religious and civil liberty which had been promised. He excused himself by declaring that the militia is made up of all sorts of nationalities and cannot be kept in proper discipline, etc. The schoolmaster complained with tears that his needed vegetables and the little buckwheat which he had sowed and which had just ripened had been trampled under foot and stolen; also that he and his lame wife had not been permitted to sleep in their own bed for several nights, nor had they been allowed to approach their hearth. But I could not help him inasmuch as I had myself had three acres of my lot near the church sowed in buckwheat, which was in fine bloom and gave promise of providing needed food for the winter, but the soldiers placed some twenty horses and head of cattle in the field and let them eat and trample it all down. If one objects with the merest word, one is told, "You are a *Tory!* Your house and home must be burned!" And those on the other side say, "You are rebels," etc.

I returned home and left the schoolmaster behind to tell the parents of the deceased child, when they arrived, that under the circumstances I could not take part in the funeral or speak a word of edification in the church. The sight of the church, etc., made me wretched. Had some visitors who asked for night's lodging and received it. Only we need servants. My poor, sick wife does what she can, and almost more than she can, but this is not enough.

OCTOBER 2. We were graciously preserved during the past night by God's protection. This forenoon all the American troops stationed hereabouts marched off down the highway. It is said that the main American army is also moving somewhat nearer the city on the Skippack road. It looks as if a swarm of locusts had been here. Bad policing. If the fences or rails around the farmers' fields and meadows are burned and their limited woodlands are cut and ruined, food for men and cattle will be reduced and starvation must follow. Before this I bought ten acres of woodland near the church; they have now been laid waste, etc. In this connection it occurred to me that we brought nothing with us into the world and we shall take nothing with us when we leave.

OCTOBER 4. The British outposts were stationed this side of Germantown. They had occupied the Lutheran church in Germantown, planted cannons in it, and fired from the windows. But on the first assault the Americans drove them out head over heels. One can well imagine what the building looks like. The fate of the Barren Hill church will hardly be better. The church in Reading has been turned into a hospital and is filled with wounded, the church in the village of Lebanon serves as a prison for captured Hessian soldiers, etc. This is a different method of preaching from the usual one in which divine goodness calls us to repentance. "Behold therefore the goodness and severity of God!"

OCTOBER 5. From early in the morning until noon the soldiers who marched off from here on October 2 came back again in troops and singly with their wagons to occupy their former places here. They were tired, hungry, and thirsty. They will consume all that is left. It was reported that they were only to reassemble here. In fact, they moved off in a side direction during the afternoon. The militiamen complain that they were not supported in yesterday's attack by the regular troops of the American army. The militiamen were egged on like young heroes and then watched from a distance. The British, on the contrary, reinforced their outposts. The result was that the militiamen had to withdraw. There were dead and wounded on both sides. Such a tragedy Germantown has not experienced since it was founded.

OCTOBER 6. Since yesterday the main American army was back again and encamped somewhat to one side of the road about five miles from our house, where they buried their dead and fired a salvo for each one. We could hear this, especially because it continued so long. At night there was an alarm in the American camp, as if the British were approaching, but it was only a false alarm.

OCTOBER 7. Received news that some of the Americans who were wounded last Saturday were taken to the Lutheran church in New Hanover and were bandaged by the physicians; that the losses of the American army amounted to about one thousand wounded, dead, or missing; and that several officers fell or died of wounds and were buried today in our neighborhood according to military usage.

OCTOBER 17. Toward evening several additional companies of militia arrived here in Providence to spend the night, some of them from Maryland and some from Reading. In peacetime, when one inn was more than enough, we used to have three large inns on the road in Providence; now, at this time, we have none. For this reason the soldiers go here and there to private homes and trouble the inhabitants for food, drink, and lodgings, for it has become too cold and raw to lie on the open ground without tents or shelter. The locusts [i.e., the soldiers] have already consumed the hay, straw, milk, butter, vegetables, etc., and have left little to be gleaned.

NOVEMBER 3. Some of the old Indians, who do not have the benefit of a higher revelation and do not understand Machiavellian principles, are astonished when they hear that German mercenaries are brought here to wound and kill the usually peaceful inhabitants of this land who have never done them any harm, to scourge defenseless and helpless women and children, and to burn their houses, crops, etc. The Indians think that these troops would do more wisely to remain here, to beat their spears and swords into axes, mattocks, shovels, plowshares, scythes, and sickles, and to cultivate the land, for there are still many millions of acres which are uncultivated—as many as there are hairs on one's head, to put it as the Indians count. Or if this did not please them, they would do better to return quietly to their homes and live there where the Great Spirit had raised them up out of the earth and where they would reap what they had planted and sowed, etc.

DECEMBER 1. In the evening *Commissarius* Robert Dill came from the American camp to say that he had heard that we had, under our house, the largest and best cellar in this neighborhood, and since he had to lay in stores for the winter he asked for permission to use it. I did not dare refuse, for it is a duty to serve friends and foes as one can.

DECEMBER 9. At night, when everyone was asleep, a half-drunken marauder knocked at the door. When I opened the door, he asked to be allowed to come in to warm himself. I said that all the fires were out; but he forced his way into the cold room and insisted on staying. He became more and more presumptuous and demanded something to eat and drink; I gave him what I could lay hands on. Kind words only made him bolder, so I had to call the watch to get rid of him. I am alone among helpless, weak creatures, without any means of defense, and some men are so barbarous that they are embittered by hard words and are made insolent by soft words. Without any merit or worthiness on our part, God in his goodness and might has so far graciously preserved us.

The Year 1778

JANUARY 7. Early in the morning Mr. Bender told us what had prompted him to come up. He owed my wife £100 and since *Congress* money no longer has any value in Philadelphia and he had some of this money left, he wanted to pay off his debt with it. We are the losers, of course, because we cannot loan out the money again. Nevertheless, we had to accept it because the *Independent* side metes out severe punishment for refusal to accept its money as valid. The trouble is that when one is able to buy a bushel of produce for 5s. in silver or gold coin, one has to pay three times as much in *Congress* paper money, and in most cases the country people would prefer to keep their goods rather than sell them for paper money. They say they have nothing for sale and, as usual, it is the poor who suffer most by it. Since we do not know yet which side will gain the victory, the people are fearful. If the *Independent* side should win, their notes of credit will retain their value, but if the British should win, the paper money will lose its value. Silver and gold coins retain their intrinsic, proportionate value, as the saying is among the children of this world who in their generation are wiser than the children of light.

JANUARY 13. The name of Muhlenberg has been made a highly suspicious one among the Hessian and English officers, and they are very angry; they threaten imprisonment, torture, and death as soon as they catch the old fellow. As far as possible I have stood between both parties, and I could not have done otherwise, for I have had no vocation to meddle in political controversy. But in times and conditions like these, envious persons and enemies, who at other times would be secret, rise up as accusers and vent their petty rage because they never had a chance to do it before. So be it. There is One who rules all things.

FEBRUARY 11. Last night a heavy rain fell upon the deep snow, and it still continues to rain today, which will result in high water and impassable roads. The people who have a roof over their heads, some grain, and some firewood are fortunate, physically speaking. There is no lack of water. In a sense, this weather also serves as a barrier, for during this time we need hardly fear an attack by the British from Philadelphia. The armies of both sides are at present fairly inactive in their winter quarters. They are forging arrows and gathering strength to shoot them where divine providence shall ordain—as King William used to say whenever he was admonished in the field not to go into dangerous places, *"Every bullet has its billet."* I cannot sufficiently magnify, much less give thanks for, God's goodness, long-suffering, mercy, and forbearance which, without any merit or worthiness on our part, has preserved us to this day, and I must attribute it directly to the intercessions of our most compassionate Mediator and the family that remains to him in Europe.

FEBRUARY 25. Mr. Iset took the remainder of Mr. Swaine's furniture to New Hanover in his wagon. There was a party from the American camp which wanted to impress the wagon. Mr. Evans came and begged me to conduct a funeral tomorrow for his deceased neighbor, Mr. Davis, who was a faithful member of the English church. But the roads are so deep that it is almost impossible for me to do it. There is great distress again today because wagons, horses, provisions, and victuals are to be impressed, or rather grapes are to be picked from thorns and figs from thistles. Toward evening we received the dreadful news that the British light cavalry was near us and that we would be attacked tonight. I had nine weak women and four children under my roof, and I was alone and quite at a loss, so I fled secretly to Jesus Christ and stayed up until four o'clock in the morning. The Lord God was our defense and shelter, and we met with no attack. They did not carry old Muhlenberg away with them.

FEBRUARY 26. It began to rain heavily early in the morning,

and this made the roads utterly impassable. Mr. Evans sent me a horse to ride the seven miles to the funeral, but it was impossible for me to proceed in such weather, so I sent the horse back. It grieves me, for I would be glad to do it, but I cannot. Things look black for me, for I am caught between two fires and I still am unable to foresee the outcome which divine providence will ordain for me. Last night the passage from C. H. von Bogatzky's *Schatzkaestlein* and his meditation thereon were reviving: Psalm 102:17, "He will regard the prayer of the destitute," etc.

The British cavalry is coming nearer and nearer and is taking captive former officers of the American militia. Toward evening came a report that they were nearby and were going to take me. I cannot flee, much less leave my sick wife behind, so I must await whatever God's holy providence and governance, which doeth all things well, has ordained for me and commit it to him, the Lord of lords, in humble prayer.

FEBRUARY 27. The flesh and the spirit are struggling within me. The flesh tells me that I should flee or seek protection from the commander-in-chief of the British. The spirit says: Seek protection from him who has all power in heaven and on earth; he can and will save all who come to him. Reason says: One must nevertheless also make use of all means that are permitted and not simply wait for supernatural protection. This is true, but in circumstances like these, if one accepts protection from one party, one exposes oneself to mortal hatred, revenge, and ruin; and lofty human reason certainly cannot foresee how God's secret counsel will decide the outcome, which side will be on top and which below. If this were a struggle for the honor of God and the welfare of religion, then each one would turn and hold to his own party; but this is not at all the issue which is being fought *pro* and *contra* now. At any rate, daily experience shows that this is an extraordinary war in ancient, heathen, barbaric mode, which manifests little or nothing that is humane, much less Christian, and which aims at the ruin of both the so-called mother and the children. Therefore it cannot be looked upon as anything else but a necessary, severe chastisement and grave punish-

ment laid upon both England and America by God, the supreme
Ruler. I prayed the almighty and gracious Redeemer for his
gracious protection, and this at least gave me a quiet and peaceful sleep *pro tempore.*

MARCH 2. In the evening we had more visits from a number
of fugitives; we were able to give lodging to only two; the others
went to Neighbor Ried's. I feared an attack, stayed up half the
night, and was unable to sleep during the other half. Prayed
fervently to the Lord and was graciously protected!

MARCH 8. Today we have no public service here and the
roads and weather are bad. We had family devotions on the
passion of our Lord Jesus Christ, which is and remains the best
nourisher of faith and the most precious balm of life. Daniel
Mertz came back in the evening, distressed and terrified. Last
Friday he had taken his sister, Widow Baiteman, who had been
staying with him for several days on a visit, down to Kensington
with two horses and had gotten through safely without mishap.
His relatives had given him a bushel of salt and some tea and
sugar. But on his way home, about ten or eleven miles from
here, several highwaymen captured him, seized all the above,
and let him ride on home, but gave him to understand that he
would be fetched from his home early tomorrow morning. I
always stay up, the last one in the family, to say my poor prayers
in private. Toward eleven o'clock someone knocked loudly, and
when I opened the door it was a huge Negro with a horse. He
pretended that he wanted a couple of tobacco pipes. I advised
him that such things could not be found here and that he must
look for them at the shopkeeper's. He begged my pardon and
rode away. Whether he had in mind an attack, or what he really
wanted, I do not know. With the almighty and most gracious
protection of the Saviour of the world we have as yet suffered
no evil. O if I could only be thankful enough for it!

MARCH 15. The Reformed minister, Pastor John Philip
Leydich, had service here today. Since the war began, both
warring parties no longer observe Sunday. The roads are never
free of wagons, etc. It is pitiful how the poor, patient animals

are cudgeled and beaten in the quaggy roads! We had private devotions. Toward evening twenty-three freight wagons, loaded with equipment from New England for the American army and accompanied by an escort, pulled up at our place. They made a fire near our orchard with rails from my fence, and a subaltern officer came up to me and wanted to impress a horse and weapons, etc. I gave him to understand that my horse was a rattan cane and that my weapons were books. He thereupon flew into a temper and began to curse violently. But when I gently reproached him, he ceased cursing and sent several armed soldiers into the neighborhood to achieve his end. He said that the convoy was poorly supplied with arms and that it was reported that the British and *Tories* were behind them to cut them off, which would entail a great loss. I feared that we would have a terrible night, so I took in hand the *arma ecclesiae,* namely, prayer, etc. They broke up between ten and eleven o'clock and turned toward the Schuylkill in order to get somewhat nearer the American camp. As it had been reported that the British cavalry was not far away, I stayed up.

About eleven o'clock someone hammered on the door, and when I opened it, it was an Irishman who was unknown to me. He whispered into my ear that the British cavalry was already near and that he would stand watch in front of my house, and when they arrived he would fire a shot as a signal for me to flee out the back into the bushes and hide. I thanked him for his kindness, forbade him to stand watch, and told him that if he would come to me in the daytime, I would discuss the matter further. I stayed up until after four o'clock and gladdened my heart with von Bogatzky's meditation on the passage, "Verily thou art a God that hidest thyself," etc. I found refuge under the all-gracious protection of the almighty Saviour of the world. It rained steadily from midnight on. Some of the militia also stood watch.

MARCH 30. The ground is covered with snow. Had a visit from a woman from the city who brought me a printed *piece* entitled *Lamentation of the Congress.* The author employed the style of the Old Testament and ran the *Independent* Americans down to the ground and exalted the *Dependents* to the skies, introducing my name and unworthy person in mockery. My daughter sent word that, if I desired to write a reply and send it to her, she would have it printed in the English newspaper. I do not deem it advisable, however, to reply under present circumstances; it is much better to be quiet and commit the matter in humble prayer to the God who rules all things and await whatever the all-wise and all-gracious providence of God may ordain.

Today I also had a visit from Pastor John L. Voigt, who reported something unpleasant to me, namely, that the American soldiers had evicted him from his residence, located in part of the old church, and seized the new church which was built in Pikestown only two years ago, tore out the seats and pews, and placed sick soldiers in it. He said that the deacons had sent petitions to the general at the camp, but these had been ignored, etc. The congregation is still about £400 in debt for the church building. This reminded me of what a boy once said to the police spies in the Palatinate when they were taking away the Protestants' books, "You may take my Catechism, for I have its contents in my head and heart." He who has gathered well in years past may now bring out of this treasure things new and old and enjoy them. Also had visits from hungry and thirsty soldiers.

APRIL 19. Easter Sunday. Lovely weather. In the forenoon I dragged myself to Augustus Church and found there a fairly numerous gathering to which I set forth a threefold testimony of the truth of Christ's resurrection. (a) The antecedent divine prophecies concerning Christ's death and resurrection. (b) The eye-witnesses. (c) The powerful effects upon and in men. Afterwards baptized two children. As English service had been appointed, I remained at the church until after two o'clock, when a considerable number assembled and I preached to them on the festival Gospel. The singing is hardly tolerable any more among the English people because it is so little practiced among them and the young people have no instruction in it at all. The hearers were attentive. I was weak and tired and preferred to go home through the woods instead of on the open highway. I tried to leap over a ditch, but came short and fell in, so that I had to wash myself before I was able to hobble on home. The spirit is willing, but the flesh is weak. In the evening a violent windstorm arose which shook our whole house. Not long afterward we saw a flaming fire several miles away on the road toward the Schuylkill River, and it continued for a long time.

APRIL 28. Since last night I have been so tormented with catarrh in the head that I was almost bereft of my senses. In the forenoon a man and his daughter from our congregation in Philadelphia stopped in after he had visited his son here in the country. The daughter received the Lord's Supper for the first time with others last Sunday from Pastor Kunze and said that he was still quite well. Zion Church is still full of sick soldiers and is badly ravaged. Victuals are rare and expensive there. Recently a shipload of *potatoes* arrived from Ireland, and they were sold for 15s. a *buschel*. Garden vegetables cannot be planted and raised because the garden fences and hedges have been torn down and burned for several miles around the city. Psalm 80:14, 17. Ezekiel 34:18, 19. Mama sent her yarn (fifteen pounds) to the weaver, Caspar Rahn, today. Around noon today our people heard many cannon shots from the vicinity of Philadelphia. What was up, time will tell.

APRIL 30. Today it is just thirty-three years since I was married to my wife in Tulpehocken. Very few of the wedding guests on that occasion are still living.

MAY 5. My ailing wife ventured for the first time to walk out a quarter of a mile with a neighbor woman to visit another sick woman. In the evening one of the poor women we have under our roof as fugitives went into labor and gave birth to a son during the night. God grant that he may be consecrated to his Redeemer!

MAY 7. The inhabitants of the region several miles around the American camp are experiencing and now also lamenting something which is altogether strange to them, namely, after having their hay, corn, wheat, oats, wood, straw, and horses taken away from them and sold last fall and throughout the winter, the many horses of the army are now being put out to pasture in their fresh wheat and corn fields and still bare meadows, which will thus be so denuded that it will be hard to find bread. "Man shall not live by bread alone," etc. The good God shows us a blessed harvest from afar in the gorgeous blossoms of the fruit trees, should it please him to preserve them and give the harvest. For the past two years we were shown the blossoms, but each time they were killed by the frost in May. The Lord giveth and taketh away according to the precepts of his supremely wise and good governance. "What God does is well done," etc.

Yesterday, in the American army, they marched three times around a bonfire. If the morals of the Saviour of the world were suited to the so-called world of society, a far more powerful effect would be produced at this time if America could join in a devout threefold prayer of repentance and with a believing heart three times sing, "Glory to God in the highest, and on earth peace," etc. But it depends mostly upon the leaders of the great world; when they cry, "Crucify," the multitude gives the echo with all the strength of its belly! These ancient customs borrowed from the heathen are better suited to the world of society and must be retained; so it would be vain to expect grapes from thorns and figs from thistles.

Today I was offered salt at £8 per *buschel*. How artfully do greed and material interest twist and turn! Just a short time ago a *buschel* was worth from £16 to £20, and even then was hardly to be had because the sellers were unwilling to take the *Congress* paper money and preferred to hold on to their goods. But no sooner does a hint appear, given by the two acts of Parliament on February 19, *a.c.*, which shows an inclination to offer peace and pardon because, through God's permission, the British have now vented their wrath and fury upon us and would be glad to stop and draw fresh breath, and no sooner does news arrive that the French court has concluded an alliance with the American *independent* states, etc., then the *Congress* money gains greater esteem and the sellers begin to sell off cheaply the stores they have been withholding. This is the work of the Lord God, who hears the prayer and cry of the poor and needy and helps them.

I heard a fine example today, namely, that His Excellency General Washington rode around among his army yesterday and admonished each and every one to fear God, to put away the wickedness that has set in and become so general, and to practice the Christian virtues. From all appearances this gentleman does not belong to the so-called world of society, for he respects God's Word, believes in the atonement through Christ, and bears himself in humility and gentleness. Therefore the Lord God has also singularly, yea, marvelously, preserved him from harm in the midst of countless perils, ambuscades, fatigues, etc., and has hitherto graciously held him in his hand as a chosen vessel. II Chronicles 15:1-3.

MAY 13. Today heavy cannonading was heard on the road to the Delaware River. It is said that the English made an attack from Philadelphia upon the New Jersey side of the Delaware, burned the American galleys near Trenton, and plundered and burned houses farther up in that vicinity. Poor Philadelphia, what will happen to you if the Lord God does not watch over the city? A party of allied Indians is encamped here in the neighborhood and there will, no doubt, be some hot fighting before the lion will let his prey be taken from him.

MAY 14. God in his goodness bestowed a little rain upon us last evening. Garden and field produce are retarded for lack of rain, and food for man and beast is scarce. The farmer says: A cool and showery May makes farm and vineyard pay. Cool it has been, but showers are lacking. We feared that the Indians would give us a restless night but, God be thanked, it was altogether quiet. During the day their captain spread the word that his people were not to be given any alcoholic liquor, which was easy to obey, for it is very scarce and too expensive. Their young men shot some squirrels and birds with their bows and arrows, and these they cooked over a fire in the evening and devoured without any European ceremony. One of the Indians came to our house and asked for milk. As my wife still knows a few words of their language which pertain to eating, he was delighted, and when he was given bread and milk he expressed his sentiment of joy in song. I could not understand the poetry. The *company* of Indians left here early today and went on toward the American camp.

MAY 17.   A man told me that now the rest of the Lutheran and Reformed churches across the Schuylkill in Pikestown and Pikeland have been taken over by the Americans and turned into hospitals. We heard cannon firing again this afternoon from the direction of the Delaware. Toward evening an upright member of the Philadelphia congregation arrived at our place. He wept for joy that the Lord had helped him to get this far. As the English in and around Philadelphia are taking the young men by force and putting them on ships, he fled because he is still single. Amid all the clamor and confusion one can still perceive a special providence watching over those who fear and love God.

MAY 20.   In the forenoon we heard three cannon shots, fired from the American camp, and the beating of drums, from which we surmised that something must be up. Around noon news arrived that a strong corps, ten thousand men, of the English army had gone forth from Philadelphia and were destroying everything, and that they were now only seven miles from our house. This brought fresh terror. Several settlers rode down the road to find out what was happening. In the meantime all sorts of reports kept coming in: that they were robbing all the cattle, plundering houses, taking boys, youths, and men prisoners, and that they would be here in Providence before evening, or certainly by night. I was at a loss to know what to do, so I first took refuge in prayer to the almighty and all-ruling Redeemer, and then sent up to a kind friend, four miles up, to ask whether he would send his light wagon and two horses before nightfall and give lodging to me or my family. I thought that I might at least get my sick wife, daughter, and a bed which Mrs. Kunze had left here out of the way of the first attack and leave the rest to its fate. Toward evening the neighbors who had gone to investigate returned and brought news that troops from the American camp had moved in ahead of the English and prevented them from advancing any further. The English therefore hastily withdrew toward Philadelphia with their booty and some losses. As was heard, the English moved quietly out of Philadelphia last evening, took a circuitous route, first toward the east, from there northeast, and then northwest so that they would not be immediately discovered. In the evening the man sent his wagon, but we sent it back empty. This was the third time that attacking parties have been near to Providence for the purpose of wreaking wanton revenge, and who turned them aside? Not the hand of man but of God. And why? Were they sinners above all whose blood Pilate mingled with their sacrifices, or those upon whom the tower in Siloam fell? No, they were like us, our representatives, an example. If we do not improve, the same thing, or worse, will happen to us. Turn thou us, O Lord, or we shall not be turned. Purge us with hyssop, and we shall be clean: wash us, and we shall be whiter than snow. Such domestic, civil wars are really the most horrible of all wars. Micah 7:1-9.

MAY 23. At noon our eldest son [Brigadier General] John Peter, came with two other officers and their servants from the American camp for a brief visit with us. We received from him a more exact account of the action which took place last Wednesday, May 20. The greater part of the English army moved quietly out of Philadelphia in two columns on the night of May 19. One column marched toward the west-northwest in the direction of the Barren Hill church, where a French general with two thousand and several hundreds of men and seventy Indians of the American army were posted as an observation corps. The other column of Englishmen took its way out of Philadelphia toward the east, through Frankfort on the New York road and then northwest. Thus both columns were to affect a junction, putting the observation corps in the middle and cutting it off on this side of the Schuylkill.

The main American camp was on the other side of the Schuylkill, about seven or eight miles from the Barren Hill church. The two English columns had already drawn their circle so far that the American corps was cut off from its retreat over the bridge to the main American camp. But the French general retired with his corps across the Schuylkill in an unaccustomed place, and though the water was chest-deep, they got safely through to the main camp.

The Indians were the last to get over, and they were surrounded in a small thicket by the English light cavalry, but they retired behind the trees in accord with their custom and let loose their usual hideous war whoops, which threw the horses and riders into confusion and sent them flying; whereupon the Indians shot several of the cavalrymen and gathered up their lost cloaks. In the main camp they were not aware of the attack and the approach of the English until about nine o'clock in the morning, when they fired cannons of alarm, leaped to arms, and prepared for battle.

Before they were ready to march, however, the English were already seven or eigth miles on their countermarch to the city, taking with them the booty they had seized from the defenseless inhabitants, namely, young and aged men; household goods, cows, horses, swine, poultry, etc.

MAY 28. Last Saturday several hundred volunteers from New England arrived here in New Providence on their march to the American camp. Some of them stayed overnight in our barn, but they did no damage. They left again on Sunday. The New England troops have a good reputation; they do not curse and swear like others, nor do they rob and steal.

MAY 29. Now many of the inhabitants are again in a predicament, especially the Quakers, Baptists, etc. who have been hoping all along that the might of England would conquer the land and protect these sects in their former liberties and accumulated possessions, leaving them undisturbed and settled on their lees, while only the Protestant church people would be turned into slaves. But now that it has become common talk that the British troops are about to withdraw from Philadelphia, and the independent government of this united republic has passed a new law requiring that adult male inhabitants over eighteen years of age must swear an oath of allegiance to the republic not later than June 1, *a.c.,* failing which they will be deprived of all rights or even lose all their goods and chattels and be banished from the country, their predicament is made more acute. Then there is the added circumstance that the so-called *Tories* have been at great pains to exchange and buy up, at high rates, the paper money which was issued under the authority of His Britannic Majesty, and now the government of the republic promulgates a law stating that the old paper money is to be canceled or declared void. That really is a hard pill for the shrewd lovers of money to swallow!

JUNE 3. My wife busied herself distilling some rose water and also mending clothes. Woolen and linen goods are so scarce and exorbitantly dear that they are hardly to be obtained at all; so one is obliged to cut up old clothes, stitch the rags together, and be clothed in harlequin fashion. Fortunately I still have left an old preaching gown with which I can cover up the rest of the heterogeneous ensemble when I have to conduct acts of worship in the churches.

JUNE 4. Toward evening I had an unexpected visit from the *Rev.* Thomas Barton, the Episcopal missionary who has been living in Lancaster for many years and is salaried by the Society *de propaganda fide* in London. He read to me a document which he had submitted to the *Assembly* in the name of all the Episcopal missionaries in this country, in which they state that, though they pledge loyalty to the new republic, they cannot, in the form of oath, renounce allegiance to the king of Great Britain and his heirs and successors because of their calling, etc. To which the *Assembly* replied that they could allow no exceptions and referred them to the petition submitted by the Moravian Brethren and the Schwenkfelders. Accordingly, the good missionaries are in a dilemma. If they renounce the king, etc., they will lose their support from the society. If they refuse to swear allegiance to the republic, they will not be tolerated, etc.

He gave me a more exact account of what had happened to

the Rev. Mr. Duché, the rector of the Episcopal church in Philadelphia. He was appointed chaplain by the *Congress* and was
required to preach at their ceremonies. When the English army
occupied Philadelphia in September, 1777, he was taken prisoner and held under arrest for twenty-four hours as one who had
served the rebels, etc. His Excellency General Howe was prudent
and gracious enough not to permit him to be tried by court
martial, but rather gave orders that he was to be released from
imprisonment on parole with the condition that he journey to
England, surrender to the archbishop or ecclesiastical court, and
submit to their judgment and punishment. Before he set out
for England a long letter came out in print which he had written
and sent to His Excellency General Washington, expressing his
regret that he had permitted himself to be misled into serving
the *Congress* as preacher, etc., and admonishing His Excellency
to forsake the cause and also to repent and implore God's forgiveness, etc. The good man probably thought he would extricate
himself from a precarious position with one side and also mitigate
his expected punishment in England, but it only increased the
bitterness on the other side, and it probably would have been
better if he had not published anything and rather kept still and
in humble prayer committed his plight to the Redeemer, who
rules and directs all things for the best. He then had to go to
England in accord with the parole granted him, and he set out
from Philadelphia in winter in a ship escorting General Lord
Cornwallis. When they reached the sea a storm arose and the
ship was driven out of its course. With great difficulty they
reached the island of Antigua, where a vacant English Episcopal
congregation engaged him as its minister and where he is said
to receive an annual salary of £600 sterling. But since the said
congregation is under episcopal jurisdiction and since he must
appear before the ecclesiastical court in England in accord with
his parole, it is still a question how the matter will turn out.
Missionary Barton said in closing that he would like to sell his
goods and move away, but as yet he did not know where. Mr.
Duché's name is on the register of those who have been accused

as traitors and cited to appear. So it goes, like a wheel on a cart; now one half is in the mud and mire and the other half up in the air and so on until it breaks in pieces, upsets the cart, and spills the freight.

JUNE 21.   Zion Church is said to be so devastated that it will cost a great deal before it can be used again for divine services. The gallery and pews cost several thousand pounds in times when things were cheap. Nothing happens by chance. The Lord God allows it, not without good reasons, and, to the extent that it has been allowed, the wicked one has, through his tools, wreaked his vengeance upon the innocent and vented his fury upon religion, like the mad dog that violently attacked the poor beggar and bit his wooden leg. The meetinghouses of the rich Quakers and the chapels of the holy pope were spared because they seemed to the wicked one not to be doing any harm, but rather giving him support, and they may expect a more severe judgment from the most high Ruler in the time fixed by God's infallible Word.

They also told me that a German in Philadelphia, who had been raised to the office of jailer during the recent English military rule, has been arrested by the American garrison because he, like Saul, breathed threatenings and slaughter, betrayed a great many so-called rebels and had them imprisoned, and inhumanly abused them as long as they had the misfortune of being under his hands. The cruelties this jailer committed upon the hapless prisoners are indescribable. When charitable citizens, moved by pity, prepared soup, vegetables, or bread from their scanty stores and brought them to the prison, the heartless jailers and their subordinates would either refuse to take the food with cursing and swearing or dump it on the ground in the yard and say to the prisoners, "Come on, you dogs, and lick it up." Dead were found who still had in their mouths grass which they had pulled up in the yard of the prison to still their hunger. The said jailer was also so embittered against my own humble person that he declared that he would yet get me into his keeping and that if no one else could be found to hang me he would do it himself. Several times he had even decided to come to Providence with a band of men to fetch me, but had been prevented. To my knowledge I have never done anything to harm the man; on the contrary, I have helped him.

JULY 9. Last Saturday, July 4, the Honorable *Congress* or high council of the United States made its entrance into Philadelphia after having sojourned in York, across the Susquehanna, since September, 1777. On the same day, last Saturday, there was also held in Philadelphia a public exhibition which cost less and was more profitable than the present-day comedies of the more refined taste. A number of years ago an absurd, atrocious style of high headdress took hold among the ladies, which was spread during this miserable war, carried to the most extreme lengths by the dames who were followers of the British army, and imitated by the American apes. The philosophical moralists wrote against it, and there was no lack of satires in the newspapers and calendars. Some of the preachers pointed out the soil from which these and other tares spring and recommended Isaiah 3 and I Peter 3:1-6 as a warning against the style, but it was of no avail and it grew worse and worse. These headdresses required skillful wigmakers, much time, and materials such as wool, false hair, oil, and quintessence of wheat, etc., with which the poorer families must supply their barest wants. The simple country folk, who are more accustomed to concrete than to abstract ideas, have some wonderful definitions or descriptions when they see such dressed-up pictures in the city or the country. They say they look like a big pile of hay on a hayfork. A depraved female dressed in this manner was led around the city with drums, etc.

JULY 10. At three o'clock in the morning the deacon, Mr. Keimle, set out with me in his *chaise* to drive to the city. Pastor Kunze decided to go with the other *chaise* to his brothers and sisters-in-law in New Hanover on this same day. As we approached the city—in fact, on the whole way—we saw with sadness the footprints of God's chastisement and punishment, and it made us remember Lamentations 3:22ff., "It is of the Lord's mercies that we are not consumed, because his compassions fail not," etc. This time the Lord God permitted an army, which did not heed the law of Moses, much less the laws of the Saviour of the world, to be his rod; otherwise the army would not have destroyed the many thousands of fruit trees for several miles about the city, Deuteronomy 20:19. For, after all, the soldiers had the city in their possession and did not need to besiege it; still less did they have to convert and despoil the houses dedicated to the worship of God. Matthew 7:12. Mark 4:24. The former St. Peter's Church at Barren Hill, in Whitemarsh Township, was an apple of discord for both fighting parties. The pulpit, altar, table, benches, seats, doors, and window shutters were burned, the panes of glass in the windows were smashed, the empty space between the four walls was alternately misused as a horse stable by the cavalry and filled with manure; the inhabitants and members of the congregation were, for the most part, driven away and scattered by the constant raids and plunderings, and those who remained were plunged into such bitter poverty that they can scarcely keep themselves alive. The schoolhouse still has its roof and four stone walls and looks like a lodge in a garden of cucumbers. We reached the city near eleven o'clock in the forenoon and found my daughter and her child tolerably well. I had several visits from poor members, and toward evening had to bury, in our cemetery, a twenty-five-year-old married woman who had died of burning fever. During the funeral a fearful storm arose with two dreadful claps of thunder, but no damage was done, thank God!

JULY 25. The deacons requested that the preachers make their sermons shorter. This they promised to do, though with the understanding that it could not always be done, depending upon the subject to be covered. I cannot entirely disagree with these friends for the following reasons:

1. There are indentured servants, male and female, who belong to the congregation, and when the morning service lasts even a little longer than twelve o'clock and they are not at hand to prepare the table and wait on their employers, they are

scolded, etc., or they are even kept away from divine service, which gives the corrupt flesh a ready excuse to stay away altogether.

2. The afternoon service falls right after the noon meal. Physicians say that when the stomach is full, nature is busy with digestion, preparing the chyle and sending everything to its proper place, and we know from our own feeling and experience that the mind is able to feel, apprehend, think, and meditate better when one is empty than when the stomach is full.

3. In a congregation where there is preaching twice every Sunday and feast day besides *Kinderlehre* and weekly prayer services, it very easily becomes a mere habit; indeed, it may become loathsome and be trampled underfoot, especially when too much is served up all at once. One must not always trust those who out of flattery or hypocrisy say, "It is not too long for me; I could listen with pleasure two or three times as long, even the whole day," for these generally turn out to be hearers and not doers of the Word.

To give just a few examples, Pastor J. C. Hartwick usually could not or would not cut his sermons down to less than two hours because he preached according to the mathematical method, and whenever he listened to someone else preaching who spent a half-hour on equally weighty truths, he would become annoyed, shuffle his feet, cough, or make motions for him to stop. In Holland Count Zinzendorf once preached a long sermon, which was customary with him, in the presence of a wealthy merchant whom he was seeking to win over, and when it was over, he asked the merchant privately what he thought of his address. The merchant replied very shortly and dryly, "Sir, it appears that you like to hear yourself talk." In country congregations, where there is preaching only once every two, four, or six weeks, the situation is different. There the people like long, powerful, and meaty sermons, and one finds from experience and investigation that attentive hearers, who seldom have an opportunity to hear preaching, often grasp more, take more to heart, and retain more of a sermon than those who hear preaching every day and to excess.

JULY 26. Toward evening, after five o'clock, I had a burial to conduct in our cemetery. It was that of a young man who was to be buried in military fashion. The colonel of the regiment had a battalion march up, and the battalion accompanied the procession with drums and fifes in mourning. I had to march with them. Since most of those attending were English, I read the English prayers at the grave and also said a prayer in German. When the prayers were over, the soldiers fired three salvos over the grave. I stood on the left side toward the wall of the cemetery, and the soldiers fired from the right side; the report reverberated against the wall and rebounded with such force that it injured my hearing in both ears. From there I went on to visit a very sick person; the father had to shout into my ear to tell me his sick daughter's concern that I might lay her condition before the throne of grace in my prayer. Instantly I felt a roaring in my head as though I were standing beside a waterfall or milldam. In the evening I wrote a letter to my wife and children in Providence and New Hanover. I informed them of my mishap and also reported that two German soldiers had received the sentence of death for desertion, would be shot within a few days, and had requested pastoral consolation.

JULY 27. Toward evening I married a couple for whom the banns had previously been regularly proclaimed. Further than this I could do nothing but grieve for lack of hearing and the buzzing in my head. I cannot determine whether something may have been disturbed in the delicate structure of the ear, whether the tympanum may be either relaxed or ruptured altogether or pierced. When I speak I am unable to distinguish the tone, and it sounds to me as though I am speaking from an empty barrel. When I hear the organ, it sounds like nothing but reed stops and tremolo which shatter the head. The cries of children and the crowing of cocks sound to me like the scratching of nails on glass and hurt me. The ceaseless buzzing and humming in my head make me somewhat dizzy. I have not been hearing very well with my right ear for several years past, and have had some ringing in it, and last winter I sat up many nights and had chills, so it may well be that the shooting at the grave may not be the only cause. Nature is gradually breaking down the mortal tabernacle piece by piece until it finally collapses altogether into utter decay.

AUGUST 12. In the afternoon a visit from Dr. Martin. I had a vein opened in my arm in the hope that it might abate the humming in my head, but I have felt no relief.

SEPTEMBER 13. Through Pastor Voigt I received from Dr. Bodo Otto a letter in which he gives his opinion concerning the case of my hearing, submitted to him, as follows: "The auditory nerves were irritated by detonation of the shooting. The patient should keep his head and feet warm and take frequent foot baths before going to bed. One drop of oil of anise on cotton placed in both ears. In the evening one scruple of antispasmodic powder baked in a loaf mixed with caraway, anise, and fennel seeds and a slice thereof bound upon the ear, warm, before retiring."

The Year 1779

FEBRUARY 15.   Toward evening Messrs. Francis Swaine and John Schaefer arrived at our house with their horses and stayed overnight. They wish to go to New Hanover tomorrow, God willing, to fetch my son Frederick to the city because the governor desires to speak with him. Frederick, however, has gone off on a journey to Lebanon. The matter in hand strikes me as very doubtful and dreadful and drives me to the sixth petition of the Lord's Prayer: Let us not be entangled in hurtful temptation. It is said that the *Assembly* now in session wishes to appoint three additional members to *Congress,* and some of them have proposed Frederick Muhlenberg because he understands both English and German, etc. It could turn out to be the same story as that of Mr. John Adam Treutlen in Ebenezer, Georgia. At first he was a schoolmaster in the late Pastor Bolzius' times, later a merchant, a justice of the peace, then a member of the *Assembly,* and during the present *Revolution,* a *Colonel,* a *Counselor,* and finally His Excellency the Governor. Where is he now, since November of last year, with wife and children in sackcloth and ashes? The Saviour of the world rewards his faithful servants in the evening of life infinitely better than the great world rewards its servants on the little planets. I would much rather that the Swedish *corporation* called him as preacher at Gloria Dei Church in Philadelphia or that Ebenezer were free again, etc.

FEBRUARY 22.   Today God in his goodness bestowed a blessing upon our house, namely, two calves from our two cows, a blessing which goes a long way toward providing for our daily nourishment and is a part of our daily bread. The Lord make us thankful for all his benefits, which are innumerable! God's all-wise and all-gracious providence extends to the very least of his creatures. Psalm 145:9.

MARCH 4. Mr. Kucher returned from Philadelphia and took with him the letter I had written to Pastor Schultze. He said that on the day before yesterday Frederick Muhlenberg had been elected by a majority vote of the *Assembly* as a *delegate* or member of the *Congress* and that yesterday he had already taken his seat in *rump-parliament*. I say once more: The Lord and Father of the vineyard rewards faithful laborers in the evening of life infinitely better than the so-called great world rewards its servants. O Father in heaven, preserve us from, or in, temptations which are harmful to the soul! Frederick Muhlenberg did not seek this critical service but was drawn into it by well-meaning intermediaries and their worldly motives. In the end it will appear whose tune is right, says the musician. If I were to give my judgment concerning the matter, it would be expressed somewhat like John 9:21, "He is of age; ask him: he shall speak for himself."

MARCH 5. Today I bought for the household thirteen pounds of veal at 2s. 6d. per pound, a total of £1 12s. 6d. What will be the end of this? We must have our taste for butter and meat removed and learn to eat a hermit's diet. People born and raised here think one cannot live without meat, butter, and sugar. They must learn to do what the poor soldier did who could not eat his bread ration dry. He ate it in front of a cook-shop so that he would at least have the smell of it.

MARCH 25. Deep snow is now lying on the ground, and we have as severe cold as in the middle of winter. A hundredweight of flour costs £20 in the city and is hard to obtain. Wood, salt, and clothing are still scarcer. Physical distress increases from day to day, and the spiritual judgment grows even clearer, but only a few pay any attention. I have not experienced such weather in March in all my thirty-seven years in America. The scourge of hunger is the second scourge of war. Now if the next harvest should fail, as it appears it will, men and beasts will suffer as never before.

APRIL 5. The Reformed pastor held divine service here today, and the rest of the day there were great assemblages in the

taverns, and throughout the day and night the people engaged in
calf-worship and the sins of Jeroboam. Godlessness and self-
confidence are growing apace, as in the days before the flood
and before the downfall of Sodom and Gomorrah, etc. God's
Word and the preachers who proclaim it are despised and mocked
by the fickle crowds; yet the Lord will still have left a few who
do not bend the knee before Beelzebub.

MAY 31. Dr. Sarninghausen gave me the following advice
with regard to my hearing: (a) diet; (b) bloodletting from the
foot; (c) keep bowels open; (d) morning and evening several
teaspoonfuls of the following put warm in the ear and kept there
for several minutes: a gill of milk boiled with garlic, the garlic
pressed out. A piece of cotton soaked in the same fluid placed
in the ear overnight. (e) Later a fluid made from fresh *ground*
ivy, the same way as the milk and garlic, might be tried.

AUGUST 4. Memorized an English sermon. Last night I
again had a foreboding in a dream. I was lost and confused
among strange people and old buildings, and could not find my
home. Various persons tried to direct me but did not give me the
right directions. A certain man took me by the hand and pretended to lead me out of the labyrinth and home, but in vain,
and finally took me to various families whose children I was to
baptize.

AUGUST 31. I have found it to be an old rule of experience
that when things were going well in my fellow ministers' congregations, they never wrote to me. But as soon as they became
involved in strife and trouble I received one letter of complaint
after another. So I am still obliged to swallow polemical chaff
and straw, mixed with bitter herbs, instead of green and pleasant
food, which is the more difficult for me now that I have lost
my teeth.

OCTOBER 5. My deafness detracts from the delight of conversation because I cannot understand softly spoken words, and
loud speech sounds more like angry quarreling and displeasure
than friendly and kindly conversation. Nor can anyone speak to
me privately of some secret matter without being heard at a

distance. Writing is the one means left by which friends can secretly reveal to each other their minds without shouting aloud, and also the means by which lovers can dispute and quarrel with one another.

NOVEMBER 14. In the evening my son Frederick sent the newspaper and wrote the following lines: *"I am again unanimously chosen a Delegate, but should have been left out, like two of my Colleagues, but a Junto in the Assembly was afraid if they put me out, they would lose the German Interest, which perhaps will be the Occasion of my Resignation. F. Muhlenberg."*

NOVEMBER 15. In the evening Pastor John Christopher Hartwick appeared unexpectedly; he had left his horse at a nearby tavern and stayed with us overnight. He had come from Virginia, and latterly from Lancaster, where he preached on the tribute money last Sunday. He complained that several persons left the church during the sermon and that the people seemed to be indifferent as to whether they had a minister or not. The learned man still cannot see whether it is he or the people who are at fault when they do not care to listen to him. He had heard in Virginia that the French ambassador, *Seigneur* Gerard, had inquired about him, and he was going to Philadelphia on this account. He came too late, however, for the ambassador sailed several weeks ago; otherwise he might have had an opportunity to get away. I was glad to hear this because I presumed that His Excellency the Ambassador might assist him to secure a position, or dress him up, or take him to Europe, or make some sort of provision for him, because Mr. Hartwick has told a number of people that his gracious lord, His Serene Highness the Duke of Saxe-Gotha, had sent him here as superintendent to exercise supervision over the Lutheran congregations in America. This is apparently the reason why he has wandered around America all these years, building castles in the air, etc. As I learned later, the story was that "His Excellency the Ambassador had been asked by His Serene Highness the Duke to inquire about one of his subjects in America, Preacher Hartwick, who was said to own great landed estates and have no heirs." It is true that in former

210

times he acquired, with great shrewdness, many thousands of acres of land, but he also lost them again. So my wish that he might obtain material support, and not become a burden where he had sown no spiritual seed, came to naught.

NOVEMBER 16. Early in the morning our daughter, Maria Swaine, who is living with us, was seized with birth pains. Her husband was still away on business in Philadelphia. We went at once for a midwife and the neighbor women, and she gave birth to her firstborn son (George Washington Swaine) between eight and nine o'clock in the morning after having been married for almost five years. I would have been glad to have assisted her with counsel and some medicine, but Mr. Hartwick kept holding me up with some new schemes he had thought up, since he has no feeling for anyone but himself and has no heirs. I offered him a little money for traveling expenses, but he did not accept it. After nine o'clock our son Henry and his parents-in-law came from New Hanover on their way to Philadelphia. Pastor Hartwick took leave and continued his journey, and our relatives also went on.

About one o'clock in the afternoon Pastor Voigt arrived with his betrothed, Widow Anna Maria, wife of the late Mr. Conrad Soellner, to be married. They delivered to me for safekeeping their signed marriage contract. I married them in the presence of witnesses, Mr. Diehl and his wife, Frederick Marsteller's wife, and my wife, and gave them a marriage certificate. Before the ceremony I also made some comments based on Genesis 24. My wife had prepared for them a patriarchal meal, as good a one as we could scrape together in these times of dearth when travelers must pay £3 apiece for a poor meal. To all appearances Pastor Voigt has entered upon a happy marriage, if he can and will adapt himself to it. It is sometimes no easy matter for such old bachelors, who have been revolving around their own axis and aeolipile for so many years, to have any sympathetic feeling toward anybody but themselves, much less the weaker sex. The majority of them are despotic, stubborn, and suspicious. To mention only one example among many for illustration, many years ago an old bachelor, a learned *artium magister* and preacher from Europe, married a person from his congregation in Jersey and had several children by her. He separated from her to the great offense of his congregations and I was chosen as one of the arbitrators to investigate and determine the case. He submitted his reasons, couched in Ciceronian Latin, *methodo demonstrativa,* and, among others, there was one important reason why he had separated from his wife, the reason being that once his wife had in his presence cleansed his infant son after the child had soiled its diaper. On another occasion he had pasted a piece of paper over the keyhole of the outer door of the house in order to find out whether anyone might be coming in secretly to his wife while he was asleep, and when the paper disappeared, probably because of rain, dew, or wind, it was not only possible but, to his pure intellect, already a fact that his wife had been unfaithful. On a third occasion his wife had addressed him in the second person singular instead of the third person plural. In short, his reasons were so weighty that we were unable to heal the breach but were obliged to let him remain in his atmosphere to his own undoing. If he had been a Jew, his divorce might have been valid because of the hardness of his heart. He who has the spirit of unction does things in a better way.

DECEMBER 18. Today the commissary, Mr. Elisha Davis, came to me and required that I give him, on oath, an accounting of the valuation of my property. I declared the following: (a) Real estate, seven acres, *more or less,* on which the house and barn stand, ten acres of wooded land, and a lot of three acres next to Augustus Church on which there is nothing. (b) Movable property, two cows. Occupants, one family; Daniel Croesman in the adjoining cottage.

The commissary desired to know from me what amount of cash money I still had in my possession. I produced a packet of paper money containing £172 and also showed him some loose paper money which had not been counted. I asked him to count it, and I also told him that besides this I had a Spanish silver dollar and one eleven-pence piece. He refused to count it, however, and only required the oath that I had declared all my property, which I did in obedience to the powers that be. He said that the salaries of ministers and schoolmasters were not assessed, but that if they owned property as citizens of the state, they were to be assessed and taxed. Hence the question remained whether I should have rendered to the civil authority an account of the charitable gifts which were presented to me for my necessary support and swear an oath to the same, since I no longer receive any salary as a preacher or schoolmaster. As long as I have any possessions of my own, I do not refuse to pay taxes, for it is right to pay taxes on these like other citizens. But that I should render a sworn account of income, expenditures, and balance to the government or its officials for the voluntary and uncertain gifts which come in for my necessary support, seems to me to be stretching it too far.

DECEMBER 29. In the afternoon my two oldest sons came back from New Hanover in the company of the third. Henry lamented that he had suffered much damage to his furniture and books from the storm yesterday since the old parsonage is too full of holes to withstand snow and rain. The oldest son gave me a present of a pair of breeches and a warm scarf, which I need and which fit me well because they are made of English material, although I cannot present the figure of a general in them and am happy if I can cover my nakedness. It is true that Pastor Kunze had already presented me with a scarf made of French stuff, but it is too *complaisant* to the raw winter. I am not Job, but I have cause to imitate him and offer burnt offerings for my children, Job 1:4, 5, for I have nothing else with which to compensate them.

The Year 1780

FEBRUARY 21. I read the Rev. John Wesley's "Conferences." It appears that the good man made fine gifts, plans, designs, and arrangements to further the cause of active Christianity in the English nation and to give it better order and form, but unfortunately he lacked the desired laborers and instruments. As the blessed John Arndt said, "Many hired servants but few followers."

FEBRUARY 29. The wild pigeons are already returning here. Some of the natural scientists make varying observations concerning this, though they will have to leave their various opinions to the decision and final judgment of the Philosophical Society. Some prophesy that the pigeons will bring an early spring, which is so much desired after such a hard winter; others think the pigeons signify a desired peace; and some others conjecture that the great fleet of warships which sailed south from New York frightened the pigeons and drove them here. More sensible persons see in it something similar to the story in Exodus 16, where the Lord God sent quails to the murmuring people. For the people here are also murmuring about the lack of food and the scarcity of meat. But the pigeons cannot be caught except with nets or with powder and shot. The latter method is too costly for the poor and middle-class people, and those that the rich catch in nets are first used to fill their own bellies and the rest are sold at high enough prices; so the poor get no benefit from them, for the rich have not yet learned to make to themselves friends of the mammon of unrighteousness. And if they do not learn it and practice it in this time of grace, then yonder will they beseech in vain for a drop of water to cool their tongues.

Gabriel shot six pigeons, which were unusually fat. Our young *nobility* must be suffering greatly because they can get no lemon juice for their trout (that is, no butter, fresh meat, sugar, rice, etc., can be obtained with paper currency).

MARCH 3.   We now have in our hostelry four draught horses and two riding horses which belong to the general; one horse, a cow, and two calves which belong to Mr. Swaine; and our two cows and one calf. The human creatures under our roof at the present time are (a) we two old folks and one adolescent daughter, Salome; (b) the general, his wife, three menservants, two children, and one negress; (c) Mr. Swaine, his wife, and one child. Twenty-seven stomachs and mouths! "The eyes of all wait upon thee, Lord, and thou givest them their meat in due season." The appendix contains twenty some chickens, three dogs, and two cats, which eat the crumbs which fall from the lord's table. The little household is crawling and teeming. It is fortunate that they are friends and not enemies, otherwise it would be quite a different matter. We were able to do without a pocket watch, since so many stomachs are accurate instruments to tell the morning, noon, and evening hours.

APRIL 11.   We had had a young maid working for us who had rendered faithful service for a year and a half, and received a wage that was fair and as much as we could afford. I gave her instruction in reading in the evenings with my own daughter, gave her fine, edifying hymns to learn by heart, required her to attend evening prayers, Sunday church services, and family worship with the rest, and tolerated no running around.

In time, however, she no longer cared for being thus held down, and last year she gave us notice that she was leaving our service because she could get more wages and live a much freer life, etc. After she had gained her supposed freedom and worked for other people by the month and the week at larger wages, she had relations too early, contrary to God's holy ordinance, with an uncircumcised Philistine who had promised to marry her, and thereby committed a wrong. Afterward she came crying and wailing to my wife, lamenting her fall and regretting that she had not followed our frequent admonitions, etc. But

I was unable to help her; though I wrote an earnest and sharp letter to the above-mentioned man.

APRIL 15.   Paid six dollars for a dove cage because someone advised my wife to keep a pair of turtledoves in her bedroom to draw her sickness to them. It is all right to try it, but hard to believe.

JULY 15.   Today I read in the English newspaper that a formal *actus promotionis* was held at the new university in Philadelphia on July 4, *a.c.*, and that, among others, the *Rev.* Messrs. Kunze, Weyberg, Henry Muhlenberg, Jr., and Helmuth were declared *artium magistri*. I presume that none of them desired or sought the honor, but that it was bestowed upon them with good intention, for, if they had coveted such an honor, they could have obtained it long ago at the ancient universities in Europe. In Saxony it is quite generally the custom to call the minister *"Herr Magister,"* and in England the ministers of the Episcopal Church are generally called "doctor," even though they have not actually had degrees conferred upon them or received them in course. I was only a *diaconus* in Grosshennersdorf, and yet I was occasionally called *Herr Magister* by uneducated people. This tickled me somewhat, it is true, but also gave rise to secret fear because I could not show a diploma to substantiate it, even though I probably had brought with me from the universities as many notebooks, if not more than many a *magister*. In my time, even those who were absent could get any kind of degree without trouble, according as they made their contributions. The disciples of the Lord also quarreled over the *gradus magistri et doctoris* on several occasions, before they received the unction, but our Lord flatly forbade them. After they had received the unction, one finds, in the addresses of the apostolic epistles, not the capital letters A.M., Th.D., etc., but rather, "Paul, a SERVANT of Jesus Christ," "John, Christ's SERVANT," "Peter, an APOSTLE of Jesus Christ," "James, a SERVANT of God and of the Lord Jesus Christ," etc. But when the unction gradually disappeared, the empty places were decked out with the spacious curtains of the tapestry weavers, such as *baccalaurei, artium magistri, licentiati,*

216

Th.D., mundi lumines, excellencies, magnificences, reverend, very reverend, most reverend sirs, eminences, etc., etc. And what can the making of names profit the kingdom of Jesus Christ when there is no unction? "All flesh is as grass," I Peter 1:24, 25.

> Guard us, O Lord, from doctrines strange!
> None other MASTER may we seek
> Than Jesus Christ, and never change
> Our faith in him who girds the weak.
> Kyrie Eleison!

AUGUST 1. I had hardly arrived in Reading, and was still wet and lame, when a neighbor asked that I accompany his deceased son to the grave and preach the funeral sermon. Why? Because back in 1742 and 1743 I had occasionally lodged with him in Germantown and had his little son on my lap. Adequate as the argument appeared to him, I nevertheless had to decline because there is a preacher stationed here at the present time and it is not proper to interfere in the office of another who has ministered to the deceased during illness. Besides, I cannot shake a funeral sermon out of my sleeve before such mixed, critical crowds. I promised, however, that I would attend if the rain did not continue. The funeral began at five o'clock with a large congregation of German and English inhabitants. The Lutheran and Reformed ministers put me between themselves and treated me with much unmerited honor. Our pastor requested me to preach the funeral sermon, but I firmly refused. He delivered a well-composed address on Philippians 1:23, "For I am in a strait betwixt two, having a desire to depart," etc. Proposition: The devout Christian's yearning to die and be with Christ. First he analyzed the text in the original, then set forth the reasons how and why, and finally made the application.

I was reminded of a rule which was given us by the immortal Dr. Oporin in a homiletics class at Goettingen: In delivering sermons we should speak with a reserve appropriate to the subjects and doctrines and moderate the voice accordingly; put in the proper emphases; not swallow the final words of a sentence; not sing or get into the habit of speaking in a monotone or a howling voice; and, especially in the application, use all the powers of speech in an attractive fashion. And in general, as Melanchthon advised, we should set forth *non multa, sed multum,* at any one time, and that well digested, so that the hearers can digest it easily and not be made sick. For example, there was that candidate who preached on the text of invitation in Matthew 11, "Come unto me, all ye that labor and are heavy laden," etc., in a terrifying, thunderous voice, with fearful, threatening gestures, all the while beating the pulpit with his heavy fists, so that some of the hearers ran out of the church and the rest bowed their heads and held their ears shut. Dr. Oporin said that the scoffers of religion make fun of it when preachers pound the pulpit so furiously, and they say that such preachers have to strengthen and squeeze out their weak arguments from the dry wood, etc.

My fellow minister employed fine, attractive reasons in this funeral sermon, but his voice in the small church was so violent and extraordinarily powerful and loud that I became anxious and fearful and felt as if I were being exposed to a storm in which thunder and lightning followed close upon each other. He shouted the first words of every sentence with terrible force and then let the last words drop. With every mighty shout he also gave the pulpit such a prodigious blow that it creaked. I lodged overnight in my mother-in-law's leaky house and had little rest.

AUGUST 2. Had breakfast with Pastor Daniel Lehman and begged him to spare his lungs more, for if he continued to preach as loudly as he had yesterday he would get consumption. I asked him whether he understood music. His answer was, "Yes, a little," and I told him that music was an imitation of speech and that its harmony touched people's feelings. Therefore the composers took care to adapt the varying tones to the text, and so on. He did not take it amiss and excused himself, saying that the loud shouting had already become an inveterate habit with him.

NOVEMBER 6. I found in an English magazine a remedy for deafness, namely, a spoonful of coarse salt dissolved in a glass of spring water, a teaspoonful to be put in the ear on retiring and repeated for eight days; said to be excellent. I have tried it but have had no improvement. It may have been helpful in some cases, but the ear is so delicately constructed that it is like handing over a damaged watch to a mason for repair.

NOVEMBER 11. I meditated upon the morrow's funeral sermon and gathered together the obituary. Christian Schrack was a son of the late Mr. John Jacob Schrack and his wife, Eva Rosina, who came to this country in 1717 with four children and settled in the section called New Providence at a time when it was still sparsely cultivated. At first they built themselves a makeshift hut and dug a cave beside it, in which they did their cooking, and then established a small shop and inn for travelers.

Once, when an English inhabitant stayed too long in the cave, came home late, and had a row with his wife, he made excuses and said that he had been in the *Trap*. From that time on the section was called Trappe, and is known all over America, so that one tells travelers how far they have to go from Philadelphia to Trappe, or Providence; such learned etymologies we have here! When I arrived in Philadelphia in 1742 and inquired about New Providence, nobody could tell me where it was until I happened to run into a German who told me that New Providence was also called the *Trapp* and New Hanover was called Falckner Swamp.

NOVEMBER 21. Having learned with dismay that *vox populi, per plurima vota,* had elected my son Frederick Augustus a member of the state government, and that the Assembly had even chosen him chairman after having served for two years in *Congress,* I wrote him the following comments today:

Vox populi ex parte had chosen him as the driver to drive the heavily laden wagon in these critical times and circumstances, by night and in stormy weather and over rough roads. *Vox populi,* I said, was very changeable and often shifted to extremes. Acts 14:11-13; 19:28. If he did not by penitent supplication obtain from on high an extraordinary wisdom, a terrible crash and fall would result. To be a passenger on a post coach was not so dangerous as to be the driver in these times and conditions where even the most skillful and experienced driver would not trust himself to get through without an upset.

The Year 1781

FEBRUARY 2. In the afternoon I had a visit from a neighbor who had all sorts of things to relate. My wife was with us and, feeling some symptoms of her illness, she went out into the kitchen. A kettle of red beets was hanging over the fire cooking, and she sat down on a small bench near it. Just then she was seized with a *paroxismus epilepticus* and she fell into the boiling pot with her left hand, breast, shoulder, right arm, neck, and half of her face. Immediately afterward she came back where I was, trembling, shivering, and wet. I was horrified and called our children at once. We put her to bed, and after she had regained consciousness she felt unspeakable pain from the burns she had suffered in the places aforementioned. My daughter, Mrs. Swaine, hastily ground up some *potatoes,* soaked them in sweet oil, and made poultices in hope of killing the burn. We also sent a neighbor seven miles to fetch a well-known English doctor. The neighbor came back late without having accomplished his purpose because he had not been able to get across the swollen Perkiomen River. The injury was severe, and there is danger in delay. Not only the outer but the second layer of skin and muscles were burned. I had prescriptions but no ingredients. It was a distressing night we put in. A neighbor who has some knowledge of chemistry made up a salve for burns according to Dr. Tissot's prescription, but the swelling and inflammation increased. The patient had read in the church history several days before about the terrible tortures of the first Christians, which served to strengthen her in her pain.

FEBRUARY 3. The English physician came, and it was his judgment that the inflammation and swelling on the breast and neck were the most dangerous. He prescribed and left some English salts and anodyne to keep the bowels open and if possible induce sleep, etc. In the afternoon it looked as though the throat would swell shut and suffocation would follow, but it changed somewhat toward evening. The poor patient had many visits from women friends and neighbors who also recommended all sorts of remedies, as is the custom of such women; one complained of unspeakable pains in her eye, and the other said she had had the very same pain in a tooth and got no rest until she had it pulled. Nevertheless, several neighbor women showed unusual kindness in helping my daughter, Mrs. Swaine, watch the patient during the long nights. But none could do a better job of bandaging than Daughter Swaine, who fortunately still lives with us.

FEBRUARY 5. The English doctor, Dr. Morgan, made his second visit and examined the patient, but he could not bandage her. This our daughter had to do day and night. The patient had many well-meaning visitors who were more of a burden to her than an alleviation of her pains.

FEBRUARY 15. My daughter, Mrs. Swaine, has now been staying up almost fourteen nights with her mother and has been bandaging her wounds, which nobody else except a chirurgeon is able to do. First she had a constant toothache, and yesterday her face swelled up so that last night both her eyes were swollen shut, which makes our difficulties worse. We have engaged a nurse who knows how to care for the sick but cannot bandage the wounds. We were also fortunate enough to secure a maid to take care of the cows and the rough housework. Had a day laborer to split wood because we must keep the rooms warm day and night, especially for the patient.

APRIL 9. We had day laborers for work in the garden. My wife used to be an industrious gardener, but now she cannot work in the garden any more on account of her still unhealed wounds and the old, deeply rooted illness.

MAY 10. An unmarried papermaker, complaining of melancholia and seeking aid, came to see me. He felt that he was possessed of an evil spirit and wished to stay with me and pay for his lodging, etc. I put him up gratis for a night and a day and had to pray with him frequently at his request. I found, however, that his much complaining infected my wife, too, and made her more sick, so I asked him to go to his relatives in the city, where there are physicians for ills both physical and spiritual who could advise him better than I.

JULY 5. Visit from an English doctor, Mr. Morgan. I was afraid that he would present me with a steep bill because he visited my wife several times during her severe illness after being burned. However, he refused to take anything and said that he never accepted anything from ministers.

JULY 22. Toward evening I was stricken with a mental sickness which did not originate in the body but was caused by Satan, though permitted by God with the gracious reservation that it should not harm me but rather serve to my good for the sake of his holy name. As mental or spiritual illnesses have a strong influence upon the body, I first became sleepless for many nights and then lost my appetite, which brought me to fasting, meditation, and penitent prayer and supplication in secret. The saying of our Lord and Saviour in Mark 9:29, "This kind can come forth by nothing, but by prayer and fasting," was very helpful to me, especially verses 23 and 24. The troubles of my heart were enlarged and they continued from July 22 until August 9, when I received the first sign of grace and thanked my Saviour and Redeemer with tears.

OCTOBER 19. Toward evening a Reformed woman, the wife of a Lutheran man, came to our house with a child eight weeks old, having come six miles on foot, and said that she wished to visit with us because she wanted to hear and talk of something good. I first inquired concerning her parents, relatives, and home situation and received reasonable and edifying answers, especially with regard to godly things. She ate supper with us, and we spent the evening in soul-edifying conversation, spiritual song, and prayer, for which she expressed gratification. We provided her and her child with a bed, alone in the living room, and thereafter went to rest in our own places. Afterwards, throughout the night, we heard her singing and thought she was doing so on account of the child. She kept singing off and on all night.

OCTOBER 20. Early in the morning, when we came to her, she was completely out of her mind and delirious, and the child lay beside her sleeping. Concerned most of all that she might harm her child or even kill it, we called on a stouthearted neighbor woman for help to take care of the mother, and especially the child. She was unable, however, to get the child away from her because she resisted. By various ways and means we sent word to her husband to come and take her home. About ten o'clock in the forenoon a councilman arrived from New Hanover to fetch me. It was hard for me to leave my sick wife and the other womenfolk with this insane person, but there was nothing else I could do. Afterwards, however, they brought her to the point where she dressed herself and also allowed her child to be tidied. She went away with the nurse, and her husband met her on the way and with kind words brought her and the child and the nurse home. She had had an accident two years ago, brought on by fright, and has had several such severe attacks, so that they have had to lock and bind her. What a fearful creature is a raving human being! While I was away I was worried about what would happen to my infirm wife in these circumstances, with an insane person, and I prayed to God for his gracious help for the weak.

OCTOBER 25. Received from our son, Frederick Augustus, a letter, dated yesterday, October 24, as follows:

With Heartfelt Joy, with the utmost Gratitude to the Almighty for His divine Interposition, I do most sincerely congratulate You on the Capture of Lord Cornwallis with his whole Army, amounting to 5500 Landforces, 110 Vessels, and a prodigious Quantity of Artillery, Arms etc., etc. and this without much Blood being spilt. It happen'd on the memorable 17th of October, the same Day Gen. Burgoyn had a similar Fate. I am at present in too much Hurry and Confusion to give all the Particulars, but shall do it by the first Opportunity. Just now Congress, Assembly and Council are about to proceed in a Body to our

Zion Church, to return Thanks to the Lord of Hosts for this singular Mark of His Interposition in our Favor. Oh! may all the People rejoyce in the Lord, and return the most unfeigned and sincere Thanks! In the next Papers all the Particulars will be, as Col. Tilghman, one of the Gen Aids arrived 2 Hours ago.

Frederick Augustus Muhlenberg The event in Virginia clearly shows that the sublime Saviour has accepted a prevailing intercession for the unfruitful fig tree in his vineyard and has allowed that it should not yet be hewn down and cast into the fire but rather be digged and manured.

OCTOBER 26. Last evening I held a service of thanksgiving *en migniature* with my little family, us poor sinners. We sang the hymn, *"Lobe den Herren, O meine Seele,"* etc., read II Chronicles 20:1-30, and closed with prayer. In the English newspaper the honorable *Congress* published the *capitulation* between His Excellency General Washington and the French general and admiral on the one side and Lord Cornwallis and Thomas Symond on the other; it was begun on October 17 and completed on October 19. Frederick reports that the honorable *Congress,* the *Assembly,* and the Council met at two o'clock in the afternoon in our Zion Church, where several hymns were sung with music, a number of appropriate Psalms read, and an excellent prayer of thanksgiving was made by the Rev. Chaplain George Duffield. In the evening the city was also artificially illuminated, in connection with which, he regrets to say, the vulgar rabble smashed the windows, etc. of the people where they found no lights.

The end of the war brought changes in the Muhlenberg family situation. In 1782 Frederick, who could not support his family on the salary paid for his political office, opened a small country store not far from his parents' home. Sally, the youngest Muhlenberg daughter, married Matthias Richards. In this year Muhlenberg made his final visit to Philadelphia. Now retired from active service at age 71, he spent most of his time reading and writing.

The Year 1783

JANUARY 15. I began to write the preface to the hymn-book, which has been assigned to me, in somewhat altered and shortened form. Now I shall also have to spend several days selecting the hymns to be included in the new hymnbook.

JANUARY 21. I devoted time to indexing the hymns and finished it. Made the following comments in conclusion:

(1) The Reverend Ministerial Conference decided upon seven hundred and fifty hymns for the new hymnbook. (2) I have underlined five hundred and thirty-four according to the rubrics in the Halle selection; therefore, two hundred and sixteen of the required number are lacking. (3) There may be many powerful and Spirit-filled hymns in the large Halle, Wernigerode, Coethen, etc. hymnbooks which would fill out the number, but I do not have these books. My esteemed brethren will be kind enough to criticize and improve my selection, to subtract from or add to it. (4) Those which expect the last judgment of the world in the too-near future and mention the signs that precede it I have left out. I also have not included those which, inspired by the Song of Solomon, are composed too close to the verge of sensuality, and also those that dally with diminutives—for example, "little Jesus," "little brother," "little angels," etc. These appear to me to be too childish and not in accord with Scripture, even though they were intended to be childlike and familiar. The ancient and medieval hymns, which have been familiar to all Lutherans from childhood on, cannot well be left out; even though they sound somewhat harsh in construction, rhyme, etc., they are nevertheless orthodox. (5) I have framed the preface somewhat more briefly than it was at first. If it is not considered suitable, my worthy brethren will be good enough to write a better one.

225

JANUARY 23. Received a letter from Frederick Muhlenberg, in the city, the contents of which grieved me. Since he has buried the talent entrusted to him in the political dunghill, the consequences are not lacking. In the world there is no pleasure that rests the soul; he who lets it deceive him will lose his salvation. There has been no lack of warnings, but inquisitive youth prefers to grow wise through its own hurt. But someday he may be utterly consumed with terrors if he does not turn back in time.

MAY 5. The laborers digging and plowing in the gardens and fields are finding the embryos of *Lucustis,* a kind of locust, which will emerge as soon as the warmth matures them. Seventeen years ago they appeared in great swarms, spoiled the fruit trees, did much damage, and made a constant noise which might almost be described as a Turkish war cry. The caterpillars, too, are spreading over the fruit trees. So we may have a literal fulfillment of Joel 1:4, "That which the palmerworm hath left hath the locust eaten; and that which the locust hath left hath the cankerworm eaten; and that which the cankerworm hath left hath the caterpillar eaten." The thirteen American provinces experienced this passage *sensu sublimiori* in seven years of war and doubtless will not fail to practice the third verse, "Tell ye your children of it, and let your children tell their children, and their children another generation." The Philosophical Society in Philadelphia will probably make its physical observations upon the locusts, caterpillars, etc. and suggest remedies against them, as the Egyptian wise men did, Exodus 7:11; 10:12.

MAY 31. The locusts are coming more and more thickly and are consuming the best in the realm of nature. In Philadelphia there is an elegant and numerous Philosophical Society. One might have thought that the society's members would have known of an antidote to this plague, but nothing has come from them, so it appears that they have not yet reached the level of the Egyptian magi. I Corinthians 1:19-21, 3:19.

JUNE 1. No public divine service here. I am no longer able to go out and I pray God for a merciful end! A long, drawn-

out illness in bed would be a severe and difficult trial for me
because I have a sick and helpless wife beside me. God will con-
trive that things will turn out in a salutary way. He has already
helped us in and out of many afflictions, and he will also be
gracious and merciful at the last for his name's sake.

JULY 8.   Last Friday a formal *actus promotionis,* or so-called
commencement, was held at the Academy in Philadelphia and,
among others, Pastor Kunze was made a doctor of theology. He
did not desire it or seek it. Loathsome and contemptible as the
German scholars were to the English Presbyterian politico-the-
ologians here in former times, so much the more do they for ob-
vious reasons flatter them now, because the right to elect to positions of honor depends upon the people, their legal advisers,
and the majority of their votes. *Tempora mutantur,* etc. Hitherto
they compared us Germans with sauerkraut and foul cheese.
Now their taste has changed; but these are petty things. He
who observes the signs of these times in the *regnum politicum
et ecclesiasticum* and is not willfully blind, is directed by a finger-
post to the Revelation of St. John. During the *Revolution* the
refined Presbyterian leaders wrested control of the Academy and
its estate from the heads of the Episcopal church, and now they
feel obliged out of love to make friends of the mammon of
unrighteousness and to hand out titles of honor.

JULY 25.   My son Frederick Muhlenberg communicated to
me a letter from his brother, Peter Gabriel Muhlenberg, in which
he describes his material *situation* and indicates that his service
as general has ended, etc.; that the government of Virginia has
promised him twelve thousand acres of land in a region many
hundreds of miles distant from Virginia, which has hitherto
been in the possession of savage Indians. It is said that the Indians have conceded this great territory to the Virginia government for a sum of money or goods. Little trust is to be put in the
treaties and promises of the Indians. They understand and practice the maxims of Machiavelli in their *cabinets* as well as in
other refined politics. When the chiefs sell a territory or tract
of land or trade it for goods, they very quickly rue the contract

and incite their young warriors to massacre or capture the new settlers, and then give as an excuse the story that the young men did it without their knowledge and will. Only a few years ago one such example occurred in a territory called Kentucky in the Indian language, to which some forty families moved in order to settle since it was reputed to be valuable land. But they were either massacred or carried off into captivity by the Indians. It is said that the state of Virginia has bequeathed this large territory, called Sciota, which begins about one hundred and sixty miles beyond Pittsburg, to the officers and common soldiers of its contingent, who served loyally to the end of the war, as a mark of gratitude for their service. It may still cost many a life.

JULY 28.   The English newspapers contain a very grave and important farewell address which His Excellency *Generalissimus* Washington sent to the Congress, in which he resigns his high office and declares that, in accord with his longfelt wish, he desires to retire in peace and quietness. In it he gives the wisest rules as to how the new *independent* states must conduct themselves if they wish to enjoy the privileges received and the freedom won by much blood, and he closes with these words:

I now make it my earnest Prayer, that God would have you and the State over which you preside, in his holy protection; that He would incline the Hearts of the Citizens to cultivate a Spirit of Subordination and Obedience to Government; to entertain a brotherly Affection and Love for one another, for their fellow-Citizens of the united States at large, and particularly for their Brethren, who have served in the field; and finally, that He would most graciously be pleased to dispose us all, to do justice, to love Mercy and to demean ourselves with that Charity, Humility and pacific Temper of Mind, which were the Characteristics of the Divine Author of our blessed Religion, and without an humble Imitation of whose Example in these things, we can never hope to be a happy nation.

How sublime and splendid is the character of a genuine Christian! Matthew 10:32, 33, "Whosoever shall confess me before men," etc. How rare are such true professions in the present generation of this so-called great world! Already in his time the blessed Luther said, "The souls of great men of the world will be as rare in heaven as venison on the poor man's table."

AUGUST 14. Thomas Ruther, Esq., of Pottstown, stopped in and asked that I marry two of his Negroes, which I did here at home in the afternoon. The lad's name was Stephen York and the girl's was Aromina.

AUGUST 25. In the afternoon a young Englishman who served in the war came to see me. He asked for my counsel because he was possessed of the evil spirits and was tormented day and night by blasphemies. According to his account, he had had stirrings and had been awakened several years ago, but had not been faithful; he had tried to convert others and neglected himself, especially during the distressing years of war. He imagined that the evil spirit was located on the left side under the heart and that it tormented him so that he could not breathe and might kill himself. I told him that since the Saviour of the whole world had been exalted to the right hand of the majesty of God and the miraculous gifts of the Holy Ghost had ceased, there had been in Christendom no examples of physical possession by the evil spirit; though, unfortunately, he still had his work in the children of unbelief and was visibly showing his influence toward all evil. His condition appeared to me to be mixed, both a physical and a moral illness. I told him that God wished to give him a profound revelation of the abysmally deep corruption of the heart in order that he might turn weary and heavy laden to Christ and be refreshed. And as far as his imagining that he was physically possessed by the evil spirit was concerned, it appeared to be only a severe obstruction of the spleen. In regard to his moral condition, I would pray for him in secret according to our Redeemer's precept, and for the obstruction of the spleen he must take medicine, for which I gave him directions. Much admonition and direction from the Word of God is fruitless and only increases the confusion when patients are already delirious.

AUGUST 29. Had a visit from Dr. Maus from the city. He served in the war for almost eight years and has had experience in *ars medica* and chirurgery and would like to settle here in Providence. He is of German extraction and has an English wife. He desired my advice, but it is difficult to advise. (a) Both of them are unaccustomed to the rough country mode of living. (b) It is difficult to find a residence and lot for a refined family in our neighborhood, and £30, £40, and £50 rent per year is asked for a small place where one might make shift to live and keep a horse and cow. (c) Victuals are more expensive here than in the city—except firewood. (d) An English family used to living genteelly, whose members cannot work themselves and must employ servants and day laborers, and does not own its own place, cannot get along in this neighborhood on less than £200 to £300 a year. (e) The income of a *medicus* and *chirurgus* is very uncertain and precarious, and heavy taxes and assessments must be added. Most of the families get along with home remedies and advisers, the autodidacts, or seek out those who prophesy from urine. The poor families seek advice and help from their ministers for nothing because they cannot pay anything. I told the doctor that I would gladly refer to him all the patients who had hitherto sought advice from me in emergencies if he could settle here without loss.

SEPTEMBER 17. My flattering egotism builds upon the fantasy that my chaffy journal of 1711 to 1742 and 1775 to 1783 contained a few grains of wheat and might have given some pleasure and edification to my God-fearing friends in Europe and numerous descendants here in America. But my pains in making copies of them were in vain, since the box containing them has been stolen. Since my eyesight has now become dim and my right hand too shaky, I must leave off further writing and be satisfied to be able to read something edifying now and then, to pray in secret, and to perform a few emergency pastoral acts at home. Meanwhile, the original, the copy of which was lost, is still extant, and can be examined by one or another of my descendants if they think it worth while and have the time to do so.

NOVEMBER 15. Frederick Muhlenberg came up from the

city and said that the elected members of the Council of Censors had had their first meeting and elected him president. Poor worm! Your downfall is nigh. Today there was also a *township* meeting at which the residents elected Frederick Muhlenberg justice of the peace.

DECEMBER 11. This day was set aside by the *Congress* as a day of thanksgiving in the United States, but it was not published in time and is therefore receiving little observance and celebration in the country because it could not be previously announced in the churches. And as far as the sects are concerned, they consider it contrary to conscience to celebrate days which are set aside by the government, and the *mere* politicians of the gallant world would rather celebrate days of thanksgiving in the mode of refined taste in which healths and toasts are guzzled and fine dances are held. When will the gallant world ever be satiated with hocus-pocus and shadow plays?

DECEMBER 27. Mr Frantz, of Maryland, stopped in. He said concerning my son Henry, in Lancaster, that recently deputies of His Imperial Majesty of Austria had come to see him and viewed his small collection of botanical and mineral specimens which he gathered in hours of recreation. The deputies exhibited such pleasure over it that they gave him a present from His Imperial Majesty, namely, a piece of rare marble.

The Year 1784

JUNE 12. In the evening I married a freed Negro, William Wilson, and a Negress, Diana Nixon, from Downingtown in Chester *County*. He brought the following lines from Mr. John Downing: *"This is to certify that William Wilson has lived at John Downing's for some considerable time past and has behaved himself in a sober Manner and that Henry Gauph has given him his Freedom."* I took a bond signed by William Wilson and Solomon Jones. Witnesses: George Jones and Philip Philips. Gave a *certificate*.

JUNE 14. On Saturday evening I received the following letter from the *Rev.* Dr. Kunze:

Dearest Father: It is with a truly profound feeling of joy that I desire to congratulate you upon receiving the doctor's degree, though I can imagine the expression on your face when you received it. If I had had a seat among the *trustees* of the local university a year ago, the natural order would certainly not have been reversed, since the father is prior to the son. Nevertheless, be pleased now to allow yourself to remain in venerable remembrance as "Dr. Muhlenberg." The large "D" is in itself empty of significance and does not, like "Rabbi," admit of any such origin as "being great and much." If this were the case, this "D" would certainly have been thoroughly proscribed by me. However, among people who otherwise have no intimate knowledge of one, it does occasionally give one a certain advantageous reception. Your memory will never die in America, and I hope that posterity will read much concerning you.

JUNE 15. Copied the reply written to Dr. Kunze yesterday.

Dearest Brother in Christ: On June 12 I received your important letter, dated the eleventh and written in the language of the heart in painful illness. Weakness of mind and body will permit only a brief *pro memoria* in reply.

The D.D. in the address so frightened me that I opened the letter with trembling, since I knew nothing about it previously and too hastily presumed that my Jonathan must have written while suffering a paroxysm of burning fever. However, after I found the explanation in the letter, the emotion subsided and I remembered that more than forty years ago in Upper Lusatia I had been called "*Herr Magister*," according to the custom of unlearned people who were not accustomed to abstract ideas, simply because I catechized, preached, and distributed alms, and on the voyage from London to America I was called "Doctor" because I wore a *gown* and a plaited rose on my hat and had some Halle medicines to give away. But now all that has ceased and the highly learned, wise, and estimable *trustees* of a world-famous university ought properly to be more prudent and thrifty and grant their doctor of divinity degrees only to worthy candidates, as they have in the past, and not waste them on an old, decrepit, deaf, lame, and unlearned Muhlenberg, who, despite his depraved, flattering egotism and by virtue of a true self-knowledge, still does not consider himself worthy to be called an accomplished catechist, driller, or preacher, much less a D.D., because I lack the requisite qualities and gifts. As is my duty, Romans 1:7, I privately and publicly respect and honor the degrees of *Magister* and D.D. when held by deserving men. However, I earnestly beg my esteemed bosom friends to spare me from being called by this unmerited title, which is like Saul's armor, and rather refer to me by David's staff, shepherd's bag, or harp. Psalm 23.

JULY 24.   Toward evening my wife's youngest brother, Mr. Benjamin Weiser, stopped at our house on his way from Shamokin to Philadelphia and stayed overnight with us. It is said that during the past severe winter some families were without a bit of bread for a month and cooked the brayed bark of trees, but many were made ill by it and died. In a locality near Lancaster, Christian people gathered about a hundred barrels of flour and hauled them over the long road there, over mountain and valley, and distributed them free to the hungry. That sounds refreshing to one who has humane and, especially, Christian feelings; on the one hand it is pleasing because of the charitable deed, and on the other hand it is fearful because of the rod of chastisement.

JULY 26. Our American philosophers are now very much occupied perfecting balloons or flying machines to make it possible to sail in and above the atmosphere. They have already made several trial voyages. It will probably cost more than it is worth because there are no means of subsistence or treasures to be had beyond the atmosphere, nor is there any air there that is fit for human lungs. These Daedali will thus be making waxen wings for themselves and their sons, and like Phaeton will want to rule the sun. It were safest to explore and seek first the way to the heaven of heavens, cultivate the earth for bread, improve navigation on water, and let every creature live and move and have its being in the place and element to which and for which the all-wise, all-gracious, and almighty Creator has ordained it: the birds in the air, the fish in the water, cattle and men upon the earth, etc.

AUGUST 16. It is reported that the Indians on the Ohio are breaking out in hostility and committing massacres because the land is being parceled out. There are only two ways and means by which the great uncultivated territories can be conquered: the governments of the United States must either purchase the rights of the Indians through treaties or take them by the sword. It is difficult, almost impossible, because of the lack of money.

Jehovah promised the Promised Land to Israel, but how hard it was to drive the Canaanites out of their possession. The greatest heroes could accomplish nothing unless God's almighty hand gave miraculous assistance. If the magnates of the United States have as their prime purpose the propagation and spread of Christianity, an invisible, miraculous, and almighty Hand will perform it. For to the divinely appointed kings upon Zion the heathen have been given as an inheritance, and the uttermost parts of the earth for their possession.

SEPTEMBER 21. Magister Streit sent me a letter in which he reported, among other things, *"concerning old Mr. Peter Lober and his Wife whose Separation you doubtless know. He seems to be obstinately determined, never to receive her again, to live with him. I would make free to ask you, whether, if they declare forgiveness to each other before proper Witnesses, professing to retain no Enmity or Malice against each other, but yet live separate, they or either of them may be admitted to the Lord's Supper or not? — I should be glad, if you would give me your Opinion by Writing as soon as it is convenient."*

Since he asked for a quick answer, I replied under today's date that this is my unauthoritative opinion:

One cannot well refuse them the means of grace if both of them fulfill the aforementioned *conditiones*. Since both are old people, had no children by each other, and have no other children to raise, a *separation* in this *casus* is not difficult, for the *finis primarius* of marriage is the propagation of the human race and the training of children in the nurture and admonition of the Lord, and the *finis secundarius* is that the one should be the other's help, comfort, etc. Moreover, the laws of this land allow a separation from bed and board, but neither of the two shall marry again so long as they may live. In this *casus* I cannot weigh the grounds *pro* and *contra* so quickly, but I remember what our Lord and Saviour taught in Luke 5:31, 32, "They that are whole need not a physician," etc., and in John 6:37, "Him that cometh to me penitently I will in no wise cast out."

The *casus* is as follows: (1) An elder in the congregation at New Hanover had a wife with whom he had lived for many years and with whom he had children. These children they raised until they reached marriageable age. The wife was a God-fearing woman, a diligent and thrifty housekeeper, and a person who knew how to adapt herself to her husband's choleric temperament. (2) The wife died and, after the period of mourning was over, he became engaged to a widow and was married to her in proper fashion. He was over sixty years old. She was not much younger, and also had married children. The two oldsters did not live together very long when he discovered that his spouse did not have the same qualities as his former wife. He was vexed when he became convinced that his present wife was diverting some of the household money to her children. He transferred something to her as a widow's portion that she might have something in case he preceded her in death, and this did not please his children. The wife left her husband and moved in with her son. Although she regretted her hasty action, the husband would not have her back. Now they are separated from bed and board and no longer wish to live together. The marriage cannot be dissolved by divine law or by the laws of the land because there are not sufficient grounds. Matthew 19:9.

What is a faithful pastor to do in such a case? Should he deprive them of the means of grace for their salvation? Can sinners be converted and amend their lives without the appointed means? Or are they to be left to help themselves and rise from their fall with their own strength? Does not the greatest blame and responsibility rest on those who desire the Lord's Supper and receive it unworthily? Why was the man without a wedding garment not turned away by the Bridegroom's servants instead of being admitted and having the King himself judge him and eject him? Matthew 22. Ambassadors for Christ may indeed admonish and pray, "Be ye reconciled," but they may not use compulsion. II Corinthians 5:20. It is difficult to refuse confession and holy communion if there are not sufficient reasons for doing so. An opinion given in haste until further reflection compels me to alter it.

OCTOBER 15. In the evening I admonished our maid, Widow Catharine Haag, because she was invited to attend a *frolick* in the neighborhood tomorrow evening where cornhusking will be rewarded with drink, games, or dancing. Psalm 1, "Blessed is the man that walketh not in the counsel of the ungodly," etc. How difficult it is for flesh and blood to be led to the eternal good!

NOVEMBER 5. My son gave me a letter from Mr. John Christian Grotian, of Halle in Saxony. In this letter the writer reports that he had in mind to come here to Pennsylvania, where he trusted that he would be received in a friendly fashion. If I am not mistaken, I knew his father or grandfather more than forty years ago as an honest and upright friend, and it would be my duty, and that of my sons, to be of service to him if we are in a position to do so.

Our intention is good, but we may not be able to fulfill it, for the conditions here are precarious. There are so many Jewish, heathen, and Christian candidates here for positions requiring the use of head or pen that, whenever there is an opening, they knock one another over in the rush to get the position. The prisons are almost always full of loafers and debtors. Hardly anyone has better success unless he is accustomed to work hard or has learned a useful trade and is able and willing to earn his bread with the sweat of his brow. My oldest son has some land of his own, and he would be glad to give our friend, young Grotian, a piece of it if he comes, but it lies far away, is still forested, and is subject to incursions by the barbarous Indians. It would cost a great deal to fell some of the trees, clear the land, build a cabin on it, and do some planting and harvesting. Until this is done, no benefit will be derived from it. Those who come here from Europe without paying their passage are sold into service for several years. Those who come as freemen, and who as merchants bring some money with them, may succeed or fail with their goods, for in this world temporal fortune is always uncertain.

The last war brought many lost sons of Europe to our shores and left them stranded here. They do not know how to nourish their idle bodies in any other way than by pretending to be preachers and by hiring themselves out by the year until the so-called shepherds and their flocks get into each others' hair. Send faithful laborers into thy harvest, O God, and endow thy Word with spirit and power!

The Year 1785

JANUARY 13. Was troubled with cramps in my swollen legs and was able to write only a little. It grieves me that I can not be of assistance to dear Pastor Helmuth now that he is burdened. Poor sight, deafness, swollen feet, constant dizziness in the head, trembling in all my members, etc., prevent me from dressing and undressing, walking and standing, etc., without help.

FEBRUARY 7. On January 21, *a.c.,* the American Philosophical Society held a meeting and, among many other learned men, elected the *Rev.* Henry Muhlenberg, of Lancaster, a member of the said society.

> O how fleeting, O how cheating
> Is what man has made;
> All accomplishments will vanish
> And our name will fade.
> Only those with faith in God
> Ever will abide.

FEBRUARY 12. Rough calculation of annual expenses for us two oldsters, a maid, dog, cats, etc.:

For 30 bushels of flour, at 8s. a bushel	£12
For the maid's wages	12
Two cows (£12), and hay and groats for winter fodder (£10)	22
Firewood for the whole year, especially the winter	15
Candles and soap	9
Materials for maintenance of house, barn, and fences	10
For *coffee,* chocolate, and sugar	10
For necessary clothing, shoes, bedding	9
For meat, salt, spices, and beverages	12
For medicine and beggars	5
For all sorts of taxes	5
For keeping the two wells in order	2
To wage-earners, for pruning trees and gardening	3
For paper, ink, and sealing wax	2
For buckwheat flour, butter, cheese, when the cows are with calf	3

Nothing is reckoned for emergencies; besides there are several
additional small requirements for table companions.

    Total... £131

Income from our property: An empty house, empty barn and
stalls, an additional little house and smithshop, water from two
wells, two vegetable gardens which do not cultivate themselves
but require effort and work and God's blessing if they are to
produce vegetables for the kitchen. The orchard produces some
vinegar in an emergency and, in addition, it gives poor neighbors
something to munch.

Whoever wishes honestly and scantily to support himself and
his family on this place must either work at some honest craft
or must be able to live on interest. There are already more than
enough *shops* and taverns.

It would be more tolerable for me or you (Peter and Frederick
Muhlenberg) if I had an opportunity to rent Pastor Kunze's
place in New Hanover for £25 or £30 a year and have the
farmer live there to cultivate the farm for half the proceeds.
Then, in return for the £30 rent, I should at least have a free
dwelling, flour, firewood, milk, butter, cheese, half of the increase
in the horses, cows, pigs, and fowl on the place, and it would
not be necessary to hire laborers, apart from a maid to keep
house, wash, cook, take care of the vegetable garden, etc.—until
the obscure matter of the land on the frontier is cleared up. To
continue to live, as we have, out of the bag without earning
anything, will make us extremely poor before we know it.

It is futile to expect a public office here in the country, for
there are too many hungry *pretenders* and parties; according to a
bad custom the offices require more expenditure than they
produce income; persons holding office are envied, abused,
persecuted, and hated; and a house which becomes increasingly
disunited cannot stand. Under such circumstances I should not
wish my worst enemy to be an officeholder.

Anyone who wishes to support himself and his family in these
times by keeping a *store* or a *shop*, either in the country or in
a town, must have the eyes of a falcon, the alertness of a rooster,

the fluency of a Jew, the patience of a mule, capital to invest, etc. The profits are not remarkable, *they undersell one another,* it costs a great deal to keep a clerk, some of the goods will become old and lose their value, and the storekeeper may be robbed or defrauded if debtors run away or declare bankruptcy, etc. The common proverb declares that it requires no great art to become a merchant, but it does to remain one. A Quaker once told me that he had entered a business partnership in order that, if he lost everything, he might at least blame his partner for it. Ecclesiasticus 27:23. As a nail sticks between two stones in the masonry, so sin sticks between buyer and seller.

According to my humble opinion the most innocent way of living in this part of the evil world is still the patriarchal way. The so-called gallant world gives its servants the lash at the end, while the Saviour gives his servants an eternal, gracious reward when they enter upon their rest. Thus it is better to be a martyr of Christ than a victim of the dangerous world. If you two dear older sons would have such country places where you could cultivate the soil and raise cattle, where you could bring up your children in true Christianity, and where you could accustom them to continue in work and prayer, especially if you yourselves would give them a good example of Christian conduct, you would provide yourselves with a pleasant and comfortable evening of your lives. You are servants who know the will of your Lord, etc. If you do not act as it is fitting for ordinary Christians to act, you will come to a terrible end, your children and children's children will cry out against you as pitiful waifs, and the Lord will require the blood of your hands. Our transient political *independence* does not free us for a moment, either in time or in eternity, from the *dependence* and the duties which we owe to God, our Redeemer, our neighbors, and ourselves.

APRIL 26. Was able to read only a little on account of weakness. Was visited by an exile who was born in Saxony and who served as lieutenant in the last war with the Brunswick mercenaries. Since the peace he has eked out a scanty living, so he said, as a schoolmaster in Georgia. Now he would like to return to his fatherland, but he does not have the money for the journey. I was unable to give him any more help than best wishes and a mite toward his *viaticum*. Those who came to North America from Germany as mercenaries were generally taken in. Many of them fancied that, after an easy conquest, they would possess a paradise in this part of the world and amass a great fortune. But they had the same experience as the dog in the fable who snapped at the shadow and thus lost what he already had in his jaws. A bird in the hand is worth two in the bush.

SEPTEMBER 12. German inhabitants in the *independent* states are repeatedly urged with persuasive articles in the German newspapers to establish academies and high schools and so to emulate the English inhabitants of Episcopal and Presbyterian church bodies who have already established similar institutions. But where are the large means necessary for the maintenance of such schools to come from, and where are suitable men for this purpose to be secured, and how are they to be supported? Especially in states which are already deep in debt and in times in which there is such a shortage of money! The rich, young ruler (Luke 18:18ff.) still has many imitators who go away sorrowfully when they are asked to give something for good purposes. The middle class has little or nothing left after it renders unto Caesar what is Caesar's and unto God what is God's, and poor Lazarus, or the lower class, lies before the door unable to help. Nevertheless, God's hand would not be curtailed and his heart-warming power would be able to establish and support such institutions if only education for the kingdom of heaven were regarded, cultivated, and practiced in such schools as an excellent, necessary, and serviceable thing after the rule and prescription of the supreme Lord, "Seek ye first the kingdom of God," etc. But unfortunately this is neglected, regarded as a secondary matter, at best treated as an *opus operatum,* like the nun who yawned when she prayed the Psalter, etc. Practical schools in which physical and spiritual powers are cultivated would probably be more necessary and useful for the furtherance of temporal and eternal welfare.

The Year 1786

FEBRUARY 24. Early in the morning a mad dog leaped into our house and fought with our house dog. Our neighbors killed the mad dog, and we tied up our dog in the wash house in order to see whether he may also become rabid within the next nine or ten days.

APRIL 16. Pastor Voigt conducted service here. We had private devotions. In the afternoon my wife persuaded me to crawl with her once again, and perhaps for the last time, to the home of our son, Frederick Augustus. He gathered his wife and seven children about him and together they played and sang several edifying hymns, which was very refreshing to me and evoked the wish that it might please our Lord Jesus Christ in his grace to prepare some of my very numerous descendants to be fruitful seeds in order that they might be used in some future seeding in this western wilderness. "Oh, that the even might come when it shall be so light," etc.

MAY 17. Saw the following observation in the English newspaper: *"A reformation has been introduced among the Episcopal Churches in the State of Massachusetts. . . . The new Liturgy is printed in Boston of the first Episcopal Church there. . . . The prayers are addressed to God and Father only. Even the word Trinity is totally excluded. . . .*

It is to be regretted that there are parties in the so-called Christendom of today. It is apparent that our corrupt desires concentrate on this point: we wish to be independent from God and his revealed Word and will, and everyone wishes to be his own lord. Especially the plan of reconciliation appointed by God through his Son Jesus Christ is unbearable to the children of this world, both crude and fine, and is opposed by them.

MAY 28. An acquaintance who was on his return trip from

the city stopped in and related that an announcement was read a week ago in Zion Church in Philadelphia to the effect that some new preachers were crossing the ocean and were to be expected shortly.

SEPTEMBER 6. It was seventy-five years ago today that I first came into the world. "When I came I lay naked on the ground; thus I took my first breath," etc. O gracious God, grant that the atonement of Thine only-begotten and dearly beloved Son may also benefit me, so great a sinner. Let grace be for justice and mercy for judgment. Lord Jesus Christ, thou are the highest good, the source of all grace.

OCTOBER 11. The *Supreme Court* is to meet today for the first time in the town of the new *county* of Montgomery for *criminal* cases. The weather is pleasant for the farmers who are bringing in buckwheat from the fields. The Lord God still allows his sun to rise over the evil and good.

DECEMBER 15. Frederick Augustus, Esq., showed me an English letter from his brother, General Peter Muhlenberg, dated Philadelphia, December 12, *a.c.,* in which it is reported that Peter, in agreement with his brother Henry, has set in motion a proposal to establish a German high school in the city of Lancaster and has petitioned the state *assembly* which is now in session for a *charter* for the *incorporation* of the same. According to the plan there are to be forty *trustees,* of whom fourteen are forever to be Lutherans, fourteen Calvinists, and twelve from other Christian denominations. The academy is to be called Franklin. If the undertaking is of God it will come into being despite many difficulties. If it is only of man it will not succeed.

DECEMBER 25. This is the seventy-fifth Christmas Day that I have experienced in this time of testing under God's goodness, grace, mercy, long-suffering, and forgiveness. O ungrateful creature that I am! Help me, O God. How much has the selfishness of men corrupted us! Holy Jesus, source of sanctification, etc. There was to have been a Reformed service here today, but the minister was unable to come. We had domestic devotions. Gave our maid 1*s.* 10*d.* as a *douceur.*

The Year 1787

JANUARY 21. Last night there was a storm with violent lightning and thunder and heavy rain. This is an uncommon phenomenon for this time of the winter.

JANUARY 30. A heavy snow has fallen again since yesterday. A German chimneysweep stopped in from Philadelphia and swept out our kitchen chimney for 3s.

FEBRUARY 2. Dark without and within. I looked through the so-called album which I brought with me from Europe and found to my confusion the excellent greetings, admonitions, and consolations which various counts, barons, citizens, theologians, etc., inscribed between 1735 and 1742. I suppose that most, if not all, of these blessed persons have died before 1787 and are now flourishing in the joy and glory of their Redeemer, where they are enjoying what no eye here hath seen. Meanwhile I, wretched man that I am, remain here in this dangerous wilderness of temptation. Who shall deliver me from the body of this death? Romans 7; I Timothy 1:15. O word worthy of all acceptation!

FEBRUARY 12. A *politicus* offers the following remarkable advice in the English newspaper: The French will establish themselves as mediators and protectors between Spaniards in South America and the western regions of the North American *independent* states, and they will civilize the still crude independent frontiersmen and refine their religion, etc. The wheel of revolution is still turning in the kingdoms of the world.

MARCH 29. Quite naturally I looked forward to my departure from this time of trial during the equinoctial season in this month of March. However, it now appears that the Lord over life and death has not appointed it so. Psalm 39:9, "Deliver me from all my transgressions; make me not the reproach of the foolish." I must continue to be chastised on this earth and sanctified by thy Spirit. My senses must sink more deeply into thee, etc. My wife, who is now in her sixtieth year, also frequently desires that the blessed friend of sinners, Jesus Christ, may relieve her severe sickness or in his grace take her unto himself under his immediate care. Both of us are *inutilia terrae pondera,* or we are like the fig tree which consumes sap and bears no fruit.

JUNE 5. In the evening I gave my grandson, the son of John Peter, some blows with a rod because he came home late, etc., whereupon he threatened to remain out late again tomorrow evening to play. If parents do not in time break the inborn, wicked selfishness and self-will which are inherited from Adam, the children will become thorns in their sides.

JUNE 27. Today Mrs. Hanna [wife of Peter Muhlenberg] had a first visit to her table from several neighboring women according to the prevailing fashion. They drink a glass of wine or cup of tea and some cakes in the afternoon and evening and entertain one another with vain conversations. This fashion is not according to the counsel and command of our Lord.

JULY 5. A carpenter and a mason are working to build a new front porch and the scaffolding for the wall. Meanwhile the *painter* is painting inside our house. I feel harbingers of burning fever such as I had a year ago in July.

JULY 20. I was troubled with increasing dizziness and pain in my limbs as a consequence of a journey to New Hanover.

JULY 23. Ever since I took the trip to the Swamp my swelling and dizziness have increased, so that I am able to read little and write less.

SEPTEMBER 29. Baptized Anna, infant daughter of John Frey and his wife Hanna. The child was fifteen months old. The parents were sponsors.[1]

---

[1] A little more than a week after this last entry, early in the morning on Sunday, October 7, 1787, Henry Melchior Muhlenberg died in New Providence (Trappe), Pennsylvania, and was buried there on October 10.

Index

247

Date Due